STUDYING FAMILY AND COMMUNITY HISTORY: 19TH AND 20TH CENTURIES

Series editor: Ruth Finnegan

Volume 1 *From family tree to family history,* edited by Ruth Finnegan and Michael Drake

Volume 2 *From family history to community history,* edited by W.T.R. Pryce

Volume 3 *Communities and families,* edited by John Golby

Volume 4 *Sources and methods for family and community historians: a handbook,* edited by Michael Drake and Ruth Finnegan

All four titles in the series are published by Cambridge University Press in association with The Open University.

This book forms part of the third-level Open University course DA301 *Studying family and community history: 19th and 20th centuries.* Other materials associated with the course are:

Drake, M. (ed.) (1994) *Time, family and community: perspectives on family and community history,* Oxford, Blackwell in association with The Open University (Course Reader).

Braham, P. (ed.) (1993) *Using the past: audio-cassettes on sources and methods for family and community historians,* a series of six audio-cassettes with accompanying notes, Milton Keynes, The Open University.

Calder, A. and Lockwood, V. (1993) *Shooting video history,* a video workshop on video recording for family and community historians, with accompanying notes, Milton Keynes, The Open University.

For availability of the video- and audio-cassette materials, contact Open University Educational Enterprises Ltd (OUEE), 12 Cofferidge Close, Stony Stratford, Milton Keynes MK11 1BY.

If you wish to study this or any other Open University course, details can be obtained from the Central Enquiry Service, PO Box 200, The Open University, Milton Keynes MK7 6YZ.

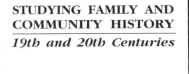

STUDYING FAMILY AND
COMMUNITY HISTORY
19th and 20th Centuries

FROM FAMILY HISTORY TO COMMUNITY HISTORY

This accessible and innovative series will stimulate and develop personal research in family and community history, and set it within a wider framework. You will find practical suggestions for research projects, activities to enhance relevant skills and understanding, and ideas about how to exploit appropriate written, oral and visual sources. The series also brings together specialist contributors who use current developments in demography, social and economic history, sociology, historical geography and anthropology to suggest new insights and lines of enquiry. With its aim of placing individual and localized cases in their social and historical context, the series will interest anyone concerned with family and community.

This volume explores population movements, spatial divisions and social structures in town and countryside, and gives pointers as to the meaning of 'community'. Regional settings, the idea of 'place', and changes over time are also examined, with special attention being paid to the *patterns* and the *processes* of all forms of migration. These themes give rise to new research ideas in family and community history.

FROM FAMILY HISTORY TO COMMUNITY HISTORY

Edited by W.T.R. Pryce

 *in association with*

06295037

Published by the Press Syndicate of the University of Cambridge in association with The Open University
The Pitt Building, Trumpington Street, Cambridge CB2 1RP
40 West 20th Street, New York, NY 10011-4211, USA
10 Stamford Road, Oakleigh, Melbourne 3166, Australia

First published 1994

Edited, designed and typeset by The Open University

Printed in Great Britain by Butler and Tanner Ltd, Frome

A catalogue record for this book is available from the British Library

Library of Congress cataloguing in publication data applied for

ISBN 0 521 46002 6   hardback

ISBN 0 521 46578 8   paperback

7216C/da301v2pi1.1

CONTENTS

PART II: PLACE AND COMMUNITY

PART III: COMMUNITY AND TERRITORIALITY: AN ILLUSTRATION

PART IV: REFLECTING ON THE ISSUES

LIST OF FIGURES AND TABLES

Figures

Tables

CONTRIBUTORS

Peter Braham, Lecturer in Sociology, Faculty of Social Sciences, The Open University

Harold Carter, Emeritus Professor of Geography, The University of Wales at Aberystwyth

Brenda Collins, Social and economic historian; Tutor-Counsellor, The Open University in Northern Ireland; Research Officer, Lisburn Museum

Ian Donnachie, Senior Lecturer and Staff Tutor in History, Faculty of Arts and The Open University in Scotland

Michael Drake, Emeritus Professor and first Dean of Faculty of Social Sciences, The Open University; Visiting Professor of History, University of Tromsø

David Englander, Senior Lecturer in European Humanities Studies, Faculty of Arts, The Open University

Ruth Finnegan, Professor in Comparative Social Institutions, Faculty of Social Sciences, The Open University

Roy Lewis, Senior Lecturer in Geography, The University of Wales at Aberystwyth

W.T.R. Pryce, Senior Lecturer and Staff Tutor in Geography, Faculty of Social Sciences and The Open University in Wales

Monica Shelley, Lecturer in Community Education, School of Health, Welfare and Community Education, The Open University

PREFACE

Many thousands of people are currently exploring their family trees or investigating the history of their localities. It is an absorbing hobby – and more than just a hobby. It combines the excitement of the chase and the exercise of demanding investigative skills. It also leads to personal rewards, among them perhaps an enhanced awareness of identity, achieved through the process of searching out your roots within the unending cycle of the past, and something to hold on to in the confusions of the present.

At the same time scholars within a series of social science and historical disciplines are increasingly realizing the value of small-scale case studies, extending and questioning accepted theories through a greater understanding of local and personal diversities. Sociologists now look to individual life histories as well as generalized social structure; geographers emphasize the local as well as the global; demographers explore regional divergences, not just national aggregates; historians extend their research from the doings of the famous to how 'ordinary people' pursued their lives at a local level.

This volume and the series of which it is a part have as their central purpose the encouragement of active personal research in family and community history – but research that is also linked to more general findings and insights. The series thus seeks to combine the strengths of two traditions: that of the independent personal researcher into family tree or local history, and that of established academic disciplines in history and the social sciences.

Now is a particularly appropriate moment to bring these two sides together. The networks of family and local historians up and down the country have in the past had scant recognition from within mainstream university circles, which (in contrast to the active involvement of further education and extra-mural departments) have sometimes given the impression of despising the offerings of 'amateur researchers'. Explicitly academic publications, for their part, have been little read by independent investigators – understandably, perhaps, for, with a few honourable exceptions, such publications have been predominantly directed to specialist colleagues. But there are signs that this situation may be changing. Not only is there an increasing awareness of the research value of micro studies, but higher education as a whole is opening up more flexible ways of learning and is recognizing achievements undertaken outside traditional 'university walls'. Our hope is to further this trend of mutual understanding, to the benefit of each.

There are thus two main aims in these volumes, overlapping and complementary. The first is to present an interdisciplinary overview of recent scholarly work in family and community history, drawing on the approaches and findings of such subjects as anthropology, social and economic history, sociology, demography, and historical geography. This should be illuminating not only for those seeking an up-to-date review of such work, but also for anyone interested in the functioning of families and communities today – the essential historical background to present-day concerns. The second, equally important aim is to help readers develop their own research interests. The framework here is rather different from traditional genealogy or local history courses (where excellent DIY guides already exist) since our emphasis is on completing a project and relating it to other research findings and theories, rather than on an unending personal quest for yet more and more details. It differs too from most conventional academic publications, in that the focus is on *doing* research, rather than absorbing or reporting the research of others. These volumes are therefore full of practical advice on sources and methods, as well as illustrations of the kinds of projects that can be followed up by the individual researcher.

Given the infinite scope of the subject and the need to provide practical advice, we have put some limits on the coverage. The timescale is the nineteenth and twentieth centuries, a period for which the sources are plentiful and – for the recent period at least – oral investigation feasible. (The critical assessment and exploitation of primary sources within this timescale will, of course, develop skills which can be extended to earlier periods.) There is no attempt to give a detailed historical narrative of nineteenth- and twentieth-century history. Rather, we present a blend of specific case studies, findings and theoretical ideas, selected with a view to giving both some taste of recent work, and a context and stimulus for further investigation.

In terms of area, the focus is on the United Kingdom and Ireland, or, to put it differently, on the countries of the British Isles (these and similar terms have both changing historical applications and inescapable political connotations, so since we wish to write without prejudice we have deliberately alternated between them). This focus is applied flexibly, and there is some reference to emigration abroad; but we have not tried to describe sources and experiences overseas. Thus, while much of the general theoretical background and even specific ideas for research may relate to many areas of the world, the detailed practical information about sources or record repositories concentrates on those available to students working in England, Ireland (north and south), Scotland and Wales.

The emphasis is also on encouraging small-scale projects. This does not mean that larger patterns are neglected: indeed, like other more generalized findings and theories, they form the background against which smaller studies can be set and compared. But small, manageable projects of the kinds focused on in this volume have two essential merits. First, they link with the emerging appreciation of the value of research into diversities as well as into generalizations: many gaps in our knowledge about particular localities or particular family experiences remain to be filled. Second, they represent a form of research that can be pursued seriously within the resources of independent and part-time researchers.

This second volume focuses on population movements, communities and aspects of community life. It can be read on its own, but it is also linked to the other volumes in the series which complement and amplify the topics considered here. The companion volumes (listed on p.ii) turn the spotlight on individual families and the broader patterns of family history revealed by recent research (Volume 1); on family- or community-based activities that can be studied at a local level such as work, social mobility, local politics, religion, or leisure (Volume 3); and, in Volume 4, on some of the many sources and methods that can be used to conduct and communicate research in family and community history.

This book forms one part of the Open University course DA301 *Studying family and community history: 19th and 20th centuries* (the other components are listed on p.ii). DA301 is an honours-level undergraduate course for part-time adult learners studying at a distance, and it is designed to develop the skills, methods and understanding to complete a guided project in family or community history within the time constraints of a one-year course – comparable, therefore, to the dissertation sometimes carried out in the final year of a conventional honours degree. It also looks forward to ways in which such a project could be extended and communicated at a later stage. However, these volumes are also designed to be used, either singly or as a series, by anyone interested in family or community history. The introduction to recent research, together with the practical exercises, advice on the critical exploitation of primary sources, and suggestions for research projects, should be of wide interest and application. Collectively, the results of such research should not only develop individuals' investigations but also enhance our more general understanding of family and community history. Much remains to be discovered by the army of amateur and professional researchers throughout the British Isles.

Since a series of this kind obviously depends on the efforts of many people, there are many thanks to express. As in other Open University courses, the material was developed collaboratively. So while authors are responsible for what they have written, they have also been both influenced and supported by other members of the course team: not just its academic contributors, but also those from the editorial, design, and production areas of the University. There was also the highly skilled group who prepared the manuscript for electronic publishing, among them Molly Freeman, Maggie Tebbs, Pauline Turner, Betty Atkinson, Maureen Adams, and above all Dianne Cook, our calm and efficient course secretary throughout most of the production period. For advice and help on various points in this volume we would especially like to thank Don Breckon (on local bus and railway systems); Richie Burman of the London Museum of Jewish Life (for guidance on photographic archives); Professor Harold Carter (for advice on central place theory and its applications); Dr Douglas Lockhart (migration research in Scotland); Dr Deirdre Mageean (Irish emigration to North America); Trevor Parkhill and the Public Record Office of Northern Ireland (for advice on Irish sources); Hywel G. Thomas and King's Cross Welsh Chapel, London (for advice on religious sources and the London Welsh community); and Sally and Peter Brander, Anne Goodman and Sheila Lucks (for additional information used in Chapter 8). For the series generally we are greatly indebted to four external critical readers who provided wonderfully detailed comments on successive drafts of the whole text: Brenda Collins, particularly for her informed advice on Ireland; Janet Few, both in her own right and as Education Officer of the Federation of Family History Societies; Dennis Mills, with his unparalleled command not only of the subject matter but of the needs of distance students; and Colin Rogers of the Metropolitan University, Manchester, for sharing the fruits of his long experience in teaching and furthering the study of family history. Finally, particular thanks go to our external assessor, Professor Paul Hair, for his constant challenges, queries and suggestions. Our advisers should not be held responsible for the shortcomings that remain, but without their help these volumes would certainly have been both less accurate and less intelligible.

Our list of thanks is a long one and even so does not cover everyone. In our case its scope arises from the particular Open University form of production. But this extensive co-operation also, we think, represents the fruitful blend of individual interest and collaborative effort that is typical in the field of studying family and community history: a form of collaboration in which we hope we can now engage with you, our readers.

USING THIS BOOK

Activities
Many chapters in this volume are designed not just as texts for reading or reference but also for active study. They are therefore punctuated by a series of activities, signalled by different formats. These include:

(a) *Short questions*: these provide the opportunity to stop and consider for a moment before reading on. They are separated from the surrounding text merely by being printed in a different colour.

(b) *Exercises*: these are activities to be carried out as part of working through the text, requiring anything from ten minutes to an hour to complete. Follow-up discussion comes either immediately after the exercise in the main text or (when so indicated in the exercise) in the separate comments and answers at the end of the book.

(c) *Questions for research*: these are suggestions for longer-term research projects to follow up selectively according to personal interest or opportunity *after* working through the relevant chapter(s). Note that although there are frequent references to 'your family' or 'your community', in practice any family or community in which you are interested will do equally well. In fact, taking one on which there are *locally* available records may be more practicable, as a first stage at least, than chasing the details of your own.

Schemas
These are lists of questions, factors or key theories which can help in formulating research, providing a kind of model or template against which research findings can be compared.

References

While this book is free-standing, there are cross-references to other volumes in the series which appear, for example, in the form 'see Volume 3, Chapter 6'. This is to aid readers using all the books.

The lists of books or articles at the end of chapters or sections follow the scholarly convention of giving details of all works cited, rather than being intended as obligatory further reading. The asterisked items in these lists are useful starting points for those wishing to go further into the subject.

RUTH FINNEGAN
(Series editor)

INTRODUCTION

by W.T.R. Pryce

'From where did I come?' This is the question that has made researching a family tree the major hobby that it has become in recent years. Compulsive and time consuming, tracing your ancestry demands considerable personal commitment and application, and calls for patience and expertise, especially in archival work. Though usually raised in the context of ancestral origins (meaning the family links of blood and marital relationships), this question also involves place origins, migration and the context in which movements occur. Very few of us can reconstruct a family lineage that, over several generations, turns out to be confined to just one or two particular districts. In Britain, no family has remained unaffected, in some way or other, by the consequences of living in a country that, starting in the early nineteenth century, was to experience the world's first substantial urbanization. Even in 1851, as Anderson discovered, less than half the population were still living at their place of birth: indeed, one in six had left that community by the time they were two years of age (Anderson, 1983, p.3). Recent estimates indicate that well over 16 million people left the British Isles to settle in countries overseas in the century ending in 1914 – a series of huge emigrations that included some 4 million from Ireland.

Thus, since the early 1800s, in a very real way migration has touched the lives of most people. It has long been an integral part of family life, bringing significant changes for individuals, and amongst families and communities. Small wonder, therefore, that migration is a major research theme in family and community history. If we all lived at the same location then migration would not have been of importance because no significant movements could have ever occurred! The real world is a territorial world, characterized by the spatial and the territorial differences that are inherent to reality.

A widely used definition revolves around the idea that, reduced to its essentials, migration involves a permanent change of residence. Such changes may involve movement from one part of a country to another, or to new places overseas. But does a move across the street to a new house constitute migration? Because of the inherently spatial nature of these movements, questions of place and location are key themes in much migration research – and 'place' does have meanings other than just location. Migration, and its effects, also mean changes in the cultural and social milieux – both in the sending areas as well as at migrant destinations. These may have been (and, in the past, sometimes were) of profound significance – an impact, indeed, that could have been much more pleasurable or traumatic than just the financial cost of moving to a new domicile. Normally, both the *spatial* and the *socio-cultural* considerations involve processes that are complementary. Yet, in some investigations in family and community history, the one or the other may assume more dominance in its effects.

All this seems very difficult and challenging, doesn't it? How, then, can we unravel all the complexities that are involved? This is the main purpose of this volume. In it we offer practical guidance and suggestions as to how these and related themes can be explored.

In *From family history to community history* we aim to transport you from a prime focus (as in Volume 1 in this series) on individual families and family history to concerns involving the study of community, its social make-up and history. In doing this we do not seek to deprecate the findings of traditional family history and genealogy: rather, here we provide a context and some settings to enrich our understanding of individual families and their inter-generational linkages. But we do have other objectives as well. These aim to equip you with an understanding of different approaches: guidance on the sources that can be explored; introductions to the analytical tools for serious research investigations in migration studies; and the techniques for exploring the nature of a particular locality, a local organization or a specific community – including 'communities' that may not be tied to any particular place or locality.

Chapter 1 presents an overview of key concepts and ideas in migration research – a basic framework that receives further elaboration in the exemplars and case studies discussed later in the volume. Similarly, in dealing with the nature of towns and their regional settings, and with the changing internal social structures of urban communities (large and small), villages and rural areas, Chapters 5 and 6 offer useful conceptual perspectives on the meaning of 'place' and 'community'.

Throughout the volume you will find a strong 'how-to-do-it' emphasis on methods of research investigation – on the approaches that can be adopted, on the evaluation of sources, on the ways in which data can be analysed; and on appropriate modes for the presentation of your results as text, in tabular format and/or in map form and as explanatory diagrams. You will find, too, that, here and there, we try to practise what we preach by using carefully chosen old photographs, prints and pictures to illustrate salient topics.

There are two important methodological matters that arise on numerous occasions throughout this book, namely (1) the use of models and theories as explanatory devices; and (2) issues of scale.

A *model* (or *theory*) can be regarded as a 'simplified structuring of reality', helping us to understand abstract or intangible phenomena. Only the essential data are selected: social scientists (and others) often refer to these activities as 'building' a model; or, when applying them to particular circumstances, to 'fitting a model' or the 'modelling' of a specific pattern or process. Many of these ideas are first introduced in Chapter 1 where we discuss those migration theories and explanations that are useful research templates for work in family and community history. Thus, the more successful a model is as an explanatory tool, the greater the likelihood that it will have general validity in a range of different circumstances.

Traditionally, historians and social scientists have tended to focus attention on the aggregate, on large numbers; and they have attempted to identify the general patterns and processes affecting migrants and places. This is the *macro level* approach. In recent years, increasingly this has been found unacceptable for detailed work. Quite apart from the 'ecological fallacy' (explanations based on the overall local context that may not apply to specific individuals), it is now realized that some explanations of human behaviour – not least in migration studies – are to be found at the individual or *micro levels* of investigation. Consequently, there has been a reaction against large-scale cross-national surveys and their somewhat rigid research designs. On the other hand, as the case studies in this volume reveal, because significant processes involving wider arenas are at work, not everything can be explained simply in terms that are strictly individual and local. Clearly, there is a prevailing need for researchers to evaluate these apparent contradictions. This remains a challenge of central importance for researchers.

The contributors to this volume explore a wide range of different research strategies that, at the same time, are both complementary and contrasting in style. A substantial number of our case studies are of a *qualitative* nature, drawing on a number of different research approaches. Some, such as the interesting examples of the immigrants Hermann Schulze, Samuel Abramson and the Hyman family (Chapter 3), are straightforward narrative 'histories' – but the authors are careful to interpret the migrations of their own ancestors, and their settling downs, in the context of wider events and processes. Other contributions, particularly some of the studies dealt with in Chapter 2, and in Chapters 4, 5 and 6, demonstrate the use of *quantitative* and *cartographic analytical techniques* – approaches that often enable us to explore qualitative source data in new and original ways. Finally, drawing on a number of different approaches and techniques, in Chapter 8 we provide an illustrative example of an extended in-depth study in community history.

A large number of well-honed *local* research investigations, drawn from many different types of locality and community throughout the British Isles, including Ireland, appear in this volume. We are very aware that not all our readers live in the heavily populated regions of south-east and midland England, nor, say, in central Scotland! Our case studies include an examination of the role of the family in migration processes in rural Essex; a detailed investigation of in-migration to north-east Wales; aspects of the urban social geography of Wolverhampton and of Edgbaston in Birmingham; the impact of the Great Famine and the ensuing rural exodus from parishes in western Ireland; Jewish settlements in Dublin, Manchester and London's East End; urban hinterland studies of Reading, Newbury, Driffield, Carmarthen, Haverfordwest and Maidstone; Pakistani settlement patterns in Manchester; economic and social conditions in the Scottish Highlands and out-migration to Glasgow; ways of measuring population turnover in rural Yorkshire; chain migration between parishes in western Ireland and specific destinations in Canada and Australia; and the roles played by cultural institutions (Welsh nonconformist chapels in England; Jewish synagogues in London) in the migration process, in settlement and in community-building functions. Each case study illustrates particular research themes as well as ways of initiating new investigations; and each contains numerous practical suggestions for further work or for research in new directions.

Invariably, because of the specific personal interests of researchers, more work has been completed on some particular topics, localities, nations, ethnic or social groups than others. The themes pursued in this book are not intended to cover all parts of the United Kingdom, nor the whole of Ireland. Rather, in terms of location, we have had to be selective in order to be reasonably comprehensive in our treatment of different sources, techniques and research topics. We intend to leave you, our readers, equipped to embark on new investigations in your own localities. Alternatively, you may decide to replicate one or other of our case studies for a new location or apply the analytical methods to different circumstances. If carefully planned, cross-fertilizing studies of this kind can enrich personal interests and, at the same time, contribute meaningfully to the scholarly literature on family and community history.

REFERENCE

Anderson, M. (1983) *What is new about the modern family?*, Office of Population Censuses and Surveys, Occasional Publication 32, pp.2–16. Reprinted in Drake, M. (ed.) (1994) *Time, family and community: perspectives on family and community history*, Oxford, Blackwell in association with The Open University (Course Reader).

PART I

PEOPLE ON THE MOVE

❖ ❖ ❖

CHAPTER 1

STUDYING MIGRATION

by W.T.R. Pryce and Michael Drake

From the very start of this book we are making a strong plea for the adoption of rigorous intellectual approaches in migration research – with the emphasis placed as much on analysis as on description. This chapter offers much, too, on research approaches for the volume as a whole, functioning as a theoretical background for the case studies discussed later.

We begin, therefore, in sections 1 and 2, with a brief review of key terms, concepts and sources needed for any research into the migration history of your family or community. Next, in section 3, we examine some theories and explanations, which will help to focus your work. Finally, in section 4, we apply and extend some of these ideas in a broad-brush treatment of overseas migration since 1815.

1   FUNDAMENTAL IDEAS AND CONCEPTS

1.1   SOME BASIC TERMS

Migration involves the permanent or semi-permanent movement of individuals, families or groups from one place to another. The concept is fuzzy at the edges but normally a permanent change of residence is involved. Thus, whilst the daily journey to work, holiday travel and military call-ups are not usually regarded as migration, a seasonal movement (e.g. Irish labourers harvesting crops in mainland Britain) would be. Migration is more likely to occur at certain distinctive stages in the life cycle – for example, at marriage, on starting a new job, on retirement. The various terms used in migration studies are summarized in Schema A.

Schema A: Key terms in migration studies

Migration	movements of individuals/families involving a permanent/semi-permanent change of domicile.
In-migration	movements of people *within a nation state* arriving in a new community.
Out-migration	movements of people *within a nation state* who leave a community.

Emigration	movements of individuals/families to take up permanent residence *in another nation state* which, for British emigrants, means a foreign country overseas.
Immigration	movements of individuals/families *from a foreign country* who arrive and settle in a nation state, taking up permanent residence – in the case of Britain, from countries overseas.
Gross migration	the *total number* of migrants moving into and/or from an area.
Net migration	the net balance of movements left after the numbers of in-migrants have been subtracted from out-migrants or vice versa. These balances will be *negative* or *positive*, depending on whether, in net terms, an area is losing or gaining population by migration.

Note: the phrase 'nation state' is used here as a reasonably intelligible term in the modern period; but it is worth noting that, until latterly, the world was not divided strictly into nation states. Therefore, for earlier periods (including the colonial era), the term needs to be interpreted rather more liberally and the equivalencies – though reasonably clear – are not always exact.

Source: based on Pryce (1993) p.228

_____ **EXERCISE 1.1** _____

Using the terms given in Schema A, fill the gaps in the following:

In the nineteenth century, the Irish .... to England but .... to the USA. After 1922 they .... to England too!

Answer p.218.

_____

MIGRATION PATTERNS AND MIGRATION PROCESSES

In studying *migration patterns* our primary concern is with what happened in physical terms: the basic geography of the movements, changes in numbers over time, changes in the social structures of the sending or the receiving communities. *Gross* (or absolute) migration covers both the flows and counterflows from and to a particular place, whilst *net* migration covers only the balance of movement after *in-migrants* are subtracted from *out-migrants* in a specific place (Schema A above; Chapter 4, section 2.3).

Migration processes are more difficult to define, but it can be stated that these are related to specific circumstances. In consequence, like the man leading the pink elephant, often their identification will be a case of 'you will recognize them when you see them!'. Essentially, these cover the circumstances of movements (e.g. information flows; assistance provided by previous migrants in, say, the form of pre-paid passages; or simply the availability of a place to lay one's head), and the impact of migration, social and economic, on both the sending and receiving communities (Schema B). Sustained out- or in-migration can have a dramatic impact on a community (Figure 1.1).

Schema B: Some features of migration patterns and processes

1   The underlying mechanisms by which actual movements are accomplished (discussed in section 3 below).

2   Relative size/volume of migration flows in relation to size of the host (receiving) and sending communities.

3   Effects of movements on population structures in sending and/or receiving areas (see Figure 1.1).

4   Effects of migration flows on the social and/or cultural milieu in sending/receiving areas (including the diffusion of new ideas).

5   The effects and consequences of migration on individuals, families or communities (whether 'movers' or 'stayers').

Process also refers to changes that occur to the migrants themselves. People may migrate for a variety of reasons – adventure, work, better opportunities for their children – and may not intend to stay permanently. But individuals are changed by the experience of migration. As Joseph Hartley and his wife wrote, on 8 December 1872, to his relatives in 'old England' from his new home in Lockport, Upper New York State, 'we are Yankies now'. Admittedly the process had taken 14 years! (see Volume 1, Chapter 2, section 3).

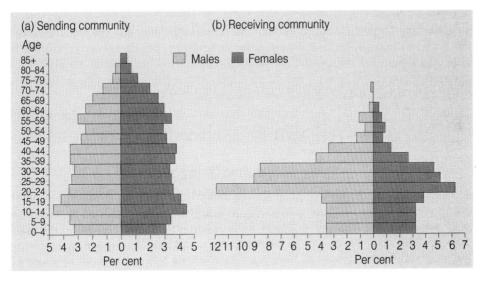

Figure 1.1   Population pyramids of (a) sending and (b) receiving communities. In (a), the population pyramid reflects the depletion of adults in the age cohorts 20–39 years due to out-migration. In (b), representative of a community receiving migrants, these age cohorts are very strongly represented, especially among men. Age pyramids such as these point towards the selective nature of migration (Source: Mageean, 1982, Figure 3, p.31)

2 SOME SOURCES FOR MIGRATION STUDIES

Until recently, researchers working on nineteenth- and early twentieth-century migration focused their attention on data collected by official government censuses and the summary tables published in the official reports. But, increasingly, the shift of interest towards micro studies has diverted attention towards the census enumerators' books (CEBs) from which these tabulations were prepared (see section 2.2 below), as well as qualitative sources (see sections 4 and 5 below).

2.1 CONTINUOUS RECORDS AND SURVEY DATA

'Continuous data' record *all* migratory moves, not just, as in life-time migration, details as to birthplace and place of enumeration. Nevertheless, even very detailed official records, such as those kept in Sweden, can pose difficulties for analysis and interpretation. For example, where records have been compiled on a local basis, as opposed to central registration, problems of incompleteness may arise for psychological reasons: whilst most migrants register their arrival in the new community, many might fail to report their departure – understandable when looking forwards to new opportunities rather than backwards to the 'old' community left behind.

Older United Kingdom residents will recall the system of national registration used during the Second World War for security purposes (Lewis, 1982, p.70). More recently, change-of-doctor records compiled by local health authorities have been used to analyse inter-regional migration flows (Stillwell, 1990). Another form of continuous migration data comes from official records of international movements such as passenger and immigration statistics (Baines, 1991, pp.7–20).

Questionnaire-based surveys have been widely used in migration research, particularly for collecting information on the characteristics of migrants, especially behavioural aspects such as the roles played by attitude and individual perceptions in the migration process. The special value of such surveys is that, unlike the standard census tables, they do provide a considerable amount of information at the personal level. Questionnaire-type methods can be adapted for research projects on the more recent past, involving in-depth interviews and the techniques of oral history (Volume 4, Chapter 6, section 7, and Chapter 7).

2.2 CENSUS-TYPE LISTINGS AND POPULATION CENSUSES

SOME SOURCES COMPILED BEFORE 1841

Because investigations in family and community history tend to be concerned with the more distant past, it is very likely that the vast majority of our potential informants have long since been dead! Sometimes, however, data collected in a local survey, conducted originally for specific purposes other than for the study of migration, may still survive. Often it is possible to 'interrogate' these data in ways that are much more helpful than with the official published census tabulations. Such sources, because they do not constitute a census in the full sense, are known as *population-* or *census-type listings*. These data may have been collected over a period rather than at one particular point in time, and the list of names may not have been comprehensive in some respect or other (for examples, see Holderness, 1971; Schofield, 1970; Tranter, 1974). A key requirement is to know as much as possible about the source. What was the purpose of the original survey? How was it planned? How had it been administered? What methods were used to complete the enumeration? What assumptions were in the minds of the investigators? And, equally important, how was the survey perceived by the respondents? Such requirements do pose stiff challenges to the present-day researcher.

Migration can also be studied from records compiled, perhaps over many years, for administrative purposes and for public regulation – sources that, in the strict sense, can be regarded neither as surveys nor as censuses (see, for example, Robin, 1980). These include marriage registers (Millard, 1982); apprenticeship returns (Buckatzsch, 1949; Patten, 1976); Poor Law settlement certificates (Pelham, 1937; Parton, 1987); and, as we shall see in Chapter 2, section 2.1, poll books, electoral registers and rate books (Gibson and Rogers, 1993; Pritchard, 1976; Werbner, 1979). In Scotland, important research findings have come from analyses of estate records (Lockhart, 1980, 1986, 1989). The problem with all of these sources is that, unlike the CEBs, their availability is limited – both in time and in terms of territorial coverage. Still, it is always worth the effort to search for them in local archives.

POPULATION CENSUSES

At the present time the census collects information on migration flows and the characteristics of migrants. In addition to the published volumes, starting with the 1961 results, special computer-printed tabulations are available for small areas – known as *Small Area Statistics* (Dewdney, 1981) (see Volume 4, Chapter 3, section 1.5).

The nineteenth-century census reports provided no such *local* tabulations as to the ages and occupations of migrants (Baines, 1978, p.148); and while the reports for 1801, 1821 and 1831 give no direct information whatsoever on migration, by comparing local and national sex ratios some indirect measures of its significance at specific locations can be obtained (see the case study of north-east Wales in Chapter 4, section 2.1). Starting in 1861, births and deaths that occurred during the previous decade in registration sub-districts were published with the main population tables, thus permitting the calculation of *net migration* balances. For earlier periods, back to the start of civil registration in 1837, it is necessary to turn to the annual reports of the Registrars General for these figures.

Birthplace tables, essential for calculating life-time migration, appear in the published census reports covering England, Wales and Scotland from 1841 to 1911 and, again, somewhat surprisingly, but for the last time, in 1951. For the intervening years total numbers are given of those born in the separate *countries* of the United Kingdom and in Ireland (Interdepartmental Committee, 1951, pp.69–79; Lawton, 1978, pp.289–319). The published tables for Ireland follow the same general pattern but the partition of the country in 1921 ushered in important differences. In Northern Ireland, birthplaces are included for 1926, 1937, 1951–71 (but not for 1981); in the Republic of Ireland they appear in the 1926, 1936, 1946 and 1951–81 returns. The detailed tables cover individual *counties* but only for persons actually born in Ireland: persons born elsewhere are shown, as in the published returns for mainland Britain, by their *country* of birth (England, Scotland or Wales, etc.).

THE CENSUS ENUMERATORS' BOOKS (CEBs)

Much work in family and community history focuses on particular localities – on individual villages, towns, streets within towns, groups of parishes – or on particular groups within, perhaps, a wider area. Therefore, researchers are always on the look-out for data that relate to small areas, particularly sources that provide information in detail. In consequence, the census enumerators' books are now the main source for local studies of migration in England, Wales and Scotland between 1841 and 1891 (later ones have yet to be released). For the Irish censuses of 1901 and 1911 (and occasionally elsewhere, see Pryce, 1973, pp.196–7), the original householders' schedules can be consulted. From the CEBs we learn the name, age, sex, address, relationship to the head of the household, marital status, occupation and *place of birth* of individuals, down to the parish level – except again in Ireland, where only the county of birth was requested (though sometimes a more precise place of birth was actually recorded). Clearly, everywhere there were both householders and enumerators who did not always do what they were asked to do: precise addresses are notoriously elusive, ages are often misstated, personal and place names misspelt. (Further information on the CEBs is available in Volume 4, Chapter 3, section 2; Higgs, 1989; and Collins and Pryce, 1993.)

EXERCISE 1.2

1 In general migrants are ....

Complete this statement by ticking the appropriate word(s) below:

    elderly
    single
    badly educated
    skilled

2 Define (a) *direct* and (b) *indirect* methods of migration measurement.

3 List two problems that arise in the use of the birthplace tables published in official census reports.

Answers/comments p.218.

---

3 THEORIES AND EXPLANATIONS OF MIGRATION

Migration in some form or other occurs in every society, in every community, in all families; and there have been many attempts to describe the nature of these movements in theoretical terms. Some explanations take the form of statements that seek to uncover the underlying reasons or motives for the decision to move. Others explore the various structural considerations involved and the processes of movement. Such theories are useful as background and as stimuli for your own research.

3.1 E.G. RAVENSTEIN AND THE 'LAWS OF MIGRATION'

By the 1840s, peak populations were recorded throughout much of the countryside in mainland Britain as well as in Ireland; and rural districts, generally, contained many more people than could be supported by the local economy so that in some localities poverty had become endemic. Population pressures were such that new opportunities had to be sought elsewhere, leading, inevitably, to the development of out-migration, especially of the young. And it was the growing towns and emergent new centres, especially those on coalfields, that became attractive as the immediate destinations for large numbers of landless men and women – some of whose ancestors had lived in the countryside for many generations. The main exceptions occurred in those districts where lead and mineral working provided supplementary or alternative employment to farming (Law, 1967; Lawton, 1968; Lawton and Pooley, 1992).

    Like his contemporaries, E.G. Ravenstein (1834–1913) was concerned about the rural exodus which, by the 1870s, was beginning to exceed natural increase, leading, in some areas, to the beginnings of *depopulation* (i.e. an ageing population where out-migration continued to exceed births). Ravenstein's famous paper 'The laws of migration' appeared in the *Journal of the Royal Statistical Society* in 1885 – sixty-seven pages of closely printed text, 41 tables and 11 maps. This pioneering and perceptive study, still highly regarded by researchers, was based on a detailed statistical analysis of the birthplace tabulations in the 1871 and 1881 census reports (Schema C; see, also, Grigg, 1977).

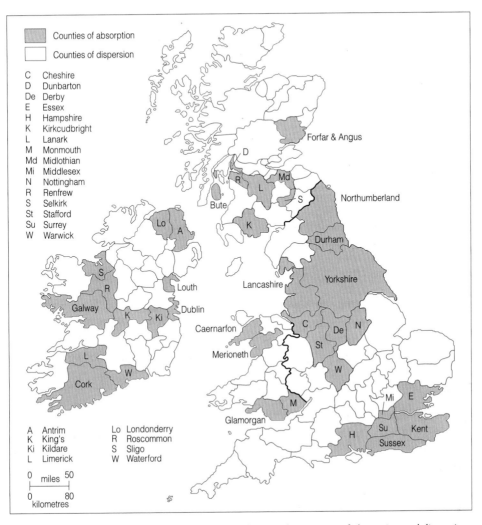

Counties of absorption
Counties of dispersion

C	Cheshire
D	Dunbarton
De	Derby
E	Essex
H	Hampshire
K	Kirkcudbright
L	Lanark
M	Monmouth
Md	Midlothian
Mi	Middlesex
N	Nottingham
R	Renfrew
S	Selkirk
St	Stafford
Su	Surrey
W	Warwick

A	Antrim	Lo	Londonderry
K	King's	R	Roscommon
Ki	Kildare	S	Sligo
L	Limerick	W	Waterford

0   miles   50
0   80
kilometres

Figure 1.2 Migration in the British Isles as at 1881, showing the counties of absorption and dispersion, according to Ravenstein, 1885 (Source: based on Ravenstein, 1885, Map 6, p.184)

Schema C: Ravenstein's 'laws of migration'

1 The majority of migrants go only a short distance.

2 Migration proceeds step by step.

3 Migrants going long distances generally go to one of the great centres of commerce or industry.

4 Every migratory current has a counter-current.

5 Natives of towns are less migratory than those of rural districts.

6 Females are more migratory than males within the county of their birth, but males more frequently venture beyond.

7 Most migrants are adults: families rarely migrate.

8 Large towns grow more by migration than by natural increase.

9 Migration increases as industries develop and transport improves.

10 The major direction of migration is from the rural areas to towns.

11 The major causes of migration are economic.

Source: devised by W.T.R. Pryce, based on Ravenstein (1885)

Ravenstein confirmed that the sustained impact of migration was to be found everywhere throughout the British Isles in the 1870s. Except for mining and quarrying communities, it was the countryside that now constituted the 'sending areas'. Conversely, the new industrial communities of northern and midland England, central Scotland, Northern Ireland and parts of north Wales, together with the capital cities of London, Dublin and Edinburgh, had become the 'reception areas' (Figure 1.2) (Law, 1967; Lawton, 1968; Lawton and Pooley, 1992, pp.117–37).

Ravenstein's first and second 'laws' (Schema C again) have been confirmed frequently by subsequent investigators, notably by Redford (1926), another pioneer in migration research whose findings, dealing with overall trends between 1800 and 1850, were based on a variety of other sources, including Poor Law records. The tens of thousands of individual step-by-step moves eventually generated, as Ravenstein had put it, 'a universal shifting or displacement of the population' that culminated in a 'series of wave-like motions', extending throughout all the countries and regions of the British Isles, reaching even the remotest of areas (Figure 1.3). Ravenstein was amongst the first to articulate the essential differences between *gross migration* and *net migration* implied in his recognition of 'compensating counter currents' (Law 4 in Schema C; Schema A, p.5).

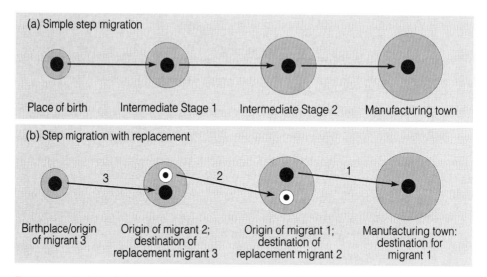

(a) Simple step migration

Place of birth   Intermediate Stage 1   Intermediate Stage 2   Manufacturing town

(b) Step migration with replacement

Birthplace/origin   Origin of migrant 2;   Origin of migrant 1;   Manufacturing town:
of migrant 3   destination of   destination of   destination for
    replacement migrant 3   replacement migrant 2   migrant 1

Figure 1.3 Models of simple step migration and step migration with replacement (Source: Pryce, 1982, p.73)

Although Ravenstein's 'laws' stem from the specific transport conditions of the late nineteenth century – when, for example, the impact of the railways was far less widespread than in the twentieth century – they do offer us a number of useful insights. Moreover, while his individual 'laws' can be adopted as hypotheses for testing at the community level, they also provide a meaningful framework for the interpretation of findings. But his 1885 findings (Ravenstein, 1885) do need to be supplemented by his later work on movements overseas (Ravenstein, 1889), and his ideas need to be seen in the context of more recent research (section 4 below; Jackson and Moch, 1989; Holmes, 1991).

3.2   PUSH–PULL EXPLANATIONS

The so-called *push–pull* models, which deal with movements in terms of the relative attractive-ness of different locations, are, perhaps, the most basic of all explanations. Such interpretations can relate to multi-centre situations as well as one-to-one centre movements (Herberle, 1938; Bogue, 1969).

Push–pull forces can be regarded as falling into two broad categories: (1) those relating to changes in the surrounding social environment or milieu; and (2) those relating to changes in individual motivation (Schema D).

Schema D: Push and pull factors

Push factors

1   Decline or exhaustion of a natural resource and/or the market demand for it.

2   Loss of employment.

3   Oppressive treatment on religious, ethnic or political grounds.

4   Quarrels, disputes (family, social, political, religious) and alienation from a community.

5   Lack of opportunities for personal development.

6   Effects of natural disasters.

Pull factors

1   Opportunities for employment, training, education.

2   Higher standards of living.

3   Personal dependency – for example, migration of married couples; movements of dependants linked to those of the principal wage earner.

4   Lure of new or different activities – cultural, intellectual, recreational.

Source: devised by W.T.R. Pryce, based on Bogue, 1969, pp.753–4

Amongst the criticisms of push–pull models are the facts that:

o   It is often difficult to differentiate between the forces involved – that is, to establish exactly where the 'push' effects actually end and where the 'pulls' begin.

o   These types of explanation tend to create a 'snap-shot' view of events – that is, migration is seen as a once-only phenomenon, rather than as a continuing and dynamic process.

Nevertheless, as we shall see in this book, in dealing with both internal migration as well as longer-distance movements involving emigration and immigration, researchers have relied, and have continued to rely, on push–pull explanations.

_____ **EXERCISE 1.3** _____

Identify any *two* specific migrations made by yourself, a relative, an ancestor, or a member of some other family that you are studying.

Write down (on photocopies of the form below) when each of these occurred (an approximate date will do) and the nature of each move (e.g. new job, marriage, unemploy-ment, promotion, to 'escape' something or other).

Evaluate the relative importance of the push and pull factors on a scale of between 1 and 10 points (e.g. 7 points for push, 3 for pull factors), both adding up to the total of 10.

Migration no.: _____

From: _____ To: _____

Date: _____

Nature of movement: _____

Evaluation of migration factors (insert points): Push factors [ ] Pull factors [ ]

Comments _____

Comment p.218.

3.3 THE GRAVITY MODEL

The *gravity model* has been widely used, especially by geographers, to account for many different types of flow pattern across territorial space, including migration. This encompasses some of the features of push–pull models as well as aspects of the intervening opportunities model introduced below.

Essentially, the gravity model postulates that migration between any two places is linked positively to population size and inversely related to the distance between these locations. Thus, the larger the cities or regions involved, the greater will be the number of interactions: these encourage population exchanges, giving rise to significant migration flows. But the greater the distance between these centres, the higher the transport costs – so reducing the volume of movements. Geographers refer to these latter effects as due to the 'friction of distance'; and the falling off of interactions between centres, as distance between them increases, as reflecting 'distance decay' considerations. The original gravity model is generally attributed to Zipf (1946) whose formulation was based on Newton's famous gravity equation encompassing notions of gravitational force, mass and distance. Modified and adapted on numerous occasions, the gravity model does provide a means of explaining migration in quantitative terms, despite suffering from some methodological problems. The underlying ideas continue to have some validity for interpretative work in family and community history. (For further information see Taylor, 1975; White and Woods, 1980, pp.39–40; Johnston *et al.*, 1986, pp.185–6.)

3.4 INTERVENING OPPORTUNITIES AND OBSTACLES

Dissatisfaction with the more ambiguous aspects of push–pull explanations and the gravity model has led to attempts to explore more realistic alternative approaches. These have included increased emphases on the ways in which potential migrants respond to real-life opportunities and/or obstacles to movement. Stouffer (1940), in his *intervening opportunities model*, drew on the fact that individuals weigh the relative costs and the more immediate benefits of a short-distance move against the potentially greater rewards from a longer-distance one. Hence, the migration process is seen as occurring in a series of steps (i.e. opportunities) during the life of an individual – not dissimilar, in many respects, to the first and second of Ravenstein's 'laws' (Schema C, p.11).

Lee (1969) took the opposite line, emphasizing the barriers to movement. His *intervening obstacles model* draws attention to economic difficulties (e.g. the cost of moving house, travel expenses), political barriers (e.g. an oppressive regime at likely destinations) and cultural considerations (e.g. religious, social class, linguistic or ethnic factors might make it hard to 'fit in'). Successful migrants, capable of maximizing opportunities, find such obstacles to be minimal and easily overcome. Migrations that can be interpreted in terms of 'obstacles' or 'opportunities' include, for example, the step-wise and selective movement of metallurgical workers and their families from Wales to Northumberland and Durham (Gwynne and Sill, 1976); and the emigration of Hermann Schulze and his family from Germany, to settle in London, before later moving on to settle in Sussex (outlined in Chapter 3, section 1).

Some factors are temporary, or intermittent, others are constant; some may strongly influence individuals or families at particular stages of their lives (see Lewis, 1982, p.101). Though easy to express in theoretical terms, the incidence of all these factors is notoriously difficult to test empirically. Nevertheless, these ideas do need to be kept in mind in any research that seeks to explore migration processes. Schema E provides a useful set of guidelines that can be adopted for identifying appropriate migration data or for arranging and categorizing data already collected.

Schema E: Factors to be considered when researching migration

1   Factors associated with the area of origin.

2   Factors associated with the area of destination.

3   Intervening obstacles.

4   Intervening opportunities.

5   Personal factors.

3.5   CHAIN MIGRATION

Chain migration is linked closely to the identification of opportunities but in a context that involves successive and multi-phased movements, often over considerable distances. The initial (or primary) movers (usually young adult men) constitute the first 'pioneers' who, having decided to seek better opportunities, find, and eventually settle, at a new location. Messages are then sent back to the home area with information on the new conditions together with details of travel arrangements and costs, etc. After due evaluation of the circumstances the migrant is joined by secondary migrants – spouse, children, parents, siblings, cousins, friends or former neighbours in the home area. The interactive nature of this feedback loop generates further migration.

Clearly, such a system is fuelled by personal information. In consequence, chain migration tends to achieve maximum development in specific families and kinship groups. The information that sustains interest in further movements can be transmitted in any media, usually by letter or information relayed by primary migrants on return visits home. Although not necessarily operating in isolation, chain migration thus tends to develop in particular circumstances and has distinctive features (Schema F).

Schema F: Distinctive features of chain migration

1   Movements tend to be long-distance, often because there are no other sources of detailed information other than personal contact.

2   Migration tends to be channelled to just one or two destinations (e.g. particular streets within a city) from specific sending areas and, over time, strong links are built up. In these areas migrants are most likely to find people with similar origins who share their own particular world view and cultural background.

3 Remittances sent back home by successful migrants can raise local living standards, place increased status on consumer goods and generate enheightened notions of the 'good life' that the successful migrant now enjoys – giving rise, in due course, to further migration.

4 Once the chain migration system has become established, it can engender significant culture modifications – for example, the view that to succeed it is essential to emigrate. In consequence, people can become caught up in self-perpetuating movements that might not be appropriate for them as individuals.

5 Potential destinations for later secondary migrants tend to be restricted to those on which favourable reports have been received.

Several of the examples discussed in later chapters make explicit reference to the significance of chain migration – especially for understanding communities in which large proportions of the population have family links and ancestors born overseas. Before the development of mass communications, no doubt it was through letters, oral messages and chain migration that distinctive movements occurred between the various regions and countries of Britain and Ireland – particularly in the later nineteenth century and during the initial processes of industrialization and urbanization. Chain migration in this context awaits further investigation.

3.6 LIFE-CYCLE STAGE AND MIGRATION

The models discussed so far can be seen as refinements of Ravenstein's 'laws' or as summaries of logically connected factors. They do not, however, offer much guidance as to *when* migration might occur. This is where personal factors linked to an individual's stage in the life cycle may play a crucial, sometimes a determining, role (see Hareven, 1991; Elliott, 1990). In reality, life-cycle factors sometimes seem to override external economic and cultural factors. For instance, migrants like the 19-year-old Joseph Hartley (Volume 1, Chapter 2, section 3) emigrated to the USA in 1858, a year in which the American economy was depressed. Was the need to leave the family 'nest' the reason for his departure?

Changes of house within growing nineteenth-century towns seem to correlate strongly with particular stages in the individual's life cycle. But, as R.J. Dennis (1972) has shown, this was but one of a number of factors affecting *intra*-urban movements. In his study of mid-nineteenth century Huddersfield, Dennis observed:

More moves were made over very short distances, for purely economic reasons, as families rented the most expensive accommodation they could afford at any moment, and moved frequently, following unpredictable fluctuations in their income. Over ninety per cent of occupiers rented their dwellings privately, with no security of tenure. The addition of forced moves, owing to eviction or changing circumstances, to life-cycle moves probably generated higher rates of intra-urban mobility than we find nowadays, especially among the poor. The concentration of the working class in private tenancies meant that the class as a whole was more mobile than the minority of middle-class owner-occupiers, whose mobility was subject to the same constraints as it is today.

(Dennis, 1972, p.230, emphasis added)

Dennis traced individuals from one census to the next through the CEBs and he paid special attention to life-cycle considerations. His techniques have been used in more recent research on other urban communities – notably in Schofield's (1991) analysis of movements of the Irish within the town of Keighley, Yorkshire, between 1841 and 1881. These same approaches can be further adapted for research on inter-regional and international movements.

3.7   A SYSTEMS APPROACH TO THE MODELLING OF MIGRATION

It is clear that migration is a complex process that, over time, is related to many different aspects of life. Though beset with some practical difficulties for the individual researcher (see Jackson and Moch, 1989, p.32), systems and network theory can be regarded as valid attempts to encapsulate all the various considerations within a logically coherent framework.

Thus, Figure 1.4 illustrates how movements can be presented as a series of cause-and-effect loops. Within this particular system, there are two influential *domains* (or sub-systems) – the rural and the urban. Within the rural domain the family and village community function as the controls; in the urban system, residential and occupation structures imply similar constraints and opportunities.

Holderness (1971), though not taking an explicitly systems approach, does alert us to its potential. He notes that inheritance considerations, tenancy arrangements and leasehold agreements functioned as important controls on the migration of farmers in rural Yorkshire in the early nineteenth century. Similarly, retailers, craftsmen and professionals were tied to a specific locality by their clientele and the need to maintain 'good will'. In contrast, labourers and unskilled workers of either sex were much more mobile, as they had fewer local ties of a legal or economic

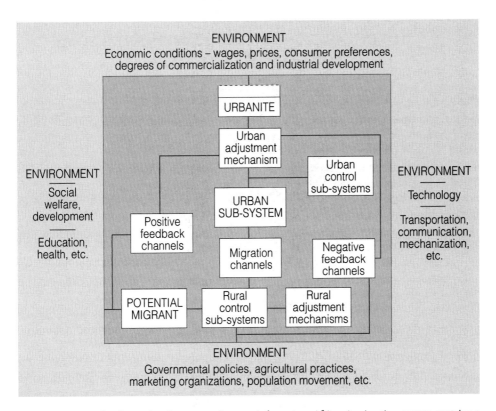

Figure 1.4   A rural–urban migration system in twentieth-century Africa. A migration system contains a number of different but interrelated considerations (shown in the boxes). Influences, which can flow in either direction, move along the interconnections (represented by the lines). The systems approach emphasizes interdependencies rather than one-way linear flows. The complete network of relationships and interactions is set within a distinctive external 'environment' or milieu which, itself, has been shaped by a number of all-enveloping influences – economic and technological factors, statutory and institutional policies – as well as by prevailing cultural attitudes and outlook. Clearly, an in-depth knowledge and understanding of the situation is essential before a systems network of this type can be drawn up to represent particular circumstances (Source: Mabogunje, 1970, p.3)

nature, but their movements were constrained by the Poor Law legislation that restricted settlement in a parish to those born there, married to someone born there, or, for example, to those who had worked in the parish for more than a year. Information flows, by letter or by word of mouth (e.g. seasonal harvest workers), as in chain migration, are essential channels of communication in the systems approach.

_____ *EXERCISE 1.4* _____

Review the various ways in which the systems network approach could aid the development of a project on migration:

1   List any adjustments you would make to the system shown in Figure 1.4.

2   Write down two advantages of applying systems analysis to projects in family and community history.

Answers/comments p.218.

4   MOVING OVER SEAS AND CONTINENTS: SOME FURTHER PERSPECTIVES

As we have seen already, the difference between migration and emigration is, in part, technical (Schema A, pp.5–6): a Mayo man moving to Manchester in 1850 was a migrant, whilst in 1950 he would have been classified as an emigrant! There is little difference, too, in the methods of analysis: push–pull, chain and step-wise movements are just as much features of *emigration* or *immigration* as of internal migration. The trauma arising from internal migration could be as great, possibly greater, than that of emigration. Thus, for example, the migration of the son of a Welsh monoglot farmer from the mountains of Merioneth to work in the coal mines of English-speaking Flintshire (see Chapter 4) probably involved a much greater change of life style than did the emigration of the young Joseph Hartley (featured in Volume 1, Chapter 2, section 3) from the quarries of Brighouse, in Yorkshire's West Riding, to the same work at Lockport, Upper New York State, where he was met by lots of other 'John Bhuls *[sic]*'.

So, often the theories developed for analysing internal migration can be applied to external movements. We can sometimes amplify them too, for looking at long-distance movements can highlight aspects which have not yet received the attention they deserve.

4.1   SUBJECTIVE EXPERIENCE AND MOTIVATION

Subjective and personal elements seldom surface in traditional migration theory. Certainly the attraction of the 'bright lights' of the city sometimes can be included among the 'pull' factors, but even then we hear little of the sheer excitement that migration – especially far-flung travel – can generate. Academic studies of migration tend to ignore these aspects. The following passage from a recent sketch of unofficial life styles within the former British Empire captures the feeling:

Think what the Empire could do for a fellow! It could take him gold-hunting in the Yukon, where the whores of Dawson City cheerfully awaited his custom, the melodies of Snake Hips Lulu and the bar-room piano rung out brassily over snowy Saturday nights, and there was at least the off-chance of making a fortune. It could take him to the bridge of a paddle-steamer chugging high up the Murray river, where the gum trees stood silent over the muddy waters, where if he wasn't careful the beer fizzed in the heat of the sun, where wallabies and aboriginals flitted away at his passing like shadows through the scrub. It could give him a flock of sheep in the far-away Falklands, where no patronizing landlord would ever bother him again, and he could build his own square stone house just as he liked it in the lee of the moors.

It could make him a planter in Ceylon, looking out from his verandah over the smiling hills where the girls in their bright saris gracefully plucked his profits in the sunshine. It could appoint him a Hooghly river pilot, and send him out immensely posh, in white gloves and gold-embroidered cap, to guide the steamships through the heat-glazed flats up-river to Calcutta. It could make him a newspaper editor in Hong Kong, or an Anglican dean in Belize, or mountain guide in New Zealand, or a dentist in Malta, or a financial advisor to the Sultan of Johore, or a tutor to the children of the Maharajah of Mysore, or an inspector of light-houses in the Persian Gulf, or a dam-builder in Nubia, or the keeper of a botanical garden in Jamaica, or an elephant trainer in Burma, or a Fijian magistrate, or a New South Wales jockey, or an engine-driver on the Canadian Pacific, or a photographer in Durban, or a draper in Singapore, or one of the Shakespearian actors, the Shakespeare–wallahs, who from time to time turned up with their wandering troupes in the paint-peeled, up-country halls of India.

Or it could make of him, very frequently, and happiest of all perhaps, one of the myriad bums of Empire, the loafers and beachcombers and itinerant philosophers, who roamed all the imperial frontiers, frequented every island strand, and turned up to shame the imperial hierarchy from Penang to Nootka Sound.

(Morris, 1982, p.205)

In spite of its imperialist, racist, sexist – and goodness knows what else – undertones, this impressionistic passage does highlight aspects of migration of central interest to historians of family and community that, often, are lost in the macro-economic models coined by researchers. What are these?

Personal choice   Migration – like marriage – is an intensely personal decision. Of course, family, social and economic factors play their part, but millions of men and women over the past two centuries have made the decision to leave their native land. Just how they got to be a quarryman in New York State, 'a dentist in Malta', or 'an inspector of light-houses in the Persian Gulf' only they can tell. Unravelling the histories and motivations that took them there is a worthwhile goal for the historian of the family.

Family traditions   Some families have a tradition of service overseas. Individuals or newly married couples may have been expected to spend part of their lives working abroad. Often, the decision to go overseas is taken at a particular stage in personal careers, or, again, at one of the distinctive stages in the family life cycle. Others may have spent much of their working lives abroad, returning for the occasional extended holiday or furlough, before finally coming back to retire at 'home'. Such traditions have continued in some families over several generations with the pattern of many comings and goings taken for granted as an integral part of their way of life. This has been particularly true of families whose members may have been military personnel, missionaries, educationalists or, for example in India, civil servants and administrators; and, increasingly from the mid-twentieth century, business men and women. Their comings and goings over the decades add up to a regular series of cyclical movements as semi-permanent emigrants with temporary sojourns at different destinations.

Whilst generated initially by administrative or business considerations, or by personal commitment, many of these moves have been shaped by processes inherent to chain migration – but in the reverse direction to those discussed in section 3.5 above.

Adventure   Another element frequently ignored in research studies, as already noted, is the sheer excitement of it – for some people! Studies of emigration often focus on the uprooting, the 'perils' of the voyage, the homesickness, the discrimination, swindling, and the sense of failure. But what about the sense of adventure many must have felt when they finally decided to make the break? This is reflected in emigrant letters (see Volume 1, Chapter 2, section 3; also analyses such as Erickson, 1972; Richards, 1991), or the short stories of Somerset Maugham, Jack London, or the *Boys' Own Paper.* Flora Thompson, too, conveys it in her novel *From Lark Rise to Candleford* in the context of the 1880s where the soldiers with homes in the hamlet were looked on as 'young adventurers who had enlisted as the only way of seeing the world before they settled down to marriage and the plough tail' (Thompson, 1968, p.283).

If you yourself have migrated from your native land, or are familiar with people who have, what role would you say was played by this 'sense' of adventure?

WHAT'S MISSING?

As you will have noticed, studies emphasizing these subjective aspects mostly draw on qualitative and personal sources rather than on the aggregate and quantitative analyses typical in many of the theories discussed earlier. It is illuminating to compare these more personal studies with the predominantly negative impression of migration in much existing academic research where 'rarely is migration seen as desirable [or] described in constructive, positive terms' (Kleiner *et al.*, 1986, p.306). By contrast, we often find *positive* views in the biographies, letters or reminiscences where migration is often presented as a 'success story' for the individuals and their families.

The insights we get from such sources into people's values, experiences and motivations – the subjective and experiential aspects – are beginning to be treated more seriously in migration studies (e.g. Jackson and Moch, 1989; Kleiner *et al.*, 1986; Pooley and Whyte, 1991). But these presentations, too, may give less than a full picture: the migrants themselves may not be fully aware of the economic and social pressures influencing their decisions, or may be reinterpreting their own experiences in hindsight (on memory processes see Volume 1, Chapter 4, section 3). *Published* migrant letters, moreover, were sometimes plainly propagandist (see Richards, 1991). So, before moving on to the specific case studies below and in later chapters, let us pause to put the personal examples into a wider context, to complement subjective accounts by some attention to general patterns.

4.2 NUMBERS AND MAJOR EMIGRATION ROUTES

During the nineteenth and early twentieth centuries, as new lands were opened up overseas, all the countries of the British Isles continued to lose population by emigration. Although the first peak in the 1850s may have been due to the passage of Ireland's rural exodus through United Kingdom ports, the losses were significant throughout the period and emigration continued to increase right up to the start of the First World War (Jackson and Timmins, 1989, p.140).

In dealing with emigration it is important not to lose sight of the world dimension. Millions left their homelands for the Americas, South Africa, Australia and New Zealand – initially from the British Isles and Germany, but later from the Mediterranean countries and Eastern Europe. But substantial population movements occurred, also, from Africa during the slave trade, from the Indian sub-continent, and also *within* countries now regarded as separate nation states (the USA, for example, or China). Clearly, all the movements of emigrant Britons and Europeans were caught up in a world system of population transfers (Figure 1.5 covers some of these).

From a British or from an Irish point of view, we can divide international migration into three periods: (1) 1815–1914; (2) 1919–39; (3) 1945 to the present.

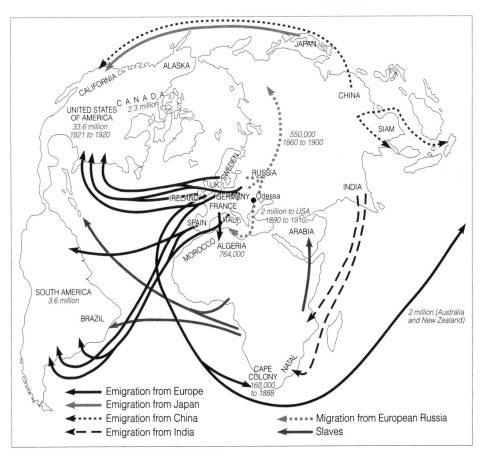

Figure 1.5   Major world population transfers, 1821–1920 (Source: Barraclough, 1978, Figure 2, p.209)

OUT OF EUROPE, 1815–1914

The period from 1815 to 1914 is dominated by the exodus from Europe. Of an estimated 90.5 million emigrants worldwide, some 52.5 million left Europe for countries overseas, principally the Americas, Australasia, South and East Africa. A further 10 million moved from European Russia to Siberia and Central Asia. Never before, nor since, in recorded history have so many people 'voluntarily' left their native countries. Some 16.4 million emigrated from the United Kingdom: to the USA (11 million), Canada (2.55 million), Australia and New Zealand (2 million) and South Africa (0.85 million). All these figures are approximate and do not allow for return or re-emigration (see Segal and Marston, 1989, p.37; Baines, 1991, pp.7–11; also, for further information, Porter, 1991, *Atlas of British overseas expansion*).

Certain features deserve further comment. First, of the 16 million who left the United Kingdom (which, at that time, of course, included Ireland, both north and south), a disproportionate number left from Ireland (4 million). Second, the British Empire took only about one-third. The USA dominated the picture, as it did for European migrants generally. Of Europeans migrating overseas in this period, 33.7 out of 52.5 million left for the USA and Canada. It is difficult to distinguish these two destinations as there was an open border between the two countries. Many crossed it, principally from Canada to the USA by a form of step-wise migration. Also, there was re-migration from the USA, especially from the north-east states to emergent countries where land grants were available – as in Latin America, especially Brazil and Argentina.

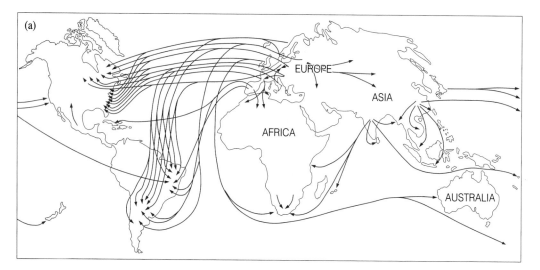

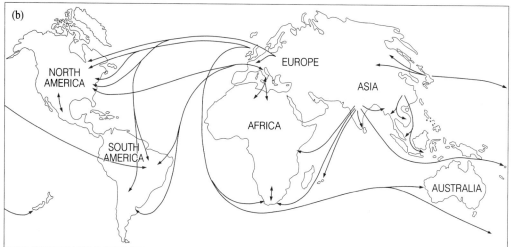

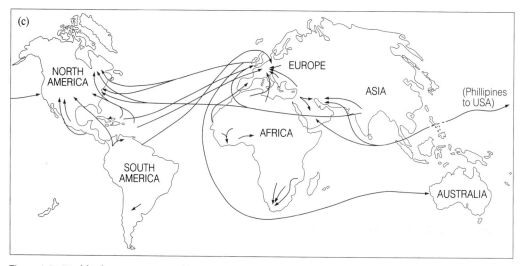

Figure 1.6   World voluntary migration: (a) 1815–1914; (b) 1919–39; (c) 1945–80. These are broad trends only, but the term 'voluntary' can sometimes be problematic (Source: based on Segal and Marston, 1989, pp.37–9)

THE SLOW-DOWN, 1919–39

The amount of emigration declined steeply in the inter-war years. The USA led the way in 1924 in legally restricting immigration: most countries soon followed. Economic depression also inhibited international migration. There were still, however, some important migrant groups – for example, Jews fleeing Nazi persecution (De Zayas, 1988).

'GUESTWORKERS, BRAIN DRAINS AND ILLEGAL IMMIGRANTS', 1945–90

Many of the movements across frontiers since the Second World War have been from the so-called 'less developed' to the 'developed' countries. As far as Britain is concerned, this resulted in the arrival here of considerable numbers from the former British imperial territories until the brakes were applied in 1962 (for some examples and discussion see Chapter 3, section 3). The post-war period has also witnessed a resurgence of Irish emigration to Britain. (For a bird's eye view of the situation in the 1980s see Pope, 1989, p.140; also, for questions that await exploration, see Holmes, 1991).

THE LONG VIEW

Figure 1.6 outlines some major directions emigrants have taken since 1815. Some paths are well trodden throughout the entire period – from Europe to North America, for instance. Others, dominant in the nineteenth century (from Europe to the colonies of the European powers, principally in the New World and North Africa) (Figure 1.6a) have witnessed a counterflow since the Second World War (Figure 1.6c).

The maps fail to pick up the probably numerically modest, though socially and economically significant, two-stage migrants, such as the migrants from India to East Africa in the nineteenth or twentieth centuries, whose descendants travelled subsequently to Britain in the late twentieth century, or those whose forebears were taken from West Africa to the West Indies *c.*1600–1800 and who later moved to Britain after 1945.

These maps, also, cover only *voluntary* migration. We must also remember forced or pressurized movement – for example, the slave trade, mainly from West Africa to the Americas (see Inikori *et al.*, 1982). Think, too, of convicts transported to Australia, internal and external migrants fleeing famine conditions in Ireland or Highland clearances in Scotland, Jews driven out by *pogroms* in Russia, paupers sent out to the colonies, refugees from war and persecution (Marrus and Bramwell, 1988). Further examples of involuntary movements – those where, at the least, there were strong pressures encouraging migration – occur in the case studies later in this volume (Chapters 3 and 8). Then there are also the child migrants shipped to North America or Australia, ostensibly as 'orphans' for new opportunities abroad, but in practice only too often without the knowledge of their families and destined for a life as cheap labourers. About 80,000 children were sent to Canada between 1868 and 1925, for instance (only one-third of them orphans), while children were being shipped to Australia by Barnardo's and others as late as 1967 (see Wagner, 1982; Parr, 1980; Bean and Melville, 1989; Constantine, 1991, p.69 ff.; for reports in 1993 about the children earlier shipped to Australia, and recent renewed family contacts through The Child Migrants Trust, see, for example, *The Independent*, 13 July 1993).

4.3   TWO CASE HISTORIES

ENGLISH TEXTILE WORKERS IN NORWAY IN THE MID-NINETEENTH CENTURY

A recent study argued that 'the transfer of operative and managerial skills were a crucial part of the diffusion of industrialization from Britain' (Bruland, 1989, p.110). This was partly accomplished by skilled workers going out to countries importing British machinery either to operate it or to instruct in its use. Bruland found, for example, that every Norwegian textile firm, bar one, in the period 1813–70 employed British workers. Some were 'mechanics who came for short periods (perhaps 2–4 months) in order to set up machinery, or to modify or repair it'; others were operatives; and, most important of all, there were 'supervisors of various types'. Some of the workers were closely related.

For instance, in March 1850 a weaving master named Joseph Kingston appeared in the books of the Hjula Weaving Company at Christiania (Oslo), as, in July of that year, did his son John (on wages half those of his father), whilst in October, his daughter Emma arrived (Bruland, 1989, pp.114–15). It is difficult, given the available records (tax lists, business correspondence, and censuses) to find out precisely how long any of these workers stayed in Norway. The modal period seems to have been 1–2 years, with a sharp fall thereafter.

A man from the village of Birstall, in the West Riding of Yorkshire, stayed longer, for five years (1863–69). George Richardson was described as 'a young man of first class abilities … teetotal and most steady'. Although primarily a weaver, he was 'also a good mechanic and [could] warp, size and do all the duties of a power-loom overlooker' (Bruland, 1989, p.121).

Mention of Richardson as a teetotaller is interesting because a number of workers were dismissed for their drunkenness. One begins to wonder, then, if these expatriate artisans were the best, or the worst, that Britain could offer. Did the emigrant who became an engine driver in India go because he had failed to get a job with the London, Midland and Scottish Railway? Had the jockey in New South Wales not found employment with Lord Derby? Length of stay does not help answer this question: short stays could indicate a short-term job well done, a worker dismissed for drunkenness, or no great enthusiasm for living and working in Norway. On the other hand, the Hjula enterprise was never without British workers in the entire period from 1849 to 1875, suggesting that, on the whole, they must have given satisfaction.

QUESTION FOR RESEARCH

Is it possible to do other studies like Bruland's?

Obviously, it is difficult, if not impossible, to access records overseas. One may, however, find interesting information in business archives in this country: for example, letters sent to machinery manufacturers, spelling out the types of people required by their overseas customers. Once individuals are located, that old standby, the CEB, could yield further information – at least for the second half of the nineteenth century.

'OPENINGS … FOR OUR SUPER ABUNDANT FEMALES'

Have you ever heard of the Female Middle Class Emigration Society (FMCES)? This operated from 1862 to 1882 and its principal function was to find work for English governesses abroad. It did so by providing both loans to cover the costs of the voyage and contacts on arrival. Because loans, not grants, were provided (governesses spurned the paid passages available to working-class emigrants), considerable correspondence has survived. Drawing on these records, Clarke (1985) has written a fascinating account of the women helped by the Society.

Again, we are dealing with small numbers from a group that was atypical. Nevertheless, these letters do provide insights into emigrant life that, no doubt, were experienced by many others. No doubt, too, internal migrants within the British Isles met with similar problems.

Why go?   What could you do if, as a woman, you were 'educated and genteel, but unmarried and unemployed' in late nineteenth-century Britain (Clarke, 1985, p.1)? You would not accept lowly work as a shop assistant or a servant. You did not want to remain an 'unpaid household drudge' living with your own family or with relatives or friends. Newly settled countries overseas beckoned, not least because, usually, they contained a surplus of men. So, despite off-putting official reports from the colonies, these women set out to try their luck as nurses and missionaries, as well as governesses.

The voyage out The voyage to Australia and New Zealand by sailing ship rarely took less than three months and often took much longer. It involved climate changes – from the intense and humid heat at the Equator to the icy gales and storms of the southern ocean. Invariably, travel across the ocean was 'uncomfortable, cramped, regimented and tedious; the food was dreary and monotonous … and severe sea sickness and serious epidemic diseases were common' (Clarke, 1985, p.24).

Despite the claims of shipping lines (Figure 1.7), such would be the prevailing impression of *all* passages from Britain at this time. And, yet, a number of the potential governesses wrote back to the FMCES saying how much they had enjoyed the voyage. There were comments on the

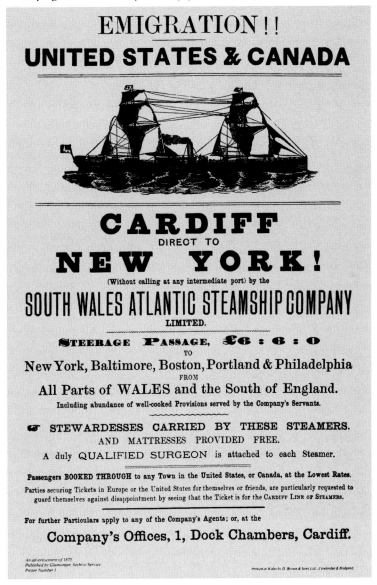

Figure 1.7 Shipping line advertisement, 1875 (Source: Glamorgan Archive Service, Poster No .1)

kindness of captains and crews: '... only a moderate amount of rough weather, pleasant travelling companions ...'; '... my fellow passengers and the captain were all so kind and attentive that the time seemed to pass quite quickly ...'; '... a pleasant voyage, although a slow one. I ... enjoyed it greatly, indeed I was almost sorry when we came to land' (Clarke, 1985, pp.25–6).

Of course, this is but one side of the picture. Others were horrified by their fellow passengers who were travelling steerage. Indeed, if there was one complaint which ran throughout all these letters it was that, by travelling Second Class, rather than First, the women sponsored by the FMCES had too much contact with the lower classes!

The reception   A pioneer group of governesses (six in all) arrived in Sydney, Australia, on 20 September 1861. Their reception was typical of subsequent experiences. The Bishop of Sydney and his wife were not present to welcome them as they had been led to expect. All but one refused to accept the accommodation in the special Governesses' and Servants' Home found for them by the Dean of Sydney, regarding it as 'more suited to servants than to governesses'; three, upon their arrival, went to their friends; one married a fellow passenger. Elements common to much emigrant experience can be noted here: disappointment at not being met by the people one expected; going off to stay with family friends (indicating the importance of networks); and the culture shock of being offered unacceptable accommodation.

Settling in   The governesses sent out by the FMCES did not, on the whole, find appropriate jobs as easy to come by as they had hoped. Their letters mention their fears of destitution after waiting several weeks for an appointment, and that 'salaries are not so high now as they were and many of these salaries in the Bush are never realized – there seem to be few situations and those persons, wishing to employ, besieged by applicants' (Clarke, 1985, p.66).

The main purpose of these women in writing to the FMCES was to repay loans or to explain why, for the moment, loans could not be repaid. However, despite personal difficulties, and sacrifices, the bulk of the loans were repaid, suggesting either some eventual success in securing a position or a strong sense of obligation on the part of the recipients.

This brief account of some aspects of emigrant experience neglects – even from the accounts received by the FMCES – much that was exciting, dangerous and colourful. It is these aspects of the letters that often are the most gripping. Here we have highlighted what happened to just a few governesses, but these experiences do seem to bear out those of much larger numbers of emigrants. Other caches of documents and the testimonies of living persons could be utilized in a similar way.

SUBJECTIVE AND OBJECTIVE

Neither of these case studies is complete. The first is strong on the official sources – but we would like to know more about the personal memories of individual migrants. The second uses letters to convey the personal experiences of individuals – but only considers briefly the social and economic situation which lay behind their decisions (for further references on this see Constantine, 1991, pp.68, 79). No one study can cover everything, but what does come through in these examples – as in those later in this volume – is that in the complexities of any given case both subjective *and* objective factors will be at play.

Indeed, just about all the theories considered in section 3 of this chapter could be reassessed and extended by bringing to bear that same dialectic between the subjective and the objective, the more personal and the more general. A *complete* analysis may be impossible within a single project, and in practice you will need to focus on particular aspects. But ultimately, whatever your chosen focus, bear in mind the wider view that:

We cannot fully understand the migration phenomena by depending on the subjective realities of individual migrants because individuals are not fully cognizant of their situations. Similarly, [we] cannot depend on the objective realities of the situation because many of these realities do not enter into the decision-making process at all, even though they may have effects on the migration experiences. A comprehensive approach that includes the subjective and objective realities provides us with a more perceptive understanding of migration.

(Kleiner *et al.*, 1986, p.316)

5   CONCLUSION

We hope that this chapter has encouraged you to do some research on migrants and the processes involved in migration in all its forms. All families and all communities have experienced this phenomenon. Much is already known but much more is still to be learned. What, then, can you do?

First, in section 2 we reviewed some key sources. The CEBs may well take pride of place for studies of movements within our own islands. But, in addition, the British Parliamentary Papers, which contain numerous reports, especially on emigration, should not be neglected. You should seek out letters and other family papers. Newspapers, too, often covered these topics, as they still do. Poor Law papers, electoral registers, and rate books can all be pressed into service. Longitudinal studies, though demanding on time and resources, can be undertaken (Robin, 1980).

For work on recent migration you could examine the possibilities of oral history. There are collections of sound recordings to be analysed (see Chapter 3, section 3); the techniques are not too difficult to acquire and apply, whilst, in contrast to relying solely on statistical sources, the chances of getting behind the anonymity of people on the move are very high. (For more on sources in general, see Volume 4; also, the useful, if somewhat dated, suggestions in Welch, 1971).

Secondly, we have tried to equip you with a variety of theories and explanations to aid you in conceptualizing, and for the investigation and presention of your findings. Ravenstein's celebrated 'laws' occupy an honoured place. But you should also consider insights and ideas from the other approaches dealt with in sections 3 and 4 above – on chain migration, for example – together with the useful categories and questions listed in Schemas B, D, E and F above (for further ideas see, also, Zolberg, 1989).

We recognize the wide scope and the length of this chapter, but this has been essential to provide a meaningful treatment of the key themes surrounding staying and moving, out-migration and emigration, in-migration and immigration. This opening chapter offers an agenda for aspirant researchers in family and community history, a framework that is fleshed out by the contrasts evident in the case studies presented elsewhere in this volume. Through exploring ways in which migration touches and involves the lives of individuals, and embraces families and groups, we are moving from a primary focus on movements within individual families towards a concern with the migration histories of communities and society in general.

REFERENCES AND FURTHER READING

Note: entries marked with an asterisk are suggestions for further reading.

Baines, D. (1978) 'Birthplace statistics and the analysis of internal migration', in Lawton (1978).

Baines, D. (1991) *Emigration from Europe, 1815–1930*, Basingstoke and London, Macmillan.*

Barraclough, G. (ed.) (1978) *The Times atlas of world history*, London, Times Books.

Bean, P. and Melville, J. (1989) *Lost children of the Empire*, London, Unwin Hyman.

Bogue, D.J. (1969) *The principles of demography*, London, John Wiley.

Bruland, K. (1989) *British technology and European industrialization*, Cambridge, Cambridge University Press.

Buckatzsch, E.J. (1949) 'Places of origin of a group of immigrants *[sic]* into Sheffield, 1624–1799', *Economic History Review*, Second Series, 1, pp.303–6.

Clarke, P. (1985) *The governess: letters from the colonies*, London, Hutchinson.

Collins, B. and Pryce, W.T.R. (1993) 'Census returns in England, Ireland, Scotland and Wales', audio-cassette 2A in Braham, P. (ed.) *Using the past: audio-cassettes on sources and methods for family and community historians*, Milton Keynes, The Open University.*

Constantine, S. (1991) 'Empire migration and social reform 1880–1950', in Pooley and Whyte (1991).

Dennis, R.J. (1972) 'Intercensal mobility in a Victorian city', *Transactions, Institute of British Geographers*, 2, pp.349–63.

Dewdney, J.C. (1981) *The British census*, Norwich, Geo Books (Concepts and Techniques in Modern Geography No. 29).

De Zayas, A.M. (1988) 'A historical survey of twentieth century expulsions', in Marrus and Bramwell (1988).

Drake, M. (ed.) (1994) *Time, family and community: perspectives on family and community history*, Oxford, Blackwell in association with The Open University (Course Reader).

Elliott, B. (1990) 'Biography, family history and the analysis of social change', in Kendrick, S., Straw, P. and McCrone, D. (eds) *Interpreting the past, understanding the present*, Basingstoke and London, Macmillan (for the British Sociological Association). Reprinted in Drake (1994).*

Erickson, C. (1972) *Invisible immigrants: the adaption of English and Scottish immigrants in nineteenth century America*, London, Weidenfeld and Nicolson.

Gibson, J. and Rogers, C. (1993) *Electoral registers since 1832; and burgess rolls*, Birmingham, Federation of Family History Societies.

Grigg, D.B. (1977) 'E.G. Ravenstein and the "laws of migration"', *Journal of Historical Geography*, 3, pp.41–54. Reprinted in Drake (1994).*

Gwynne, T. and Sill, M. (1976) 'Census enumeration books: a study of mid-nineteenth *[sic]* immigration', *Local Historian*, 12, pp.74–9.

Hareven, T.K. (1991) 'The history of the family and complexity of social change', *American Historical Review*, 96, pp.95–124. Reprinted in Drake (1994) (abridged under the title 'Recent research on the history of the family').*

Herberle, R. (1938) 'The causes of rural-urban migration: a survey of German theories', *American Journal of Sociology*, 42, pp.932–50.

Higgs, E. (1989) *Making sense of the census: the manuscript returns for England and Wales, 1801–1901*, London, HMSO.*

Holderness, B.A. (1971) 'Personal mobility in some rural parishes of Yorkshire 1777–1822', *Yorkshire Archaeological Journal*, 42, pp.444–54. (Editor's note: there is a printer's error in the title of this paper: the date was printed as 1822 instead of 1812.)

Holmes, C. (1991) 'Historians and immigration', in Pooley and Whyte (1991). Reprinted in Drake (1994).*

Inikori, J.E. (ed.) (1982) *Forced migration: the impact of the export slave trade on African societies*, London, Hutchinson University Library.

Interdepartmental Committee on Social and Economic Research (1951) *Guides to official sources, no. 2: census reports of Great Britain 1801–1931*, London, HMSO.

Jackson, J.H. and Moch, L.P. (1989) 'Migration and the social history of modern Europe', *Historical Methods*, 22, pp.27–36. Reprinted in Drake (1994).*

Jackson, S. and Timmins, G. (1989) 'Demographic changes, 1701–1981', in Pope (1989).

Johnston, R.J., Gregory, D. and Smith, D.M. (eds) (1986) *The dictionary of human geography*, 2nd edn, Oxford, Blackwell.

Kleiner, R.J., Sørensen, T., Dalgard, O.S., Torbjørn, M. and Drews, D. (1986) 'International migration and internal migration: a comprehensive theoretical approach', in Glazier, I.A. and De Rosa, L. (eds) *Migration across time and nations: population mobility in historical contexts*, New York, Holmes and Meier.

Law, C.M. (1967) 'The growth of urban population in England and Wales, 1801–1911', *Transactions, Institute of British Geographers*, 15, pp.125–44.

Lawton, R. (1968) 'Population changes in England and Wales in the later-nineteenth century: an analysis of trends by registration districts', *Transactions, Institute of British Geographers*, 44, pp.55–74.

Lawton, R. (ed.) (1978) *The census and social structure: an interpretative guide to the nineteenth-century censuses for England and Wales*, London, Frank Cass.

Lawton, R. and Pooley, C.G. (1992) *Britain 1740–1950: an historical geography*, London, Edward Arnold.

Lee, E. (1969) 'A theory of migration', in Jackson, J.A. (ed.) *Migration*, Cambridge, Cambridge University Press.

Lewis, G.J. (1982) *Human migration: a geographical perspective*, London, Croom Helm.*

Lockhart, D.G. (1980) 'Sources for studies of migration to estate villages in north-east Scotland, 1750–1850', *Local Historian*, 14, pp.35–43.

Lockhart, D.G. (1986) 'Migration to planned villages in Scotland between 1725 and 1850', *Scottish Geographical Magazine*, 102, pp.165–80.

Lockhart, D.G. (1989) 'Migration to planned villages in north-east Scotland', in Smith, J.S. and Stevenson, D. (eds) *Fermfolk and fisherfolk*, Aberdeen, Aberdeen University Press.

Mabogunje, A.L. (1970) 'Systems approach to a theory of rural–urban migration', *Geographical Analysis*, 2, pp.1–18.

Mageean, D. (1982) 'Principal themes in migration studies', in Open University (1982).

Marrus, M.R. and Bramwell, A.C. (eds) (1988) *Refugees in the age of total war*, London, Unwin Hyman.

Millard, J. (1982) 'A new approach to the study of marriage horizons', *Local Population Studies,* 28, pp.10–31. Reprinted in Drake, M. (ed.) *Population studies from parish registers*, Matlock, Local Population Studies.

Morris, J. (1982) *The spectacle of Empire: style, effect and the Pax Britannica*, London, Faber and Faber.

Open University (1982) D301 *Historical sources and the social scientist*, Units 9–10 *Patterns and processes of internal migration*, Milton Keynes, The Open University.

Parr, J. (1980) *Labouring children: British immigrant apprentices to Canada, 1869–1924,* London, Croom Helm.

Parton, A. (1987) 'Poor-law settlement certificates and the migration to and from Birmingham 1726–37', *Local Population Studies,* 38, pp.23–9.

Patten, J. (1976) 'Patterns of migration and movement of labour to three pre-industrial East Anglian towns', *Journal of Historical Geography,* 2, pp.111–29.

Pelham, R.A. (1937) 'The immigrant population of Birmingham, 1686–1726', *Transactions, Birmingham Archaeological Society,* 61, pp.45–82.

Pooley, C.G. and Whyte, I.D. (eds) (1991) *Migrants, emigrants and immigrants: a social history of migration*, London, Routledge.*

Pope, R. (ed.) (1989) *Atlas of British social and economic history since c.1700,* London, Routledge.

Porter, A.N. (ed.) (1991) *Atlas of British overseas expansion,* London, Routledge.

Pritchard, R.M. (1976) *Housing and the spatial structure of the city,* Cambridge, Cambridge University Press.

Pryce, W.T.R. (1973) 'Manuscript census records for Denbighshire', *Transactions, Denbighshire Historical Society,* 22, pp.166–98.

Pryce, W.T.R. (1982) 'Migration in pre-industrial and industrial societies', in Open University (1982).

Pryce, W.T.R. (1993) 'Migration: some perspectives', in Rowlands, J. (ed.) *Welsh family history: a guide to research*, [Aberystwyth] Association of Family History Societies of Wales.

Ravenstein, E.G. (1885) 'The laws of migration', *Journal of the Royal Statistical Society,* 48, pp.167–235.

Ravenstein, E.G. (1889) 'The laws of migration', *Journal of the Royal Statistical Society,* 52, pp.214–301.

Redford, A. (1926) *Labour migration in England, 1800–1850,* Manchester, Manchester University Press. (The second edition, revised by W.H. Chaloner, was published in 1964.)

Richards, E. (1991) 'Voices of British and Irish migrants in nineteenth-century Australia', in Pooley and Whyte (1991).

Robin, J. (1980) *Elmdon: continuity and change in a north-west Essex village 1861–1964,* Cambridge, Cambridge University Press.

Schofield, R.A. (1991) *A peculiar tramping people? Irish and long-distance British migrants in a northern English manufacturing town: Keighley 1841–1881*, unpublished PhD thesis, The Open University.

Schofield, R.S. (1970) 'Age-specific mobility in an eighteenth-century rural English parish', *Annales de Démographie Historique*, pp.261–74.

Segal, A. and Marston, L. (1989) 'Maps and keys – world voluntary migration', *Migration World*, 17, pp.36–41.

Stillwell, J.C.H. (1990) *Migration analysis based on National Health Service central register data: trends and models*, Working Paper No. 537, University of Leeds, School of Geography.

Stouffer, S. (1940) 'Intervening opportunities: a theory relating mobility and distance', *American Sociological Review*, 5, pp.846–67.

Swift, R. and Gilley, S. (eds) (1989) *The Irish in Britain 1815–1939*, London, Pinter.[*]

Taylor, P.J. (1975) *Distance decay models in spatial interaction,* Norwich, Geo Books (Concepts and Techniques in Modern Geography No. 2).

Thompson, F. (1968) *Lark Rise to Candleford*, Oxford, Oxford University Press.

Tranter, N. (1974) 'The Reverend Andrew Urquhart and the social structure of Portpatrick in 1832', *Scottish Studies*, 18, pp.39–62.

Wagner, G. (1982) *Children of the Empire*, London, Weidenfeld and Nicolson.

Welch, R.L. (1971) *Migration in Britain: data sources and estimation techniques,* Birmingham, Centre for Urban and Regional Studies (University of Birmingham Occasional Paper No. 18).

Werbner, P. (1979) 'Avoiding the ghetto: Pakistani migrants and settlement shifts in Manchester', *New Community*, 7, 3, pp.36–89. Reprinted in Drake (1994).

White, P.E. and Woods, R.I. (eds) (1980) *The geographical impact of migration*, London, Longman.

Zipf, G.K. (1946) 'The P, Pz/D hypothesis in the intercity movement of persons', *American Sociological Review*, 11, pp.677–86.

Zolberg, A.R. (1989) 'The next waves: migration theory for a changing world', *International Migration Review*, 23, pp.403–30.

CHAPTER 2

ASPECTS OF ENGLISH, WELSH, SCOTTISH AND IRISH MIGRATIONS

by W.T.R. Pryce (sections 1, 2, 3 and 5) and Ian Donnachie (section 4)

In the previous chapter we presented a number of basic concepts and methods used in migration research. In Chapter 2 the emphasis switches to a consideration of particular sources and their potential in the context of four specific case studies. Different sources yield different types of information. Some, such as official lists of named residents (nominal listings), although not fully representative of the residential population, do offer interesting opportunities for the investigation of short-term, year-to-year, movements. Others, such as the CEBs, embrace all members of the population and provide details on many more variables. However, because they were compiled only once in every decade, in reality the CEBs are a series of snapshots, widely separated in time, rather than a continuous migration record.

Apart from the nature of the data sources on which they draw, the four case studies do embrace a number of other important issues. Whilst some build on the major rural–urban movements identified by E.G. Ravenstein in the nineteenth century (Grigg, 1977), others explore the nature of population transfers between one rural area and the next or between different areas within towns. Also covered in this chapter are examples of migration involving peoples with distinctive cultural backgrounds, demographic considerations, and the role played by the family or by cultural institutions in the migration process. We hope that you will find the exercises and the check-list at the end of the chapter useful in setting up your own research projects.

1 THE FAMILY'S ROLE IN MIGRATION: AN EXAMPLE FROM RURAL ESSEX, 1861–81

by W.T.R. Pryce

The decision to migrate is not normally taken by an individual in isolation. Usually, it involves other members of the family, friends and peers. Moreover, in the past the persons who would have been consulted varied – depending on the age of the potential migrant, place in the family unit (father, mother, first son/daughter or third son/daughter, etc.), their obligations and responsibilities, and family life-cycle stage. As Schürer has pointed out, studies of internal migration (in contrast to those that have been completed of emigration overseas) have tended to neglect the role of kin in the provision of advice, practical assistance, social introductions and news of new employment opportunities elsewhere (Schürer, 1991, pp.106–7).

Later in this book, we shall also investigate the clear evidence that some cultural institutions – for example, Welsh chapels (in this chapter) and Jewish synagogues (in Chapters 3 and 8) – were active agents in the migration process.

1.1   DENGIE AND HATFIELD PARISH GROUPS

To explore the nature of migration amongst families in rural England, Schürer (1991) selected two areas in Essex (Figure 2.1). Each comprised a group of contiguous parishes which, in the second half of the nineteenth century, remained overwhelmingly rural in economy and social structure. No rural industries, of any kind, existed in either of these localities. Dengie, comprising four small parishes (total population 2,507 in 1871), was the more isolated. Here, the low-lying heavy clay lands of the Essex coast supported grassland farming, with the traditional concentration on the fattening of livestock for London markets. Falling land values and depressed rents in the 1870s caused the abandonment of some farms.

In contrast, the five contiguous inland parishes in the Hatfield area enjoyed good communications to nearby towns, such as Bishop's Stortford. Here, the settlement pattern was dominated by large villages, arable farming was important, and alternative opportunities for work existed in horticulture and animal husbandry. Unlike Dengie, therefore, as grain prices fell, there was alternative local employment and the population remained remarkably constant – 3,149 in 1861 and 3,157 in 1881.

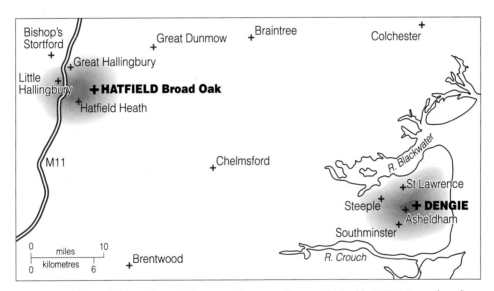

Figure 2.1   The Hatfield and Dengie, Essex, parish groups (Source: devised by W.T.R. Pryce, based on Schürer, 1991, p.109)

1.2   RESEARCH QUESTIONS

On the assumption that migration decisions were family decisions, Schürer explored a number of related issues. Clearly, long before the nineteenth century (when peak populations occurred) migration had been important in maintaining local demographic structures. Schürer reminds us that migration can be regarded as 'a mechanism for balancing out the chief resource of the pre-mechanized countryside: people. It was a way of accounting for natural population imbalances: evening out sex ratios; finding a potential marriage partner; learning a trade or skill; taking up an inheritance' (Schürer, 1991, p.114).

There are signs that an extensive communications network was essential to ensure that news of new opportunities could be diffused throughout neighbouring communities. Families as well as friends appear to have played crucial roles in the exchange of information that led, eventually, to migration. Movements usually occurred at distinctive stages in the family cycle: for example, when an individual took up a new job or married, or after children left the parental home (see Chapter 1, section 3.6). Therefore, there is a need to examine patterns of movement, in specific localities, in the context of family groups.

Although in the nineteenth century country people moved, increasingly, to live in the growing towns and in the developing industrial areas, movements continued to occur between neighbouring rural communities. However, the significant change, as Schürer himself states, is that fewer and fewer people were involved in these rural-to-rural moves. The prime cause of rural depopulation in the nineteenth century, he emphasizes, was not that levels of out-migration from rural parishes increased, but simply that *a change in the direction of the migration flows occurred* – to the towns, rather than to and from other rural communities (Schürer, 1991, p.114).

1.3 DATA SOURCES, NOMINAL RECORD LINKAGE AND METHODS OF ANALYSIS

Schürer drew his data from the 1861, 1871 and 1881 CEBs covering his two areas in rural Essex. Individuals and families were traced from one census to the next by linking names, ages, birthplaces, and place of enumeration, through the technique of *nominal record linkage* (see Schürer, 1987; Schürer and Pryce, 1993). Marriages (so that women could be traced despite their change of surname) and burials (as death certificates could not be consulted) were linked to the data in the CEBs. Information on burials was important because otherwise the failure to trace an individual could imply that he or she had migrated in this world, not to the next! To test the extent to which linked burials understated deaths, estimates of the latter were derived from regional life tables (published in the annual reports of the Registrars General, 1839 onwards). The results indicated a shortfall that was most significant amongst children under five years (Schürer, 1991, pp.111, 138–9). By using these techniques, a series of *longitudinal records* for individual families was produced, from which further new information could be derived. In order to illustrate the methods, here we have selected three themes. More detail is presented in Schürer (1991).

1.4 MIGRATION AND LIFE-CYCLE STAGE

After examining the enumeration of individuals, identifying individual nuclear families, and comparing the entries with those in previous CEBs, Schürer allocated each family to a single migration status from one of the following:

1 *All gone*: no record of the family occurs in the second set of CEBs and no burials are recorded. Such families are assumed to have migrated out of the study area.

2 *All stay*: all family members are recorded in the second set of CEBs: nil migration.

3 *Mixed*: some family members are not recorded in the second set of CEBs (excluding those appearing in the burial records), therefore partial migration has occurred.

Schürer presented his findings in tabular form (see Tables 2.1a to 2.1d) with the added refinement of the family heads being placed in one of five age categories (ages at the first census date):

o   25–34 years   – young families with dependent children.

o   35–44 years   – early middle age with dependent children.

o   45–54 years   – middle age, mostly without dependent children.

o   55–64 years   – late middle age, no dependent children.

o   65 + years   – old age, no dependent children.

Each of these family life-cycle stages represents a set of conditions embracing all individuals within the family, notably the presence or absence of dependent children. Table 2.1 shows both the percentages, and the absolute numbers involved (indicated by 'n' at the head of the appropriate columns): a useful convention, especially when numbers are small and it is possible that the percentages are not statistically significant. Moreover, this has the added advantage of allowing the data to be checked or rearranged by other researchers.

Table 2.1   Movements of families: Hatfield and Dengie, 1861–81

(a) Hatfield, 1861–71

Age of family head	All gone		All stay		Mixed	
	(%)	(n)	(%)	(n)	(%)	(n)
25–34	29.9	23	53.2	41	16.9	13
35–44	23.0	28	29.5	36	47.5	58
45–54	22.1	27	21.3	26	56.6	69
55–64	19.0	22	34.5	40	46.6	54
65+	37.2	42	37.2	42	25.7	29
Total	**25.8**	**142**	**33.6**	**185**	**40.5**	**223**

(b) Dengie, 1861–71

Age of family head	All gone		All stay		Mixed	
	(%)	(n)	(%)	(n)	(%)	(n)
25–34	34.0	17	46.0	23	20.0	10
35–44	34.5	38	30.0	33	35.5	39
45–54	27.0	31	24.3	28	48.7	56
55–64	22.4	15	29.9	20	37.8	32
65+	48.3	28	25.9	15	25.9	15
Total	**32.2**	**129**	**29.7**	**119**	**38.0**	**152**

(c) Hatfield, 1871–81

Age of family head	All gone		All stay		Mixed	
	(%)	(n)	(%)	(n)	(%)	(n)
25–34	38.1	32	47.6	40	14.3	12
35–44	27.9	38	29.4	40	42.6	58
45–54	20.3	27	21.8	29	57.9	77
55–64	24.7	23	23.7	22	51.6	48
65+	42.9	57	35.3	47	21.8	28
Total	**30.6**	**177**	**30.7**	**178**	**38.7**	**224**

(d) Dengie, 1871–81

Age of family head	All gone		All stay		Mixed	
	(%)	(n)	(%)	(n)	(%)	(n)
25–34	59.7	40	26.9	18	13.4	9
35–44	46.5	47	16.8	17	36.6	37
45–54	31.5	34	14.8	16	53.7	58
55–64	28.0	23	19.5	16	52.4	43
65+	46.4	39	33.3	28	20.2	17
Total	**41.4**	**183**	**21.5**	**95**	**37.1**	**164**

Note: in all four tables families are classified according to the age of the head at the first census date.

Source: based on Schürer (1991) Table 6.3, pp.124–5 (rearranged and simplified by W.T.R. Pryce)

It is clear from the four tabulations (Table 2.1) that Hatfield recorded higher proportions of 'stayers' than did Dengie in all age groups, and that Dengie lost even more families in the second decade 1871–81. When each stage in the family cycle is examined, evidently it was the younger families (heads in the age group 25–34 years) who tended to be the stayers. Why should this be so? This may relate to the fact that younger families benefited most from starting life near their own kin, especially parents. Alternatively, these may have been new arrivals in the community who were beginning to put down roots. Clearly, further independent evidence needs to be linked to the data in the CEBs. As the tables reveal, the differences between the two areas increased in the 1870s, reflecting the greater economic problems in Dengie with its narrower economic base and consequent lack of alternative employment.

1.5 MIGRATION AND OCCUPATION

By classifying families according to the occupation of the family head it is possible to examine the impact on migration of employment and levels of skill. It has been shown that, in the Vale of York, for example, during the eighteenth and early nineteenth centuries, persons with hereditary ties, leaseholders and those dependent on a local clientele (landowners, farmers, professionals, shopkeepers and other traders) tended to remain in the community over successive generations. Conversely, unskilled workers and general labourers, especially the young, dependent on selling their muscle power to the highest bidder, were more likely to move in search of fresh opportunities. Married labourers with cottages and family responsibilities were much more settled (Holderness, 1971).

Table 2.2 Family migration and occupations: Hatfield and Dengie, 1861–81

		All gone (%)	All stay (%)	Mixed (%)	Total number of families (n)
Hatfield					
Crafts	1861–71	26.2	33.7	40.0	32
	1871–81	25.3	29.3	45.3	34
Farmers	1861–71	27.3	40.0	32.7	55
	1871–81	38.9	29.6	31.5	54
Labourers	1861–71	23.0	32.4	44.6	352
	1871–81	25.1	32.2	42.8	367
Others	1861–71	38.3	27.1	34.6	107
	1871–81	49.2	27.0	23.8	126
Dengie					
Crafts	1861–71	25.8	40.9	33.3	66
	1871–81	43.3	23.9	32.8	67
Farmers	1861–71	35.9	20.5	43.6	39
	1871–81	41.0	10.3	48.7	39
Labourers	1861–71	32.8	26.7	40.5	232
	1871–81	42.7	20.3	37.0	246
Others	1861–71	36.6	30.5	32.9	82
	1871–81	39.3	23.1	37.6	117

Note: families have been classified according to the occupation of the head at the first census date stated in each line.

Source: based on Schürer (1991) Table 6.4, pp.128–31 (rearranged and simplified by W.T.R. Pryce)

To explore aspects such as these, Schürer tabulated his data in terms of three broad occupational categories, implied levels of skill, and general social standing; that is: (1) craft workers, (2) farmers, (3) labourers. Inevitably, a fourth group, labelled 'others', had to be added (Table 2.2).

Thus, while in Hatfield (1861–71) there seems to have been little variation in the 'all gone' category amongst craft workers, farmers and labourers, it was the farmers who recorded the lowest proportion (32.7 per cent) with a 'mixed' migration status. By the end of the 1870s, however, the proportion of 'all gones' amongst farming families had increased to 39 per cent, whilst that of craft and labouring families remained at around a quarter. Farming was the major economic activity that depended on all members of the family. Thus, Hatfield's farming families tended to stick together, taking decisions as a family group rather than as individuals – either moving all together or all staying put. These patterns of movement are somewhat different to those of families in other occupational categories and also are in contrast to migratory trends amongst farming families in the Dengie area. Further work may well confirm that these migrational trends were determined as much by the ways in which farming families were bound together through tenurial arrangements as through the experience of jointly working the land.

In Dengie (1861–71) the proportion of 'all gone' migration was higher than in Hatfield for farmers (36 per cent as against 27 per cent) and labourers (33 per cent as against 23 per cent), but not for craft workers (26 per cent in both areas). Yet, as Table 2.2 shows, probably due to difficult local conditions, Dengie farming families recorded higher proportions of 'mixed' migration and significantly lower proportions (21 per cent) of 'stayers'. In contrast, larger numbers of families headed by craft workers (41 per cent as against 34 per cent) stayed in Dengie than in Hatfield, but the severe problems affecting the local grass-farming economy in Dengie during the 1870s led to increased levels of out-migration amongst all occupational groups. The dramatic collapse of farming in Dengie resulted in a mere 10 per cent of families in the 'all stay' category by 1881.

EXERCISE 2.1

In this section we have looked at migratory trends amongst families classified according to the age and occupation of the head of the family. Note down briefly what other aspects of migration you think can be examined drawing on the CEBs as the main data.

Comment p.218.

QUESTION FOR RESEARCH

Schürer (1991) considered the extent of migration in two rural areas, over two decades (1861–81) by age and occupation of family head and by family size. As some tables are based on small numbers, it may be wise not to read too much into them. To enhance the value of this kind of data you can:

1 Increase the number of families under observation by taking a larger study area.

2 Combine categories by amalgamating areas or variables (e.g. age groups), though this leads to a loss of fine-tuning.

3 Use correlations rather than just percentages for comparative purposes. This involves using 'goodness of fit' statistical tests like *Chi-square* or *Kolmogorov–Smirnov* (see Chapter 4, section 4; especially Ebdon, 1985).

Be warned, however! These suggestions (especially no. 1) could turn out to be very time consuming and should not be accepted lightly – particularly if only a few weeks can be devoted to the research.

---

2 HOW DO WE STUDY SHORT-TERM POPULATION MOVEMENTS? TWO CONTRASTING ENGLISH EXAMPLES

by W.T.R. Pryce

Much historical research on migration has focused on specific isolated dates, especially the work based on the CEBs. But where enquiries are concerned with short-term population turnover, there is a need to explore other sources, especially lists of named residents. Specific names can be cross-checked between dates, so producing the three categories, *stayers, movers* and *arrivals*. These terms are purely descriptive in nature: whilst implying origins, none should be accepted as an explanation linked directly to particular categories of migration behaviour.

What types of data can the researcher seek out in the hope of further refining this information?

There are four basic conditions that an appropriate source needs to fulfil:

1 *Named individuals:* all individuals need to be listed unambiguously by name – usually Christian/personal name(s) and surname/family name.

2 *Comprehensive coverage:* ideally, all members of the population need to be included but, as a minimum requirement, the list should contain the names of the heads of individual families and/or households.

3 *Specific to territory:* the names should relate to people living within a defined territorial unit or area – parish, township, village or street.

4 *Data need to be comparable over time:* for example, lists of all members of the population will not be comparable with lists of householders.

Providing all these criteria can be met, any two or more nominal lists can be compared and used for the study of population turnover and migration research. Thus, for example, estate records offer interesting possibilities – but, of course, only when all the houses and land properties within a particular area are in common ownership. For example, the Registers of Sasines (in the Scottish Record Office, Edinburgh), chartulary books (held by solicitors) and estate records have been analysed in studies of movements to estate villages in Scotland (Lockhart, 1986, 1989, 1991).

In some areas purely *local* records may come to light but there are two major series of records which, like the CEBs, should, in theory, be available everywhere. These are the local property *valuation lists* (compiled in the administration of local taxes) and the *rate books* based on the evaluations. In addition, *electoral rolls* or *electoral registers* list individuals qualified to vote in local and national elections (Gibson and Rogers, 1993; see also Volume 4, Chapter 4).

Information gathered from rate books has been used in studies of urban structures and the changes that occur over time (Davies *et al.*, 1968); their analysis does need to be approached with considerable care, however, particularly in relation to methods of property assessment. Early rate books merely listed names and payments: therefore, while not very appropriate for studies of urban morphologies, these sources have been explored by Holmes (1973), and others, for the study of migration and population turnover within specific urban communities (for a brief review see Carter and Lewis, 1990, pp.12–17).

The use of such nominal list records will now be illustrated from two case studies involving contrasting dates in rural as well as urban locations.

2.1   MOVEMENTS WITHIN LEICESTER, 1871–72

In his book *Housing and the spatial structure of the city*, Pritchard (1976) identified distinctive social areas within Leicester, and changes over time. By the early 1870s, an internal migratory system had developed within the town, which, with some 100,000 people living in an area of less than 2.5 square miles, constituted a relatively small, compact urban community.

DATA SOURCES

Since Pritchard's research involved the study of movements from street to street as well as between one year and the next, very detailed local information, relating to individual houses, was needed. This can be derived from the rate assessment books, revised annually, for the purpose of levying local taxes. However, because full coverage of all rateable properties in Leicester ends in 1855, Pritchard had to turn to the electoral rolls as the next best alternative source.

The borough's electoral rolls had been compiled under the legislative provisions of the Reform Act, 1867. This brought voting rights to (a) *male* householders resident in the area for at least one year, and (b) all their male lodgers paying at least £10 per annum in rent. Note the particular conditions under which the lists had been compiled: only 70 per cent of male householders qualified for inclusion on the electoral roll; a further 15 per cent of householders were excluded because they were women. Also excluded were recent in-migrants (resident for less than 12 months), and a small proportion of men whose names had been left out through error, personal objections to registration or, as Pritchard puts it, 'just plain disinterest' (Pritchard, 1976, p.49).

DATA PREPARATION

From the outset, Pritchard recognized that all the relevant information in the electoral rolls would have to be extracted, broken down and simplified in terms of four major themes needing close examination:

o   The creation and dissolution of households.

o   Movements by established households to new locations within the town.

o   Movements of households into Leicester.

o   Movements of households to locations outside the town.

To obtain these details, the electoral rolls covering 1871 and 1872 were examined closely to find out: (1) how many persons were recorded *at the same address* in both years; (2) those whose names appeared in 1871 but not in 1872; and (3) names appearing for the first time in 1872. In 1871 these lists contained 12,802 names, and, in 1872, 13,337, reflecting the rapid growth of Leicester.

POPULATION TURNOVER

In addition to his analysis of the electoral rolls, checks had to be made against registers of marriages and deaths. Twenty-one per cent of the names disappeared from the 1871 roll, of which 457 (3.6 per cent) had died. Of the 3,620 new names on the 1872 list, 856 (26.3 per cent) were newly married men. Clearly, marriages, and the setting up of new homes, were important elements in fuelling the relatively high rates of population mobility within the town.

To squeeze out still more information, Pritchard prepared further detailed lists, which involved the cross-tabulation of individuals by name, area by area. Be warned! Such a task can turn out to be very time consuming and tedious! To reduce errors, further independent verification is needed. In addition, Pritchard devised standard rules to avoid errors from double counting. For example, only one person was counted when the rolls had listed two individuals with exactly the same name in both years.

The final results indicate that 1,424 internal moves occurred within Leicester between 1871 and 1872, accounting for 52 per cent of the losses from the 1871 electoral roll and for 44 per cent of the gains in 1872. After taking into consideration deaths, marriages and moves to new locations, 980 households still remain unaccounted for. Some 844 householders left Leicester during this period but these out-movements were more than counterbalanced by the 992 persons who had arrived in the town from elsewhere. This apparent inflow does not match up with the overall migration trends as revealed by independent census and registration data. Pritchard observes that at least some of these may, on further investigation, turn out to be married couples who had been living with parents up to 1872 before setting up new homes of their own elsewhere in the town – thereby qualifying, for the first time, for inclusion on the electoral register.

Overall aspects of population turnover, as revealed from this analysis of the electoral rolls 1871–72, are summarized in Figure 2.2. In *net* terms the numbers of households grew as a consequence of marriages, and significantly more migrants arrived in Leicester to replace those who had left. Leicester in the early 1870s was, therefore, something of a boom town, growing rapidly, with substantial numbers moving within the town. It is to this latter important feature that now we turn.

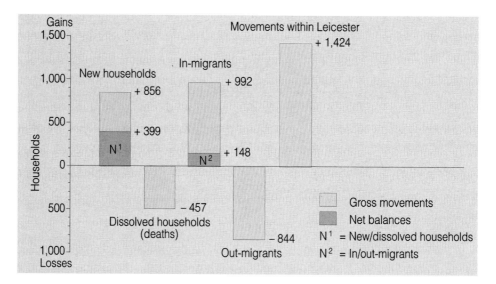

Figure 2.2 Components of mobility, Leicester, 1870–71 (Source: compiled by W.T.R. Pryce, based on Pritchard, 1976, pp.50–4)

MIGRATION WITHIN THE URBAN AREA

To deal with migration in spatial terms, Pritchard divided the built-up area of the town into 26 territorial units, based on the subdivisions used for local elections. With between 200 and 600 entries on the electoral roll, these were 'areas of approximately similar geographic and demographic scale constructed within the framework of the old parish boundaries in Leicester and the lines of the main thoroughfares'; and, he contended, each subdivision had 'some validity in terms of housing and social characteristics' (Pritchard, 1976, p.54). Movements in each area were expressed as a percentage of the total names recorded on the electoral rolls. This approach standardizes the volume of migratory flows and enables the information to be presented in ways that emphasize the interconnections within the migration system. Finally, the volume of migratory flows was mapped, using proportional flow lines (or arrows) for movements *between* areas and square 'point' symbols to represent the movements that occurred *within* each area (Figure 2.3).

Mobility within Leicester tended to reflect two overall trends:

1 Movements showed a moderate, inverse correlation with the social status of an area – higher rates of movement occurred in lower status areas.

2 Areas with new house building 1871–72 recorded slightly higher rates of mobility than did old, established housing districts.

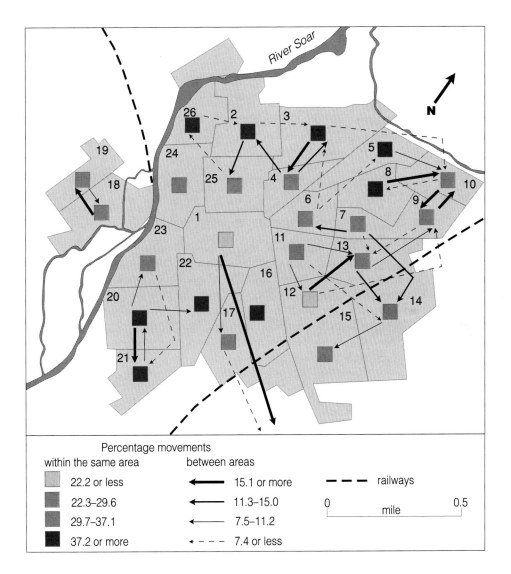

Figure 2.3 Internal movements within Leicester, 1871–72, based on names listed in electoral rolls. Reference numbers identify each of the 26 areas used for statistical purposes. Railways and the River Soar have been included as location indicators. Further guidance on map-making techniques is available in Mills and Pryce (1993) (Source: based on Pritchard, 1976, p.58, modified by W.T.R. Pryce)

In most localities, over 40 per cent of moves were restricted to the same neighbourhood, involving short-distance migration to a new address across the street or just around the corner: 'When one remembers the small size of these areas and the very high rates of mobility indicated, these figures suggest an extraordinary close mesh of movement, a fact which is reinforced by the great majority of moves which do not cross boundaries, only going into neighbouring districts' (Pritchard, 1976, p.57).

Most significant is the fact that all these moves added up to a closely integrated migration system, operating in every district, whose overall effects embraced, eventually, all districts. In many respects, this migration network is comparable to that which operated on a regional scale within north-east Wales up to 1851 (see Chapter 4, section 2.3). Many of the short-distance moves themselves were simply stages in a whole series of population shifts that were progressive in nature. Ultimately, all these moves were linked to changes of social status, increased social aspirations, and, in response, the development of new housing areas. So, as we shall see in Chapter 6, in these respects patterns of migration can be related to the more widespread processes of urban growth and change.

2.2   MOVEMENTS IN RURAL YORKSHIRE, 1930s

In his research into migration trends in rural Yorkshire, Dickinson (1958) faced similar problems to Pritchard concerning the nature of source data. The electoral rolls do offer the important advantage that they are available year by year, thus allowing us to make short-term as well as longer-term studies of population turnover – but their survival rates can vary enormously from place to place (Gibson and Rogers, 1993; see also Volume 4, Chapter 4).

NATURE OF THE SOURCE DATA

In 1928 the electoral franchise was extended to include women aged 21 years and over. This meant that the returns used by Dickinson are much more representative of the adult population than were earlier listings. In urban areas, individual entries tend to be listed in alphabetical order, street by street. However, in rural areas qualified voters are listed alphabetically and it is necessary to use the address information to regroup names into specific villages or townships. These records, still updated each year, are kept by the Electoral Registration Officer in local council offices. The lists for years gone by can be consulted either in this same office, in local reference libraries, or in county record offices.

Dickinson's investigations explored migration in eight villages on the western edge of the Vale of York, lying east of Pontefract, selected because they represented a cross-section of rural conditions (Dickinson, 1958, p.95). His researches covered the 1930s as well as the years between 1949 and 1954, but, to demonstrate methods, here we shall deal only with trends in the 1930s.

DATA PREPARATION AND REFINEMENT

Adopting much the same approaches as Pritchard, Dickinson first checked for errors of compilation. Next, data had to be collated for purposes of verification. Thus, information from registers of church banns, marriages and deaths was linked to the names on the electoral rolls. In addition, baptismal registers covering the previous 21 years were scanned for details as to the cohort of persons qualifying for inclusion on the electoral roll in specific years during the 1930s. After the Second World War, the electoral registers identified newly qualified voters by printing the letter 'Y' against their names. Dickinson adopted this as a cipher for all new electors who had qualified on grounds of age (today the age of majority is 18 years; then it was 21 years) and to distinguish these voters from the other new voters who had moved into the community.

Table 2.3 Gross in-migration to eight villages in Yorkshire, 1931–38

(1) Settlement	(2) Names listed 1931	(3) Names listed 1938	(4) New names	(5) 'Y' names (known)	(6) 'Y' names (estimated)	(7) Residuals (errors etc.)	(8) Total in-migration
1 Balne	185	173	124	21	2	4	97
2 Beal	234	215	184	22	7	13	142
3 Birkin	76	66	92	7	4	1	80
4 Eggborough	257	273	256	21	10	7	218
5 Heck	128	117	111	7	8	3	93
6 Kellingley	18	102	115	3	2	0	110
7 Kellington	189	207	229	16	9	10	194
8 Whitley	265	295	263	25	17	7	214

Source: compiled by W.T.R. Pryce, based on Dickinson (1958) p.101

Table 2.4 Gross out-migration from eight villages in Yorkshire, 1931–38

(1) Settlement	(2) New names	(3) Deaths (known)	(4) Deaths (estimated)	(5) Residuals (errors etc.)	(6) Total out-migration
1 Balne	136	20	2	4	110
2 Beal	202	18	5	12	167
3 Birkin	102	6	2	1	93
4 Eggborough	239	21	4	6	208
5 Heck	122	20	3	3	96
6 Kellingley	31	1	1	0	29
7 Kellington	214	16	3	13	182
8 Whitley	231	26	4	5	196

Source: compiled by W.T.R. Pryce, based on Dickinson (1958) p.101

A series of estimates as to the adult population was then produced for the period under examination. This revealed interesting details as to the nature of underlying movements (Tables 2.3 and 2.4). Thus, for example, the village of Birkin recorded the following adult population totals in each of the years between 1931 and 1936: 76, 75, 75, 75, 75, 73 (the average being 74.8 adults). Despite this appearance of stability, from Dickinson's detailed name-by-name analysis of the electoral rolls, it is clear that no less than 68 adults had left the village between 1931 and 1936 and 62 new people (excluding newly qualified voters) had arrived! Indeed, between 1931 and 1938, the population turnover in most of the villages amounted to two-thirds of their average adult population.

So, as we have seen, the electoral rolls do provide us with much more detailed information as to the underlying patterns of change than it is possible to obtain from censuses which suffer from the 10-year gap between each enumeration. After all the adjustments have been made, the data derived from lists of voters relate, initially, to overall gross migration to and from specific villages. By subtracting in-migrants (Table 2.3, column 8) from out-migrants (Table 2.4, column 6), net migration balances can be calculated for specific villages, so taking the analysis still further.

_____ **QUESTION FOR RESEARCH** _____

Electoral registers and similar nominal listings do allow us to pursue studies of population turnover year by year rather than, as from the CEBs, decade by decade. Because the listings provide information house by house, the unit of analysis can be the single street or an inner court of dwellings within a built-up area, or involve all listed persons within a whole township (townland in Ireland), ward or parish.

Moreover, *nominal record linkage* can be used to enhance the data in various ways. For example, migration according to age, birthplace (local born, born elsewhere, persons with rural or urban origins) or occupation and social class can be worked out by linking listed individuals to the entries in the CEB nearest in date to the nominal list itself. Young people can be classified according to the occupation of their father.

Whilst acknowledging that, inevitably, problems of access to appropriate sources will arise, it does seem that the scope for further data enhancement and investigation is limited only by the researcher's own ingenuity and the time available for the completion of the analysis.

Here, we have concentrated primarily on ways in which electoral registration data and similar lists of names can be exploited to yield migration statistics.

What should be the next stages in the research process?

Much statistical information can be summarized, very effectively, as graphs and in map form. You will find many examples of these in this volume and in the three associated volumes in this series (Volumes 1, 3 and 4; see, also, Mills and Pryce, 1993). Further analysis, but of a different kind, is still needed if the results are to be meaningful. This can involve a number of different approaches. For example, the migration statistics can be linked to other forms of *quantitative* information such as employment or production figures. Most successful research projects in family and community history draw on detailed knowledge of local events. Personal experience of a particular family or community and an understanding of local changes and what these mean in the context of wider issues (that is, *qualitative* information) will endow most studies with important contextual frameworks and will add further to knowledge enrichment.

3 WELSH CHAPELS IN ENGLAND AND THEIR ROLE IN MIGRATION

by W.T.R. Pryce

In this section we examine some of the approaches that can be used to explore movements of people belonging to a distinctive cultural group. The cultural identity of the people of Wales can be measured through the well-established surrogates of language and religion – more so in the past, perhaps, than today (see Hume and Pryce, 1986). Moreover, migrants leaving Wales took with them that very distinctive nineteenth-century badge of Welshness, the nonconformist chapel. These institutions retained direct links with all the major religious denominations back in Wales itself. When used in conjunction with the birthplace information recorded in the censuses, chapel membership books and committee minutes can provide key information on migration and the settlement process – especially the role played by chapels as facilitating institutions.

The problems of becoming a migrant and moving into a new cultural setting were not unique to the Welsh. Aspects of that experience would have been felt by many another migrant moving from a traditional homeland to settle in new emergent towns and cities. The regional English themselves, as well as the Scots and the Irish, went through the same sorts of process (see, for example, King *et al.*, 1989). Moreover, as we shall see in Chapters 3 (section 2) and 8, Jewish institutions played significant roles in the settlement of migrants from mainland Europe in east London.

3.1 PATTERNS OF MOVEMENT

Overall trends in the migration of the Welsh and their settling in the 58 'principal towns' of England in 1871 (as defined in official census reports) have been examined by Pooley (1983). In 1851, only two major centres, London and Liverpool, recorded more than 10,000 people born in Wales. Nearly a generation later, in 1871, whilst these cities still maintained their large numbers, many more had settled in smaller towns, including locations that would have involved considerable travel.

In general, Pooley's research confirms many aspects of Ravenstein's 'laws of migration' (Grigg, 1977). Mid-nineteenth century Wales remained substantially a rural country and migratory trends amongst the Welsh conformed closely to the standard models of rural–urban movements discussed earlier in Chapter 1 (Figure 2.4). (See, also, Pryce, 1993.)

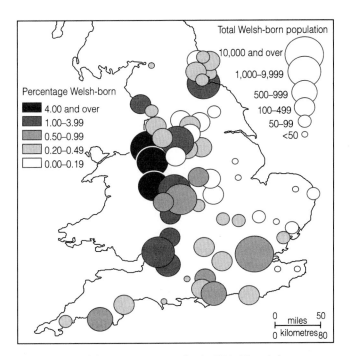

Figure 2.4 Welsh migration to England, 1871. The circles are proportional to the numbers born in Wales. The shadings indicate Welsh-born migrants as a percentage of the residential population in specific towns (Source: based on Pooley, 1983, Figure 2, p.290)

3.2 THE CHAPELS AND THE MIGRATION PROCESS

Moving into a new and different world posed a number of challenges, particularly in the context of community life and religion. In nineteenth-century Wales the split between the ordinary people and the then Church of England (not finally disestablished in Wales until 1920) had become so complete that nonconformist religious bodies – strongly Protestant, and substantially indigenous in origin – were flourishing. Although enjoying strong links with Methodism in England, the new denominations had built up their own organizations; and, by 1851, when the census of religious worship was conducted, these were fully established. So, when people left Wales they took with them not only their language but also their religion; and their chapel buildings were to become outward signs of their distinctive cultural identity.

From the work of Emrys Jones (1981, 1985), it is clear that, by the early 1800s, the Welsh had been settling in London for over four centuries. Their numbers increased steadily, reaching 17,572 in 1851, 35,421 in 1901 and 59,751 by 1931 (1.4 per cent of London's residential population). Drawing on birthplace information, trade directories and chapel membership records, Professor Jones has been able to chart occupational structures and the pattern of settlement. From the seventeenth century onwards, the Welsh occupied high positions in the established professions (especially law and education), but during the nineteenth century they cornered, also, much of the dairy trade, especially in central districts such as Islington. Out of the 1,450 dairymen-farmers in London in 1895, over 500 had distinctively Welsh family sur-names: 103 of them were Joneses, 83 Davieses, 63 Evanses, 38 Williamses, 36 Morgans, 30 Jenkinses, 29 Edwardses and a further 22 families carried the name Lewis!

During the nineteenth and twentieth centuries more than 30 Welsh meeting houses, school rooms and chapels (overwhelmingly nonconformist rather than Anglican) were established in central London to serve this substantial in-migrant population. These were to become centres for secular as well as religious activities – nurturing, in effect, a distinctively Welsh corporate and social life. Moreover, it is not without significance that several of these chapels were built at central locations: most were within easy walking distance of the major railway termini that connected with different regions in Wales. At the same time, the site for each chapel had been chosen so that it was easily accessible from the northern inner suburbs where the great bulk of the Welsh-born population had settled.

In a very real sense these chapels, and the social life that revolved around them, were transplants of cultural institutions from Wales itself. This is evident from the published memoirs of the son of a London-Welsh milkman and reminds us of the close-knit nature of the Welsh community. The parents of Gwilym Griffiths, both from rural Ceredigion, had met, and were married, at the Welsh chapel in King's Cross (Figure 2.5).

Figure 2.5 Members leaving King's Cross Welsh Congregational Chapel, London, after the 11 am service, Sunday, 6 June 1993 (Source: photograph by M.G. Levers, Open University Photographic Department)

With father busy on his milk rounds, Mr Griffiths recalls that it was 'a bit of a rush' on a Sunday morning to get six children washed and dressed to catch the no. 173 bus for the service at King's Cross at 11 am:

> We sat in pew number 56. At the end sat Mr. & Mrs. Tudor Evans and daughter Marie; next to them the Griffiths crowd, then Mr. & Mrs. Williams and son John (Mill Hill later), then Bessie Davies and her mother; and later on, Mr. & Mrs. Elwyn Owen … . In front … quite often Mr. & Mrs. Hopkin Morris, then a barrister and Liberal M.P. … . Across the aisle were the J.R. Thomas family; Mr. & Mrs. Tom Davies and daughter Gwenllian and son Trefor – I could go on and on, naming rows upon rows of families.
> … Very often the chapel [at the evening service at 6 pm] was packed to capacity and extra chairs had to be brought into the aisles to cope with the crowd … . The gallery was likewise packed, with a full choir in place.
>
> (Griffiths, 1989, pp.130–2)

After the evening service, many of the young went on to social gatherings and supper at the homes of established Welsh families. It is clear that chapel members played a key role in the migration process:

> … A phone call from Wales would be met by the command to 'send him/her up'. This young person would be met at Paddington or Euston and taken to a home where 'digs' were provided, pending instructions to someone who would offer the youngster employment and a chance in life. There are many alive today who have never forgotten this good Christian witness of long ago.
>
> (Griffiths, 1989, p.134)

The importance of the chapels as reception points for new migrants is highlighted by Emrys Jones. His analysis of the records of the chapel at King's Cross indicates that, at first sight, this particular institution recorded a stable membership of about 800, which peaked at some 1,000 in the early 1930s (during the depression in south Wales) and for a second time during the 1939–45 World War (Figure 2.6, upper graph). But, as the lower graph in Figure 2.6 shows, a very different situation emerges when the numbers of newcomers are compared against the departures. From this, it is clear that, despite high overall membership, each year recorded a substantial number of comings and goings: in reality, the numbers of new arrivals were more or less balanced by those whose membership had lapsed.

What is the underlying significance of these trends?

In making a plea for further research, Professor Jones concluded, provisionally, that the membership records suggest that the chapel was playing a key role for new migrants in the assimilation process. New arrivals had had their membership transferred to Tabernacle, King's Cross, by a chapel in their home district in Wales. For a time this membership was maintained until the migrant had become settled in London. Later, when they had became more assimilated into London life, some migrants transferred, on their own initiative, to another Welsh church elsewhere in the city; others joined an English congregation. Their places at King's Cross were filled by more new faces from Wales until, eventually, either the migration stream began to dry up or migrants were coming from communities in Wales where, already, chapel-going was on the decline. Therefore, as Jones pointed out, with all its comings and goings, in some respects, Tabernacle, King's Cross Welsh Congregational Church, resembled King's Cross Railway Station!

Emrys Jones concluded that the experience of the Welsh cannot be regarded as unique and specific to one nation:

> Welsh assimilation into London Society has few barriers, unlike those facing the many monoglot Welsh of the last century or the majority of new ethnic groups in London today [he was

writing in 1985]. What the Welsh needed was a temporary place of refuge, where once a week or so they could have a little cultural renewal, speak the [Welsh] language again, sing the familiar hymn tunes, and alleviate a little of the hiraeth [i.e. longing for the homeland], which is a natural effect of leaving home. Sooner, rather than later, the majority dispense with this.

(Jones, 1985, p.166)

Further information on the roles played by Welsh chapels in the migration process comes from Liverpool. By the 1890s, over 50 chapels, school rooms and missions (including two Anglican churches), catering for Welsh-speaking people, had been established on Merseyside. As in London, migrants found that a very warm welcome awaited them in the chapels – a welcome,

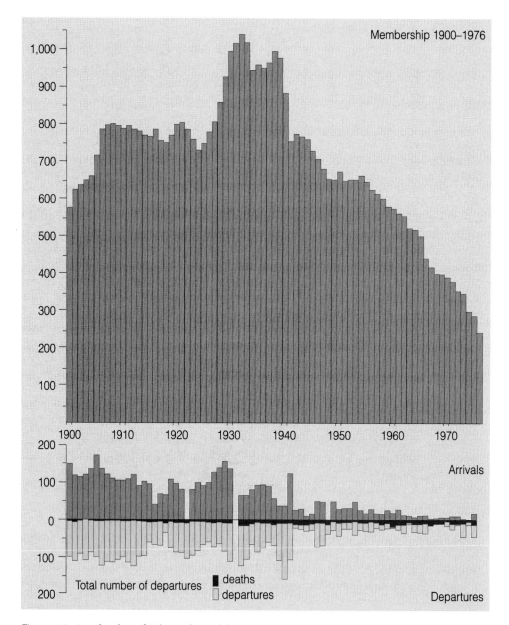

Figure 2.6 Membership of Tabernacle, Welsh Congregational Chapel, King's Cross, London, 1900–76 (Source: Jones, 1985, p.165)

moreover, articulated in their native language (Figure 2.7). From membership records and their committee minutes, it is clear that the Liverpool chapels, also, acted as agents in finding homes for migrants (lodgings for young people, houses for married couples) as well as employment. It is not without significance that at this time Welsh house builders were prominent on Merseyside (Jones, 1946).

The chapels seem to have functioned as the hub of a communications system that embraced and integrated all the Welsh congregations and societies in the city. Moreover, as in London and elsewhere, this network reached back to the sending areas within Wales itself. Despite differences of social class, the majority of the out-migrants from rural Wales shared an identity based, not, as at home, on kinship and proximity, but now, in the English city, based specifically on the more universal and common linguistic and ethnic bonds of Welshness. The impact of the migration process was such that, in their new cultural milieu, many became much more conscious of their Welshness in ways not possible in their home areas: 'To be Welsh in Wales was unremarkable: to be Welsh in Liverpool was to be visible, and to be conscious of that position' (Jones and Rees, 1984, p.34).

Marriage between in-migrants from different parts of Wales consolidated and heightened this self-awareness. And the chapel, together with its satellite literary and cultural societies, was an active agent of community building and, ever aware of the secular as well as the spiritual needs of individuals, seems to have provided discrete opportunities for the bringing together of potential partners (Jones and Rees, 1984, pp.23, 34).

Ultimately, however, despite the intense feelings of kinship, and of Welshness, for many, the move to the city meant a conscious breaking away from the relative isolation and parochialism of the traditional rural life in the old homelands of rural Wales. There was an urgent need to build a new identity and this could be done most easily by consolidation and enhanced development away from the old foundations. Again, as we have seen in the context of the London Welsh, this experience was not, is not, unique to the peoples of Wales. Amongst other migrants, there must have been many parallels: these still await exploration.

Figure 2.7   Waiting to welcome the migrant. The Rev. John Hughes, minister, (centre) and the deacons of Fitzclarence Street Presbyterian Church of Wales, Liverpool, *c.*1865 (Source: National Library of Wales)

This section has reported on the ways in which membership records and the committee minutes of Welsh chapels in the cities of England can be used to reveal the roles played by a distinctive cultural institution in the migration process.

Similar approaches can be explored for studies of movements amongst members of the other old nations of Britain, in particular the regional English, as well as members of newer ethnic groups from overseas (see, for example, Pooley, 1989; Townsend and Taylor, 1975). The roles played by such agencies as trade unions, major employers, and landlords in the recruitment of workers and their settlement at new locations are topics that can be explored by researchers in family and community history. The relationship between labour skills and the distances over which people migrated, and the ways in which some particular destinations may have developed migration links with specific towns and sending regions, are topics that offer considerable scope for further exploration.

4   SCOTS AND IRISH ON THE MOVE

by Ian Donnachie

Like the Welsh, the Scots and Irish have maintained a strong sense both of national tradition and of religious and family ties long after their absorption into the communities in which they have settled. They enthusiastically transplanted themselves to other parts of the British Isles, as well as overseas, and some of their institutions have maintained archives which can be useful as starting points for research projects on family and community history. Although many became totally assimilated, some migrants made a distinctive impact in their new homelands – apparently, it seems, out of all proportion to their numbers. Success stories (male-dominated, inevitably) are generally well documented, so, as with other migrants, historians have tended to overlook the failures. Movements amongst both the Scots and Irish are the themes of this section. As we shall see, some similarities and some differences emerge.

4.1   PERSONAL BEGINNINGS AND SCOTTISH CONDITIONS: A POSSIBLE FAMILY HISTORY PROJECT?

Just north of Pitlochry in Perthshire is the Clan Donnachaidh Museum and Centre. Historically, this part of the Central Highlands around Rannoch and Atholl was home to one of the many Gaelic-speaking Scottish clans whose names were Anglicized at a relatively early date, the parent branch becoming Robertson. Apparently, the first to use the Anglicized name was William of Struan, who became Chief in about 1509. During the sixteenth century the name of Robertson became quite general with some clan members, but in Gaelic they still continued to be called Clan Donnachaidh. Few of the clan converted to the reformed religion and during the civil and religious wars many rallied to the Stuart banner. The clan seat was at Dunalastair in Kinloch Rannoch – and the Rannoch Barracks, built by Hanovarian troops after 1745, were partly intended to control the Clan Donnachaidh. It is said that Anglicized forms of the name were then widely adopted 'in order to conceal their identity after the events of 1745' (Martine, 1987, p.186). Presumably, some of the clan retained the original name, which has passed, through the generations, to my own family (Moncreiffe, 1971, p.21).

Fascinating though this unsubstantiated clan history may be, more to the point is the fact that, after 1745, clan lands were forfeited to the crown and only restored in 1784. In the meantime, another important external force was at work: agricultural modernization began to impact on the central Highlands, with black cattle and sheep being introduced from the 1750s. The new agriculture, largely geared to supplying emergent urban markets in the Lowlands rather than to subsistence, changed clan life, as it did everywhere in the Highlands, and began to scatter Clan Donnachaidh from Rannoch and Atholl. There is no direct evidence of eviction by the Chief, and indeed, the story is told that the 18th Chief sold one of his largest estates, Struan, in 1854 allegedly 'in his efforts to look after his Rannoch folk' (Moncreiffe, 1971, p.21).

Here is yet another example of a recurrent theme in the study of family and community history – the importance of social and economic background. We can take this further and find confirmation of the dramatic changes experienced by my ancestors and their kin, by looking at some descriptions by contemporary observers in these Perthshire communities (Figures 2.8, 2.9 and 2.10).

> *Population.*—In August 1791, there were living in the u-
> nited parishes, 3120 souls, viz. 1480 males, and 1640 fe-
> males. Of that number, 758 were under eight years of age.
> The yearly average of marriages, for the last ten years, was
> nearly 26; and the yearly average of baptisms, for the same
> period, was 94. Besides the number above mentioned, there
> is a considerable number of young people, belonging to the
> parish, serving in the east and west; of whom part will pro-
> bably return, and part will not.
>
> Though it cannot be exactly determined, the probability is,
> that the number of the people in this parish is diminished,
> owing to several causes. When people of small landed pro-
> perty no longer lived upon the produce of their estates, but
> followed the example of their wealthier neighbours, in the
> use of foreign commodities, they contracted debt, sold their
> estates, and went to push their fortunes elsewhere. When
> the jurisdiction act took place, and men of landed property
> could not make their tenants fight their battles, they became
> less careful of having clever fellows about them, and so began
> to consider, how they might make the most of that class of
> men in another way. Then the rents began to be raised, the
> farms to be enlarged, much land to be taken into the land-
> lord's domain, and the shepherd and his dog to be the inhabi-
> tants of farms, that formerly maintained many families;
> though this last particular is not, as yet, so much the case
> here, as it is in many other places. In consequence of these
> changes, some of the tenants are become cottagers; some have
> removed to towns, to gain a livelihood by labour; and a few
> have emigrated to America, though that spirit is not become
> very common here as yet. The return to Dr Webster, how-
> ever, being only 3257 souls, the decrease has been inconside-
> rable.

Figure 2.8 Blair-Atholl and Strowan, 1790–91 (Source: facsimile extract from *The statistical account of Scotland*, 1791, pp.466–7)

III.—POPULATION.

In 1755, the population, by the returns of Dr Webster, was			3257
1791,	by the last Statistical Account,		3120
1801,	by the census,	-	-
1811,	-	-	-
1821,	-	-	-
1831,	-	-	2495

Number of families in the parish,	. . . .	549
chiefly employed in agriculture,	. . .	197
chiefly employed in manufactures, trade, or handicraft,		75

Number of illegitimate births during last three years, **7.**

There is good reason to suspect that the last Government census is overrated. The present incumbent in his parochial visits, and more especially in 1814, found the number of his parishioners to be about 2333. The parish is divided into eleven districts, with an elder in each district, and in May 1836, according to the census of the elders, the population was found to amount to 2312.

The gradual decrease of the population is easily accounted for. In former times, the higher grounds were inhabited by numerous tenants. Their possessions were small; their supply of farinaceous food was precarious, and in the very best seasons afforded but a scanty subsistence. They had no potatoes, and their principal aliment was animal food. A system of more beneficial management has converted these dreary and comfortless habitations into sheep-walks; and greatly to their own interest, though not perhaps at first so congenially to their feelings, the people have emigrated to the large towns of the south, or to America. And though the population upon the whole has diminished, it has greatly increased in the strath of the country, which is certainly a more natural and suitable residence for man, than the bleak unsheltered wastes of the Grampian mountains. The parish is entirely landward, and it cannot be said that there is a town or village in it.

Figure 2.9 Blair-Atholl, 1838 (Source: facsimile extract from *The new statistical account of Scotland*, 1845, pp.569–70)

_____ *EXERCISE 2.2* _____

Read the facsimile extracts reproduced in Figures 2.8, 2.9 and 2.10. Complete the following exercise (looking back if necessary):

1 From the data provided, tabulate the population of the parishes of Blair-Atholl and Fortingal between the 1790s and the 1830s. Comment on the trends.

2 What explanations are advanced for depopulation?

3 What seem to have been the consequences of agricultural modernization and changes in land use?

4 List the principal destinations for migrants.

5 What types of occupation did they take up?

III.—POPULATION.

At present, no part of the parish is more populous than it was in 1790; whereas in several districts, the population has since decreased fully a half; and the same will be found to have taken place, though not perhaps in so great a proportion, in most or all of the pastoral districts of the county.

According to census of 1801, the population was	-		3875
1811,	-	-	3236
1821,	-	-	3189
1831,	-	-	3067
Number of families in the parish,	-	-	621
chiefly engaged in agriculture,	-	-	273
in trade, manufactures, or handicraft,		-	119

One of the principal causes of the decrease has been emigration. Upwards of 120 families from this parish, since the former Account was drawn up, have crossed the Atlantic, besides many individuals of both sexes; while many others have sought a livelihood in the low country, especially in the great towns of Edinburgh, Glasgow, Dundee, Perth, Crieff, &c. The system of uniting several farms together, and letting them to one individual, has, more than any other circumstance, promoted emigration.

Figure 2.10 Fortingal, 1838 (Source: facsimile extract from *The new statistical account of Scotland*, 1845, pp.552–3)

A simple tabulation, based on the information provided in Figures 2.8, 2.9 and 2.10, will look something like Table 2.5.

Table 2.5 Population of Blair-Atholl and Fortingal, 1791–1836

Year	Blair-Atholl	Fortingal
[1791]	[3,120]	ND
1801	ND	3,875
1811	ND	3,236
1821	ND	3,189
1831	2,495	3,067
1836	2,312	ND

Note: ND = no data. Reference to census returns in Parliamentary papers could fill the gaps for Blair-Atholl.

Several explanations for depopulation are advanced, including the sale or letting of estates, raising of rents, introduction of sheep farming and consequent clearance (or 'removal') of the people. There is an oblique reference to the break-up of the clan system in the first Blair-Atholl account (Figure 2.8). The later accounts are more explicit (Figure 2.9); in Fortingal consolidation of farm units is seen as the main explanation (Figure 2.10).

Former crofters and herders of cattle were forced off their traditional holdings in higher parts and many migrated to the straths (or valleys), where the potato had become a subsistence crop, accounting for 50 per cent of diet. Others took non-agricultural occupations and the rest migrated to towns, or emigrated to North America. Most went into industrial occupations. But a closer examination of the extracts provides an interesting gloss on what was actually happening in these localities. Young people from Blair-Atholl seem to have been temporary migrants to the Lowlands and some might have become return migrants. Clearly, others settled permanently. The bulk of the out-migrants apparently headed south to Edinburgh, Glasgow, Dundee or Perth, rather than across the Atlantic.

So, the 'push' and 'pull' mechanisms, discussed in Chapter 1, section 3.2, clearly under-pinned migration from this district – as they did in so many other parts of Scotland and Ireland during the nineteenth century.

From these extracts you can see that the *Statistical accounts of Scotland*, which are available in some major reference libraries, can provide vital background to migration projects (see, also, Volume 4, Chapter 4, section 6; and for statistical surveys covering Ireland, Volume 4, Chapter 3, section 1.1). Much the same story can be charted and questions posed using the valuable topographical dictionaries and their subsequent editions, edited by Samuel Lewis (Lewis, 1831, England; 1833, Wales; 1837, Ireland; 1846, Scotland) – as well as county and parish histories, including, in England, the famous *Victoria County Histories* (see Volume 4, Chapter 3, section 1.1).

What we have seen here gives some background to the family legend surrounding my own ancestors. The story goes that, in the wake of clearances from Highland Perthshire, the family migrated to Lowland Fife at the beginning of the 1800s and became colliers, moving west to Lanarkshire later in the century, when large-scale mining got underway after the 1840s and new communities sprang up on the coalfields. The story, as substantiated from parish registers, vital records, census data and the old family Bible, indicates that my great-grandfather had made an occupational shift into the textile trade as a tailor, while my grandfather continued in his father's footsteps as a textile designer. By the 1880s the Highland migrant family had become firmly established in a Lowland community. Meanwhile, other members of Clan Donnachaidh were widely scattered by internal migration to elsewhere in Scotland and into England and by emigration (some went to Canada and New Zealand) – typical of the Scottish and Irish experience since the nineteenth century.

_____ **QUESTION FOR RESEARCH** _____

If there is a history of migration in your own family, you might like to investigate further by addressing similar questions about origins, motivations and destinations.

4.2   SCOTTISH AND IRISH DEMOGRAPHIC PATTERNS

Scottish and Irish population movements are, in themselves, distinctively different, but the two countries were exposed to similar external social and economic forces. The changes and movements need to be seen in the wider context of industrialization and economic growth during the eighteenth and nineteenth centuries. The forces of economic change in both agriculture and industry certainly had a more sudden and dramatic impact in Scotland; in Ireland, the limited industrialization of Ulster was accompanied by agricultural and land-use changes that profoundly modified the existing social fabric throughout the country. Despite differences of scale, both poverty and repression, to varying degrees, are common underlying themes. As we saw earlier, explanatory models of migration take account of such important 'push' factors.

Do you think demographic changes might also have played a part in migration?

As in England, there was marked and sustained growth of population in Scotland from the late 1740s, reaching 1.6 million by 1801, 2.9 million in 1851 and 4.4 million in 1901. Losses through migration to England and emigration to North America and Australasia were considerable; though, to some extent, these were redressed by in-migration from Ireland, England and Wales and immigration from continental Europe. The Highlands experienced a persistent decline from the mid-nineteenth century following the famine of the 1840s. Although a few country communities (often market towns) continued to grow by attracting in-migrants from their immediate hinterlands, most rural areas, including many Lowland parishes, reached peak population in 1851. Thus, urbanization and industrial development were significant features in Scotland – as they were elsewhere in Victorian Britain – profoundly affecting both family and community history until the present day (Flinn, 1977; Gray, 1990).

While Scotland broadly conformed to north European norms, trends in Ireland were very different. Ireland reached its peak population of 8.5 million in 1845, having quadrupled since the 1740s. Nowhere else in Europe, with the possible exception of Finland, had growth been more rapid; Ireland seems unique in its dramatic population explosion (Ó Gráda, 1989, pp.108–33). Recent investigations of tax and census-related data, however, do suggest that the annual rate of increase was slackening from 1.6 per cent between 1791 and 1821, down to 0.5 per cent between 1831 and 1845. There were large regional disparities too: the strongest growth was in Munster and Connaught, almost twice as fast as in the region bounded by Dublin, Derry, Athlone and Waterford, the most economically developed part of Ireland.

Why did the population rise? Improved food supplies (mainly the potato) prevented and moderated subsistence crises and enabled earlier marriages with high marital fertility. Early marriage had been traditional in Irish society and an increased food supply kept the marriage age from rising. Age at marriage was low, but fertility was high – a function partly of the economic value of large families. Ó Gráda (1989, p.119) has even suggested that the potato had fecundity-enhancing powers! Note, however, that the nature of all the processes described here is still open to debate.

After 1801 the slackening rates of demographic growth were not accompanied by any significant decline in life expectancy. Even if pressures on food supplies resulted in increased mortality, this might have been offset by a reduction in child mortality. Certainly, temporary migration and emigration, both of which increased dramatically after 1815, contributed substantially to the decline in the growth rate. A further preventative check was the decline in the marriage age of women between 1811 and 1841 – by 1841 the proportion that had never married (one woman in ten) was the same as in Scotland and England.

Rapid population growth elsewhere in Western Europe was accompanied by large-scale urbanization. But in Ireland this did not occur. Dublin accounted for only 3 per cent of the total population of the country in both 1801 and 1841; and the other major centres, Belfast and Cork, did not individually exceed 80,000 until 1845. Certainly, Irish towns – like towns everywhere – acted as magnets for migrants from rural areas but they were greatly overshadowed by Glasgow and Manchester which were the main pre-famine destinations of the Irish on the move in search of a livelihood (Freeman, 1989, pp.242–64). In other words, with nothing to hold them in Ireland, the migration streams were deflected to mainland Britain.

The Great Famine or 'Great Hunger' of 1845–49, probably the most serious demographic catastrophe in the British Isles, was caused by the failure of potato crops through blight, which came to Europe from North America. The crisis was at its worst in Ireland because for a third of the population the potato was the staple food. Returns from grain and other crops were used to pay the rent, and, as folk starved, ironically, millions of pounds worth of food left Irish ports. Conditions approaching famine in other parts of Europe – including the Scottish Highlands – led to massive speculation in food and even when grain was available, the ordinary people could not afford the prices. Inevitably, as they failed to pay the rent, they were evicted. Starving people, in their thousands, wandered the countryside, seeking nourishment from berries, nettles and even grass. The pressure on the Poor Law system was unprecedented.

Public work relief schemes – employing as many as 734,000 by 1847 – alleviated but did not eradicate the problem. As the famine bit deeper, thousands succumbed to diseases of malnutrition. The lucky ones with enough strength or cash trekked to the ports in a flood of emigration to mainland Britain and to North America. Landlords began to seize corn in lieu of rents and, as inflated Poor Law rates were levied, farms were abandoned in a new wave of emigration from among the more prosperous tenant-farmers and small businessmen. There was a major outbreak of cholera in 1848–49. The census recorded the impact of these events in all their starkness when a substantially reduced population of 6.5 million was returned in 1851 in contrast to the 8.1 million of 1841. Due to famine conditions, an estimated one million more people died than were born. The remainder of the decline was due to emigration – a trend that continued, virtually unbroken, into the 1960s.

EXERCISE 2.3

Having read the above account of Scottish and Irish population trends, make brief notes on:

1 Common explanations for demographic growth in both Scotland and Ireland before the 1840s.

2 The significance of demographic growth for migration.

Comment p.219.

What then, in summary, has prompted and sustained migration? In both Scotland and Ireland, as we noted, some were pushed, some were pulled. Migration – short or long term – was under-pinned by population pressure, poverty, intervening opportunities (mainly jobs), and, in the case of emigration, the longing for land or the desire to preserve religious and cultural cohesion. Successful settlers reported favourably on their new environments and communities, encouraging others to move – often setting up new trains of chain migration (see Chapter 1, section 3.5). Government intervention also played a part.

Technological developments had a significant impact on migration into the Clyde (from both the Highlands and from Ireland) and to Merseyside in Lancashire. The first regular sea-going steamship, 'Rob Roy', began plying the Belfast–Greenock route in 1818 – followed by the Howth–Holyhead, and the Belfast–Glasgow and Belfast–Liverpool routes. This greatly encouraged passenger movement, especially of seasonal migrants such as harvest workers. In turn, the building of both the canals and railways – mainly using Irish labour – facilitated internal movements, particularly after the creation of the national networks by the end of the major Railway Mania in the 1840s (see Chapter 5, section 3.2).

EXERCISE 2.4

Before reading further, make a list of the recurrent theories and common factors mentioned above that affected Scottish and Irish migration.

Compare your list with that in Schema A below.

Schema A: Some factors in migration

o 'Push–pull' factors.

o Short- and long-term economic and social factors.

o Population pressures (see demographic trends above).

o Poverty.

o Employment opportunities.

o   Desire to own land (especially emigrants).

o   Need to preserve religious and cultural cohesion.

o   Encouragement by successful settlers (letters, newspaper reports, etc.).

o   Chain migration.

o   Government intervention (relief schemes, assisted passages).

o   Improved transport facilities (steam ships, canals, railways).

Some – if not all – of the factors shown in Schema A would be well to the forefront in any migration research project. Indeed, this is a useful check-list of questions that might be addressed about individuals, families and larger cohorts.

4.3   INTERNAL MIGRATION: STEP-WISE, SEASONAL AND PERMANENT

While many stayed at home, some Scots and Irish moved – mainly, but not exclusively, from rural to urban areas. In contrast, in England migration between one rural area and the next was still occurring (see section 1). Demand for rural skills was on the decline, so these migrants sensibly settled in other parts of Britain where they might start unskilled but could soon acquire new skills. These movements have provided scholars with some challenging projects in historical demography. Their findings set the context for further investigations of migration, thus illustrating the kinds of sources and questions that can be explored and the possible projects that might be tackled.

STEP-WISE MIGRATION: HIGHLAND MIGRANTS TO GLASGOW, 1852–98

In the past, Glasgow police officers have stood out from the crowd, not just because of their height, but by the fact that they all spoke with Highland accents! A study by historical geographers, Charles Withers and Alexandra Watson (1991), picks up on the story of what, initially, was temporary but became permanent migration from the rural Highlands to the urban Lowlands – the process referred to earlier in my own 'personal beginnings'. Most previous studies of Highland–Lowland migration had assumed movements between birthplace and place of enumeration (say, in the 1851 census) as the result of single direct moves. But, as we have seen, migration can proceed by stages or steps. Withers and Watson looked at the General Register of the Poor, as well as at the CEBs, to reconstruct the step-wise migration patterns of a cohort of Highland migrants to Victorian Glasgow, elsewhere in the Lowlands and beyond (Table 2.6).

As Withers and Watson demonstrate, migration brought an important source of cash income; it relieved population pressure; and, in the 1840s, it provided an escape from the widespread destitution brought on by the potato famine. Highland towns were important as sending areas – often the first step in the process. Lowland towns attracted the largest numbers of in-migrant Highlanders from the nearby areas, and there was a clear dividing line between east and west. The numbers of migrants from the more distant Highland origins increased towards the end of the nineteenth century, though these were still outnumbered by

Table 2.6 Migration of Highlanders to Glasgow, 1852–98

Number of moves made in migration path	Number of persons having that migration path	Number of persons as % of total step-wise movers	Average duration of complete step-wise migration path (years and months)
2	169	50.5	10 yrs 10 mths
3	78	23.3	11 yrs 8 mths
4	37	11.1	13 yrs 9 mths
5	19	5.7	11 yrs 9 mths
6	17	5.1	13 yrs 8 mths
7	5	1.5	8 yrs 4 mths
8	5	1.5	8 yrs 5 mths
9	3	1.0	10 yrs 9 mths
10	—	—	— —
11	—	—	— —
12	1	0.3	19 yrs 9 mths
Totals	**334**	**100.0**	**12 yrs 1 mth***

Note: *overall average.

Source: based on Withers and Watson (1991) Table 4, p.46

short-distance migrants. The Poor Law records contain valuable information as to the sequential steps by which individuals had moved:

> ... *Donald Ferguson, for example, an unmarried 49-year-old blacksmith from Inveraray in Argyll [applied] for poor relief on 7 March 1867 owing to 'bad health'. The parochial clerk noted 'He has been resident in Renfrew, Port Glasgow, Greenock, Dublin, Birkenhead, Chester, Partick, Govan, High St. Anderston [Glasgow] and various quarters in town and country. Not been above 3 years at one time in any parish in Scotland since he became of age'.*
> (Withers and Watson, 1991, p.40, quoting from Strathclyde Regional Archives (SRA) Barony Parish Applications D/HEW 14/31, p.25473, 7 March 1867)

Others were less mobile but still moved in steps or short-distance stages rather than direct to Glasgow. Alexander Stewart, for example, left his birthplace, aged 25, first for one month in Luss, then a year in Paisley, before getting to Glasgow. Janet Kennedy left Duirinish in 1835, at the age of 37, for Campbeltown (where she married), and was in Glasgow in 1888. Some left at an earlier age, like the domestic servants Ann Sutherland and Jessie Mathieson:

> *Their relatively young age at departure (13 and 19 respectively) and complex lifetime migration paths from rural east Scotland to Glasgow via numerous other lowland towns hint at the way these patterns of geographical mobility were, for some migrants, simultaneously processes of individual socio-cultural change.*
> (Withers and Watson, 1991, p.49)

That such movements were not unusual can be seen in Figure 2.11. Highland migration is particularly interesting because of its recurring patterns of 'return' migration and step-migration – multiple movements over time and space.

So the main picture that emerges is one that reveals the *complexity* of Highland–Lowland movements. Individual and family experiences, reconstituted not just from the census but also from other sources, such as the General Register of the Poor, do throw significant further light on the process. Looked at in more detail, it appears that the number of intermediary migration steps is related to the distances that had been covered. Moves were often related to employment opportunities and vocation, and could be quite complex. Women were just as mobile as men and the most obvious detectable pattern is the predominance of West Highlanders (Figure 2.11 again).

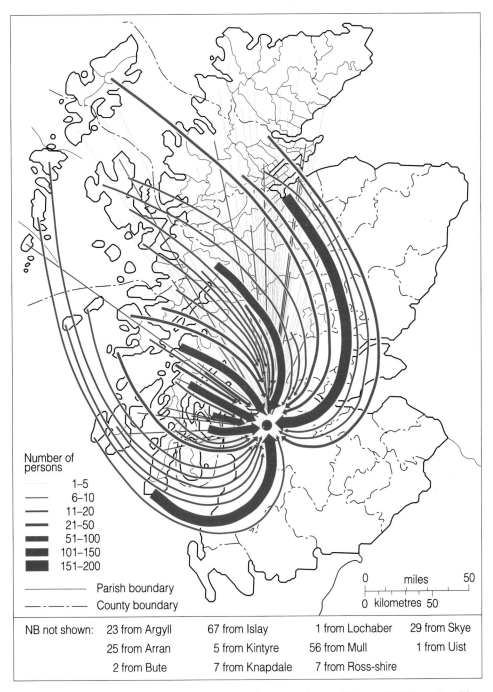

Number of persons

1–5
6–10
11–20
21–50
51–100
101–150
151–200

———————— Parish boundary
— — · — — County boundary

NB not shown:	23 from Argyll	67 from Islay	1 from Lochaber	29 from Skye
	25 from Arran	5 from Kintyre	56 from Mull	1 from Uist
	2 from Bute	7 from Knapdale	7 from Ross-shire	

Figure 2.11   Highland migration to Glasgow, 1852–98 (Source: Withers and Watson, 1991, Figure 3, p.45)

The techniques and sources used in this study have considerable relevance for reconstructing the often complex movements of individuals and families. The sources used provide data on occupational shifts and on changes, over time, in social status, as well as on the geographical movements. The study of step migration has many applications and promises the dedicated researcher challenging investigations anywhere in the United Kingdom and Ireland (see Chapter 4).

———————————— *QUESTION FOR RESEARCH* ————————————

Have your own family, or others known to you, moved much from place to place? Try to find out where, when and why, and how typical this was of others at the time. Certainly, a simplified version of the above would make an excellent project. Think about how the techniques used by Withers and Watson (1991) could be deployed in your own project, using census, Poor Law or other records.

4.4 'A CURIOUS MIDDLE PLACE': THE IRISH IN BRITAIN, 1871–1921

The Irish migrant community in mainland Britain included many of the transient folk employed as the labour force on the land, in manufacturing industry and in construction. As David Fitzpatrick has observed, transience within Britain was encouraged 'by virtual exclusion from secure housing and employment' (Fitzpatrick, 1985, p.10). Although there were no Irish 'ghettos' as such, the settlers clustered in the most decaying inner sectors of many British towns – Liverpool, Coventry, London, Glasgow and Cardiff – moving with startling rapidity from one insalubrious lodging to another (see Chapter 6, section 4.2; King *et al.*, 1989). The relative deprivation of these in-migrants is manifest in the statistics of pauperism and criminality, which revealed Irish over-representation in virtually all categories. Moreover, often the Irish were alienated because of culture and religion; their continued obsession with Irish grievances was seen in clashes between the 'Orange' and 'Green' factions, particularly in the larger towns of northern England and in Scotland where the settlers included many from Ulster.

———————————— *EXERCISE 2.5* ————————————

Examine Table 2.7 and then comment on the trends shown by the data.

Table 2.7 Irish-born population of Great Britain, 1871–1921

	Number	As % population	% female	% under 20 years of age
England and Wales				
1871	566,540	2.49	50.01	11.97
1881	562,374	2.17	48.35	NA
1891	458,315	1.58	48.81	NA
1901	426,565	1.31	47.26	NA
1911	375,325	1.04	48.88	NA
1921	364,747	0.96	51.01	NA
Scotland				
1871	207,770	6.18	47.79	14.43
1881	218,745	5.86	46.40	13.73
1891	194,807	4.84	45.71	11.99
1901	205,064	4.59	41.95	11.51
1911	174,715	3.67	42.77	10.11
1921	159,020	3.26	43.66	10.78

Source: based on Fitzpatrick (1985) Table 1.1, p.11

Table 2.7 shows that the Irish component in the population of England and Wales dropped from 2.5 to less than 1 per cent between 1871 and 1921. In Scotland, where, proportionately, the Irish had been greater in the first place, it fell from 6 to just over 3 per cent. In England and Wales women were only just in the majority of the Irish-born population, while in Scotland there was a marked male majority. The proportion of children was always small and the Scottish figures show a steady drop from 1871 to 1911.

The declining pace of migration had important demographic consequences. Irish migration to Britain during this period was dominated by young unmarried adults rather than family groups, so the proportion of children was always small. But decreasing migration compounded this by causing a general ageing of the Irish migrant population.

The Irish tended to settle where the demand for semi-skilled labour was buoyant, such as in colliery and iron-making districts. Their search for appropriate job opportunities meant that their migration trajectories included the urban and industrial networks of south Wales, northern England and the Scottish Lowlands. But the four major cities of London, Liverpool, Manchester and Glasgow have continued to be their main attractions: even in 1921 a third of the Irish-born were still congregated there (Fitzpatrick, 1985, p.13).

Temporary migration had been a traditional feature of Irish life well before the famine. Indeed, migratory labourers from Ireland formed a significant component of the British farm labour force up to the First World War (Fitzpatrick, 1985, p.16). Temporary migration is particularly hard to pin down, but from the 1880s its incidence can be traced, in part, from the returns from local constabularies and railway and shipping companies; from government reports (including an official inquiry of 1883) and Poor Law records (temporary migrants are sometimes identifiable in the communities through which they were passing); from the birthplace information in the CEBs; and from rating lists, street and post office directories and the incidence of Irish names. The great bulk of the temporary migrants came from the western counties of Ireland. In 1880 four-fifths of all migratory labourers counted by the constabulary had come from Donegal, Armagh and the counties of Connaught; later in the century the numbers greatly increased (Fitzpatrick, 1985, pp.16, 18).

What implications do you think these seasonal migration patterns might have had both for the sending communities and for the processes of migration more generally?

The accepted tradition of migration – both seasonal and permanent – was a far-reaching one in particular areas with consequences for local economies and people's way of life and aspirations there (discussed in Chapter 2, section 4, and Chapter 7, section 2), as well as for the migrants themselves. Fitzpatrick sums up the overall picture:

Seasonal migration, to a far greater extent than in pre-Famine times, was a highly localized movement between certain coastal districts in north-western Ireland and a shrinking belt of agricultural Britain. It was composed of men rather than women and farmers' sons rather than landholders, who, when they did migrate, were usually very small farmers. Thus, in a few districts, it provided an alternative to permanent emigration for the surplus population of young unmarried adult males. For many of these it was, in fact, the prelude to less easily reversible departure. It provided both a taste for life elsewhere and the means for indulging that taste. Indeed, seasonal and permanent migration were often complementary rather than alternative experiences, seasonal movement being a normal adolescent episode whereas emigration occurred slightly later in the male life cycle, when the transfer of farm occupancy between generations was being accomplished.

(Fitzpatrick, 1985, p.18)

_____ *QUESTION FOR RESEARCH* _____

A proportion of migrant labourers described in Fitzpatrick's study settled permanently in communities that previously had proved attractive to others from their country. There they made their own very special contribution to the cultural, social and economic fabric of their adopted homes and the Irish migrants have left potentially fruitful archives for historical investigations of their origins, movements, occupations and lifestyles. These and other aspects could form the basis of an interesting local project based on community or business archives. (Further suggestions relating to questions of assimilation and/or continuing cultural identity can be found in Chapter 6, sections 4 and 5; see also Davis, 1991; and for an interesting study of a more recent period, see King *et al.*, 1989).

4.5   IRISH EMIGRATION TO NORTH AMERICA: TWO EXAMPLES OF DATA SOURCES

Emigration has attracted more attention from scholars, thanks to the opportunities that exist for archive-linkage of sources, such as emigration lists, ships' passenger lists, land grant registers, census and vital registers at either end of the migration path. It is possible to identify such features as the origin, sex, age, marital status, occupation, level of literacy, ports of departure and arrival and ultimate destination of an individual. A great deal more detail can sometimes be gleaned from records. For example, my own research using sources available in the Scottish Record Office, the Public Record Office, and in local and regional archives, has dealt, amongst other things, with the Scottish–Australian connection, and looked at patterns of Scottish emigration to Australia before 1914 (Donnachie, 1992a,b).

Historically, emigrants from the United Kingdom and Ireland fall into four broad categories:

1   Those transported as convicts (mainly to Australia, but earlier to the North American colonies).

2   Indentured servants or apprentices.

3   Assisted emigrants, generally supported by the US government, colonial governments or home-based emigration societies.

4   Free or independent emigrants travelling under their own steam and with their own resources.

The majority, individuals or families, are reasonably well documented. As we have seen in Chapter 1 (section 4), the scope for research projects is considerable. The following studies – one using a primary source, the other an interpretative gloss on Irish migration from the female perspective – illustrate the kinds of sources and questions you might draw on.

ORDNANCE SURVEY MEMOIRS AND EMIGRATION LISTS: ANTRIM AND LONDONDERRY, 1833–39

Field officers mapping the first Ordnance Survey (OS) of Ireland (and elsewhere) in the 1830–40s, gathered a wealth of socio-economic information – but nowhere more so than in the counties of Antrim and Londonderry where their information included lists of named emigrants (see Mitchell, 1989; for the reprints of the Ordnance Survey Memoirs, see Day and McWilliam, 1991–). As you can see in Figure 2.12, these, virtually unparalleled, lists identify both destination and place of origin, plus age, year of emigration, the religion and (sometimes) the occupation or trade of emigrants.

Figure 2.12   Ordnance Survey Memoirs: migrants from Raloo Parish, County Antrim, 1837–39

ORDNANCE SURVEY MEMOIRS

COUNTY: ANTRIM

PARISH: RALOO

NAME	AGE	YEAR LEFT	TOWNLAND	DESTINATION	TRADE	RELI-GION
DRUMMOND, William	25	1837	Ballygowan	Quebec	Labourer	P
CRAWFORD, James	60	1837	Ballyrickard	New York	Shoemaker	P
CRAWFORD, Mary	50	1837	Ballyrickard	New York		P
CRAWFORD, Joseph	24	1837	Ballyrickard	New York	Weaver	P
CRAWFORD, James	25	1837	Ballyrickard	New York	Weaver	P
CRAWFORD, William	18	1837	Ballyrickard	New York	Weaver	P
CRAWFORD, David	14	1837	Ballyrickard	New York		P
McAREEVY, Jane	24	1837	Ballyrickard	New York		RC
McWILLIAMS, Mary	44	1838	Ballyrickard	Charlestown		P
McWILLIAMS, Nathaniel	49	1838	Ballyrickard	Charlestown	Farmer	P
McWILLIAMS, Jane	14	1838	Ballyrickard	Charlestown		P
McWILLIAMS, Sarah	12	1838	Ballyrickard	Charlestown		P
McWILLIAMS, Nathaniel	8	1838	Ballyrickard	Charlestown		P
McWILLIAMS, William	4	1838	Ballyrickard	Charlestown		P
ROBINSON, Sarah	20	1838	Ballyrickard	Charlestown	Weaver	P
ASHTON, Robert	20	1838	Ballyrickard	Charlestown	Apothecary	P
ASHTON, Alexander	40	1838	Ballyrickard	Charlestown	Farmer	P
ASHTON, Jane	36	1838	Ballyrickard	Charlestown		P
ASHTON, James	14	1838	Ballyrickard	Charlestown		P
JUNKIN, Samuel	24	1838	Ballyrickard	Demerara*	Farmer	P
McWHIRTER, David	22	1838	Ballyrickard	Demerara*	Weaver	P
McADAM, Samuel	25	1838	Ballyryland	New York	Labourer	P
ROBINSON, Andy	24	1838	Ballyryland	New York	Labourer	P
McWHIRTER, Thomas	24	1838	Tureagh	New York	Labourer	P
ORR, Eliza	20	1839	Ballygowan	Quebec		P
McCORMICK, Jane	60	1839	Ballygowan	New York		RC
McCORMICK, Mathew	24	1839	Ballygowan	New York	Farmer	P
CRAIG, Robert	20	1839	Ballygowan	New York	Labourer	P
MOORE, Isabella	20	1839	Tureagh	Glasgow	School – Mistress	P
McDOWELL, Margaret	30	1839	Ballygowan	New York		P
DUNCAN, John	34	1839	Altilevelly	New York	Weaver	P
DAVISON, Nancy	32	1839	Altilevelly	New York	Servant	P
LOGAN, Eliza	22	1839	Altilevelly	New York	Servant	P
STUART, Charles	20	1839	Altilevelly	Glasgow	Labourer	P
PENNALL, Robert	21	1839	Ballyrickard	Demerara*	Farmer	P
SNODDY, Samuel	20	1839	Tureagh	New York	Tailor	P
FERGUSON, Margaret	20	1839	Bettia	New York		P
GAULT, John	35		Ballygowan	Glasgow	Labourer	P
McFALL, Alexander	24		Ballygowan	Glasgow	Labourer	P
McFALL, Sally	35		Ballygowan	Glasgow		P
TIPPINS, Eliza	20		Ballygowan	Glasgow		P
GALLAGHER, Henry	25		Ballygowan	Glasgow	Labourer	RC

Note: P = Protestant; RC = Roman Catholic. *Demerara (now Georgetown) is in Guyana.

Source: facsimile extract from Mitchell (1989) pp.48–9

How could we use this source for research?

Such lists can provide data about how many people left each year, their age profile (in this case overwhelmingly young, it seems), and where they went (to ports in North America, to Britain – probably as seasonal labourers?). We can also use surnames to identify the numbers of apparently single unattached people leaving, and how many, like the Crawfords or the McWilliams, who left in a family group – and from what kind of background. The trades listed also give some hints about the local occupational structure. Raloo seems to have been an essentially agricultural parish in which the major industrial activity was textiles – but this would need to be checked and amplified through nominal record linkage to such complementary sources as the OS maps themselves, census and parish records, trade directories and secondary sources on the Ulster linen industry, as well as surviving domestic and industrial buildings in the locality.

A list of this kind could be used as the basis for an interesting, though more limited, local or regional study of emigration. From where and from what sort of community did emigrants come? What were their ages and occupations? Were they married or single? From which ports did they leave, and where were they bound? As pioneered in the work of Mageean (1985, 1986, 1989, 1991), shipping lists and indents, registers of emigrants, customs records and port books, together with the sources mentioned above, do provide some of the answers to such questions.

EMIGRATION TRENDS AMONGST IRISH WOMEN

From the early decades of the nineteenth century, the Irish exodus to North America included many women. As the migration streams increased, soon it became clear that women accounted for more than half of all emigrants from Ireland. Diner has emphasized that these movements eventually became 'a virtual tidal wave of human beings leaving one home and seeking another … No other major group of immigrants in American history contained so many women' (Diner, 1983, p.31).

Why should Irish male–female ratios have differed so fundamentally from those of other groups of emigrants?

This question has been followed up in Diner's study of Irish emigrant women in the nineteenth century (Diner, 1983). Her conclusion is that the famine brought major changes to family landholding patterns, forcing even more children to seek a living in non-agricultural work or to migrate elsewhere. The majority of female emigrants came from rural areas of the west that had been most seriously affected by the famine, and where (unlike Ulster and Leinster, with their major cities of Belfast and Dublin) employment opportunities for women were most restricted. Apart from the obvious reason of seeking work, the other important factor was the single-inheritance system, which cut out younger offspring, especially daughters, from any prospect of land tenure. Kinship networks were important because they promoted and facilitated further emigration. In these respects, women relatives played a key part, assisting not only other female relatives and friends, but also single and married men and their families. The favoured destinations were the east coast ports in the USA and industrial cities where women migrants – eschewing rural life – obtained employment in factories, domestic service or public work projects. Farming was more likely to be taken up by immigrant *families*, not individuals. The fact that it required capital, effectively closed farming to single men and women, except as labourers.

_____ *EXERCISE 2.6* _____

Turn back to Schema A on pp.56–7 and consider the following questions:

1 How many of the listed factors appear to be relevant to an analysis of Irish female migration?

2 Should any further factors be added to the list?

Answers/comments p.219.

This fascinating study of Irish female emigrants again stresses the importance of kin relationships in a modified pattern of chain migration and highlights the role of women in the process. It shows that the nuclear family, which was so significant in earlier Irish migrations, was less important in the later nineteenth and early twentieth centuries when individual men and women made up the bulk of emigrants to the USA. Diner's findings also have messages for wider comparative research. Although the precise details are interestingly distinctive in this particular study, the basic factors and questions to explore are, at root, not very much different from those in other migration contexts: for example, questions as to the relative importance of push–pull factors, employment opportunities, local economic structure, chain migration and the other considerations listed in Schema A. But Diner's work does bring an important added dimension on the key roles of women in the migration process.

4.6 TAKING YOUR RESEARCH FURTHER

While most communities are generated from long-stay families, migration has invariably played some role. Hopefully this section has given you further ideas as to the exciting opportunities that migration studies can open up for the family and community historian. You need not feel intimidated by problems of access to original sources, for national, regional and local archives throughout the United Kingdom and in Ireland have an enormous range of holdings relevant to such studies, including microfilms or microfiches of records from other parts of the country and from archives overseas. Joint international copying projects – including those involving the Church of the Latter Day Saints (Mormons) and local and regional family history societies – have also made some regional and overseas records available. The scope for more localized and for more firmly focused projects that draw on these sources is considerable – providing the appropriate research questions are posed.

5 CONCLUSION

by W.T.R. Pryce

The case studies discussed in this chapter cover a number of themes that are appropriate for local, small-scale research investigations and projects. Throughout, rather than present all that there is to know about a particular topic or locality, the approach has been selective. Specific lines of enquiry have been highlighted, the availability and limitations of sources have been discussed, and we have demonstrated the effectiveness of a number of useful analytical techniques. There has been emphasis, too, on ways of presenting results in texual form complemented by statistical tabulations, photographs, diagrams and maps; and, in the text itself, on the interpretation of results and the presentation of conclusions.

Our concluding exercises, which draw, in part, on ideas presented earlier in Chapter 1, are designed to assist in the consolidation of some of the key issues dealt with in this chapter. At the same time, these also provide useful check-lists as to some of the concepts and methods that might be explored in your own research project.

_____ *EXERCISE 2.7* _____

List any ten sources used in the case studies discussed in Chapter 2.

Answer p.219.

_____ **EXERCISE 2.8: MIGRATION TERMS AND CONCEPTS** _____

Each of the following deals with a particular aspect of migration research. Tick the appropriate column of the specific case study/studies in which individual topics appear in Chapter 2. *Answers p.220.*

		CASE STUDIES					
Tick the appropriate column(s)		(a) Rural Essex, 1861–81	(b) Leicester, 1871–72	(c) Rural Yorkshire, 1831–38	(d) Welsh chapels in England	(e) Scots on the move	(f) Irish on the move
1	Chain migration						
2	Long-distance moves						
3	Step migration						
4	Intra-urban moves						
5	Short-term moves						
6	Longitudinal records						
7	Push–pull factors						
8	Immigration						
9	Internal migration						
10	Emigration						
11	Return migration						
12	Temporary/ seasonal migration						

REFERENCES AND FURTHER READING

Note: entries marked with an asterisk are suggestions for further reading.

Braham, P. (ed.) (1993) *Using the past: audio-cassettes on sources and methods for family and community historians*, Milton Keynes, The Open University.

Carter, H. and Lewis, C.R. (1990) *An urban geography of England and Wales in the nineteenth century*, London, Edward Arnold.

Davies, W.K.D., Giggs, J.A. and Herbert, D.T. (1968) 'Directories, rate books and the commercial structure of towns', *Geography*, 53, pp.41–54.

Davis, G. (1991) *The Irish in Britain 1815–1914*, Dublin, Gill and Macmillan.*

Day, A. and McWilliam, P. (eds) (1991–) *Ordnance Survey Memoirs of Ireland*, Belfast, Institute of Irish Studies, The Queen's University of Belfast; Dublin, Royal Irish Academy (reprint series of 38 volumes in progress).

Dickinson, G.C. (1958) 'The nature of rural population movement – an analysis of seven Yorkshire parishes based on electoral returns from 1931–1954', *Yorkshire Bulletin of Economic and Social Research*, 10, pp.95–108.

Diner, H.R. (1983) *Erin's daughters in America. Irish immigrant women in the nineteenth century*, Baltimore, MD, Johns Hopkins University Press.*

Donnachie, I. (1992a) 'The making of "Scots on the make": Scottish settlement and enterprise in Australia, 1830–1900', in Devine, T.M. (ed.) *Scottish emigration and Scottish society*, Edinburgh, John Donald Publishers.

Donnachie, I. (1992b) '"Utterly irreclaimable": Scottish convict women and Australia 1787–1852', in Swan, P. and Foster, D. (eds) *Essays in regional and local history*, Beverley, Hutton Press.

Drake, M. (ed.) (1994) *Time, family and community: perspectives on family and community history*, Oxford, Blackwell in association with The Open University (Course Reader).*

Ebdon, D. (1985) *Statistics in geography: a practical approach*, 2nd edn (reprinted 1992), Oxford, Blackwell.

Fitzpatrick, D. (1985) 'A curious middle place', in Swift, R. and Gilley, S. (eds) *The Irish in the Victorian city*, London, Croom Helm.*

Flinn, M.W. (ed.) (1977) *Scottish population history from the 17th century to the 1930s*, Cambridge, Cambridge University Press.

Freeman, T. (1989) 'Land and people, *c.*1841', in Vaughan (1989).

Gibson, J. and Rogers, C. (1993) *Electoral registers since 1832; and burgess lists*, Birmingham, Federation of Family History Societies.

Gray, M. (1990) *Scots on the move: Scots migrants 1750–1914*, Edinburgh, Economic and Social History Society of Scotland.

Griffiths, G. (1989) 'Recollections of early childhood', in Owen, W.T. (ed.) *Capel Elfed: hanes Eglwys y Tabernacl, Kings Cross*, Llundain, Eglwys y Tabernacl, Kings Cross. (This is a history of the Welsh Congregational Chapel, Pentonville Road, King's Cross, London N1, published by the chapel.)

Grigg, D.B. (1977) 'E.G. Ravenstein and the "Laws of Migration"', *Journal of Historical Geography*, 3, pp.41–51. Reprinted in Drake (1994).*

Holderness, B.A. (1971) 'Personal mobility in some rural parishes of Yorkshire, 1772–1822', *Yorkshire Archaeological Journal*, 42, pp.444–5. (There is an original printer's error in the title of this paper. The period covered is 1772–1812, not 1772–1822.)

Holmes, R.S. (1973) 'Ownership and migration from a study of rate books', *Area*, 5, pp.242–51.

Hume, I. and Pryce, W.T.R. (eds) (1986) *The Welsh and their country: selected readings in the social sciences*, Llandysul, Gomer Press.

Jones, E. (1981) 'The Welsh in London in the seventeenth and eighteenth centuries', *Welsh History Review*, 10, pp.461–79.

Jones, E. (1985) 'The Welsh in London in the nineteenth century', *Cambria*, 12, pp.149–69. (Part I in Davies, W.K.D. (ed.) *Human geography from Wales: proceedings of the E.G. Bowen Memorial Conference*.)*

Jones, J.R. (1946) *The Welsh builder on Merseyside: annals and lives.* Liverpool, J.R. Jones (private publication).

Jones, R.M. and Rees, D.B. (1984) *The Liverpool Welsh and their religion,* Liverpool and Llanddewi Brefi, Modern Welsh Publications.

King, R., Shuttleworth, I. and Strachan, A. (1989) 'The Irish in Coventry; the social geography of a relict community', *Irish Geography,* 22, pp.64–78.[*]

Lewis, S. (ed.) (1831) *A topographical dictionary of England,* London, Samuel Lewis (4 volumes). (Subsequent editions appeared in 1833, 1835, 1842 and 1848.)

Lewis, S. (ed.) (1833) *A topographical dictionary of Wales,* London, Samuel Lewis (2 volumes). (Subsequent editions appeared in 1840, 1843, 1849.)

Lewis, S. (ed.) (1837) *A topographical dictionary of Ireland,* London, Samuel Lewis (2 volumes). (A subsequent edition appeared in 1842.)

Lewis, S. (ed.) (1846) *A topographical dictionary of Scotland,* London, Samuel Lewis (2 volumes).

Lockhart, D.G. (1986) 'Migration to planned villages in Scotland between 1725 and 1850', *Scottish Geographical Magazine,* 102, pp.165–80.

Lockhart, D.G. (1989) 'Migration to planned villages in north-east Scotland', in Smith, J.S. and Stevenson, D. (eds) *Fermfolk and fisherfolk,* Aberdeen, Aberdeen University Press.

Lockhart, D.G. (1991) 'The construction and planning of new urban settlements in Scotland in the eighteenth century', in Maczak, A. and Smout, T.C. (eds) *Wolfenbüttler Forschungen,* Wiesbaden, Harrassowitz.

Mageean, D. (1985) 'Nineteenth-century Irish emigration: a case study using passenger lists', in Drudy, P.J. (ed.) *Irish studies 4: the Irish in America,* Cambridge, Cambridge University Press.

Mageean, D. (1986) 'Ulster emigration to Philadelphia 1847–1865', in Glazier, I. and DeRosa, L. (eds) *Migration across time and nations,* New York, Holmes and Meier.

Mageean, D. (1991) 'From Ulster countryside to American city: the settlement and mobility of Ulster migrants to Philadelphia', in Pooley, C.G. and Whyte, I. (eds) *Migrants, emigrants and immigrants: a social history of migration,* London, Routledge.[*]

Mageean, D. (with Glazier, I. and Okeke, B.) (1989) 'Socio-demographic characteristics of Irish immigrants, 1846–1851', in Friedland, K. (ed.) *Maritime aspects of migration,* Cologne and Vienna, Bohlau Verlag.

Martine, R. (1987) *Scottish clan and family names. Their arms, origins and tartans,* Edinburgh, John Bartholomew.

Mills, D.R. and Pryce, W.T.R. (1993) 'Preparation and use of maps', audio-cassette 3A in Braham (1993).

Mitchell, B. (1989) *Irish emigration lists 1833–1839,* Baltimore, MD, Genealogical Publishing Co.

Moncreiffe, A.I. (1971) *The Robertsons, Clan Donnachaidh of Atholl,* Edinburgh, Johnson and Bacon.

New statistical account of Scotland. By the ministers of the respective parishes, under the superintendence of a committee of the society for the benefit of the sons and daughters of the clergy (1845), Edinburgh and London, William Blackwood and Sons, vol. X, *Perth.*

Ó Gráda, C. (1989) 'Poverty, population and agriculture, 1801–45', in Vaughan (1989).

Pooley, C.G. (1983) 'Welsh migration to England in the mid-nineteenth century', *Journal of Historical Geography*, 9, pp.287–305.*

Pooley, C.G. (1989) 'Segregation or integration? The residential experience of the Irish in mid-Victorian Britain', in Swift, R. and Gilley, S. (eds) *The Irish in Britain, 1815–1939*, London, Pinter Publishers.

Pritchard, R.M. (1976) *Housing and the spatial structure of the city*, Cambridge, Cambridge University Press.

Pryce, W.T.R. (1993) 'Migration: some perspectives', in Rowlands, J. *et al.* (eds) *Family history in Wales: a guide to research*, Aberystwyth, Association of Family History Societies of Wales.*

Registrars General (1839 onwards) *Annual Reports (births, marriages and deaths)*, London, HMSO (available in major reference libraries).

Schürer, K. (1987) 'Historical demography, social structure and the computer', in Denley, P. and Hopkins, D. (eds) *History and computing*, Manchester, Manchester University Press.

Schürer, K.S. (1991) 'The role of the family in the process of migration', in Pooley, C.G. and Whyte, I.D. (eds) *Migrants, emigrants and immigrants: a social history of migration*, London, Routledge.*

Schürer, K. and Pryce, W.T.R. (1993) 'Nominal lists and nominal record linkage', audio-cassette 2B in Braham (1993).

Statistical account of Scotland. Drawn up from the communications of the ministers of the different parishes (1791), Edinburgh, William Creech, vol. II, no. 41.

Townsend, A.R. and Taylor, C.C. (1975) 'Regional culture and identity in industrialized societies: the case of north-east England', *Regional Studies*, 9, pp.379–93.

Vaughan, W.E. (ed.) (1989) *A new history of Ireland, Ireland under the Union, I, 1801–70*, vol. 5, Oxford, Clarendon Press.

Withers, C.W.J. and Watson, A.J. (1991) 'Stepwise migration and Highland migration to Glasgow, 1852–1898', *Journal of Historical Geography*, 17, pp.35–55.*

CHAPTER 3

MOVEMENTS INTO THE BRITISH ISLES: THREE COMPLEMENTARY PERSPECTIVES

by Monica Shelley (section 1), Peter Braham (section 2) and Ruth Finnegan (section 3)

Reconstructing migration experiences and individual histories within any family poses many questions. These can turn out to be very challenging, especially in families whose ancestors came as immigrants from overseas. Ways of conducting research into these particular origins, and the questions that have to be asked, are demonstrated in the three contrasting studies presented in this chapter.

Our first two case studies deal with the immigration of a Protestant German furrier to London and the movement of Jewish families from Eastern Europe. Each of these investigations started off as deep personal and specific questions as to family origins. But, as the authors clearly demonstrate, our understanding as to the nature of the movements that actually occurred gains immeasurably when seen in a broader setting and in a wider sequence of events. These same approaches are pursued further in section 3 where a number of new methods for the collection of information are introduced – methods that are particularly useful when the research involves more recent arrivals (referred to below as the 'new' British) and the need to understand the make-up of the newer communities in which they now live.

1 WHY DID HERMANN SCHULZE EMIGRATE FROM FINSTERWALDE TO LONDON?

by Monica Shelley

In common with many other people in the United Kingdom, some of my forebears came here from another country. I have looked in some detail at the circumstantial evidence that relates to their lives and considered it in the light of wider questions. In this section you will find some exercises aimed at helping you to think about those wider issues.

1.1 THE RESEARCH CONTEXT

In my case, my grandfather, Hermann Schulze, and his wife, Anna, emigrated to London from Germany in 1899, very soon after their marriage. They both died here, paying only one or two brief return visits to the small town where they had been born. After completing a family tree, I began to wonder about my grandparents' lives here, their family backgrounds in Prussia, why they chose to emigrate and what drew them to London. The facts that I gradually uncovered were interesting in themselves, but they did not tell me much about the reasons why they undertook such a major change. While there is much that remains unknown about their personal motivation (since I have not, as yet, uncovered any family letters, or any records that might tell me more about the immediate reasons for their decision to come here) I have tried to find out more about the Germany of 1899, which they left. I hoped that this would cast some light, not only on Hermann Schulze, but also on how typical (or not) his move was.

What were the conditions in the area of Germany where he lived? What changes were taking place in Germany as a whole which might have made emigration a good idea for him? What might he have thought were the advantages of living in England rather than Germany? And why England rather than somewhere else? Why did he never go back to Germany for any length of time? And how did things work out for the Schulze family in their new country?

These are all questions that anyone with emigrants in their family might ask – though the answers will, of course, vary from case to case and country to country. But this kind of background investigation does much to fill out the picture of one's forebears, puts them into context to some degree, and gives some idea of what they were like as people, rather than just 'cardboard cut-outs' of genealogical data. Starting from one particular case (the life of my grandfather), I have extended it to set it in a wider historical context (Germany at the end of the nineteenth and England at the beginning of the twentieth centuries). So here we are concerned with one particular example of immigration and settlement in the light of wider questions – the economic, demographic, political and personal selectivity factors involved in emigration. You may well have migrants in your own family whose background and motivations could be examined in the same way.

1.2   SOME BASIC FACTS

Until comparatively recently, when East and West Germany were reunified (November 1989), access to the former German Democratic Republic was possible, but difficult and complicated. And while records and background material of different kinds are, of course, available in Germany (see Baxter, 1986), gaining access to them requires a large investment of time, money and energy. It is, in any case, a long way from England to Brandenburg! So far, the sort of field work that most family historians prefer to do has not yet been possible. In common with most other people with emigrants in their family trees, I have had to do some of my research at a distance. What have I been able to find out so far that might go some way towards answering some of the questions posed above? How much evidence is there in support of any of the theories I might have?

I built up a very basic outline of my grandparents' lives, using information gleaned from a wide variety of different sources. These included information from a verger recently retired from the local German parish church in Finsterwalde, and official channels through the former Embassy of the German Democratic Republic; the General Register Office at St Catherine's House, London; change of name records at the Public Record Office; trade directories and bankruptcy records at London's Guildhall Library; and medical records from the Middlesex Hospital where my grandmother died, as well as some family memories and the few family documents that still survive.

The Schulze family came from Finsterwalde, a small town in the Cottbus administrative area in that part of Brandenburg known as the Mittelmark, part of Prussia. The church registers show that Friedrich Hermann Schulze, furrier, the son of Christian Gottlob Schulze, a master nailmaker from nearby Kalau, married Frederike Agnes in April 1847, daughter of Ernst Louis Sheppang, a dyer and finisher. Their son, Hermann Kurt Schulze, who grew up to become a master furrier and town councillor, was born in July 1847. He married Elise Amalie Anna Scholz, and my paternal grandfather, registered as Kurt Heinrich Hermann Schulze, was born in 1873. He had three younger brothers, called (confusingly) Hermann Kurt Max, Hermann Kurt and Johann Kurt (see Figure 3.1).

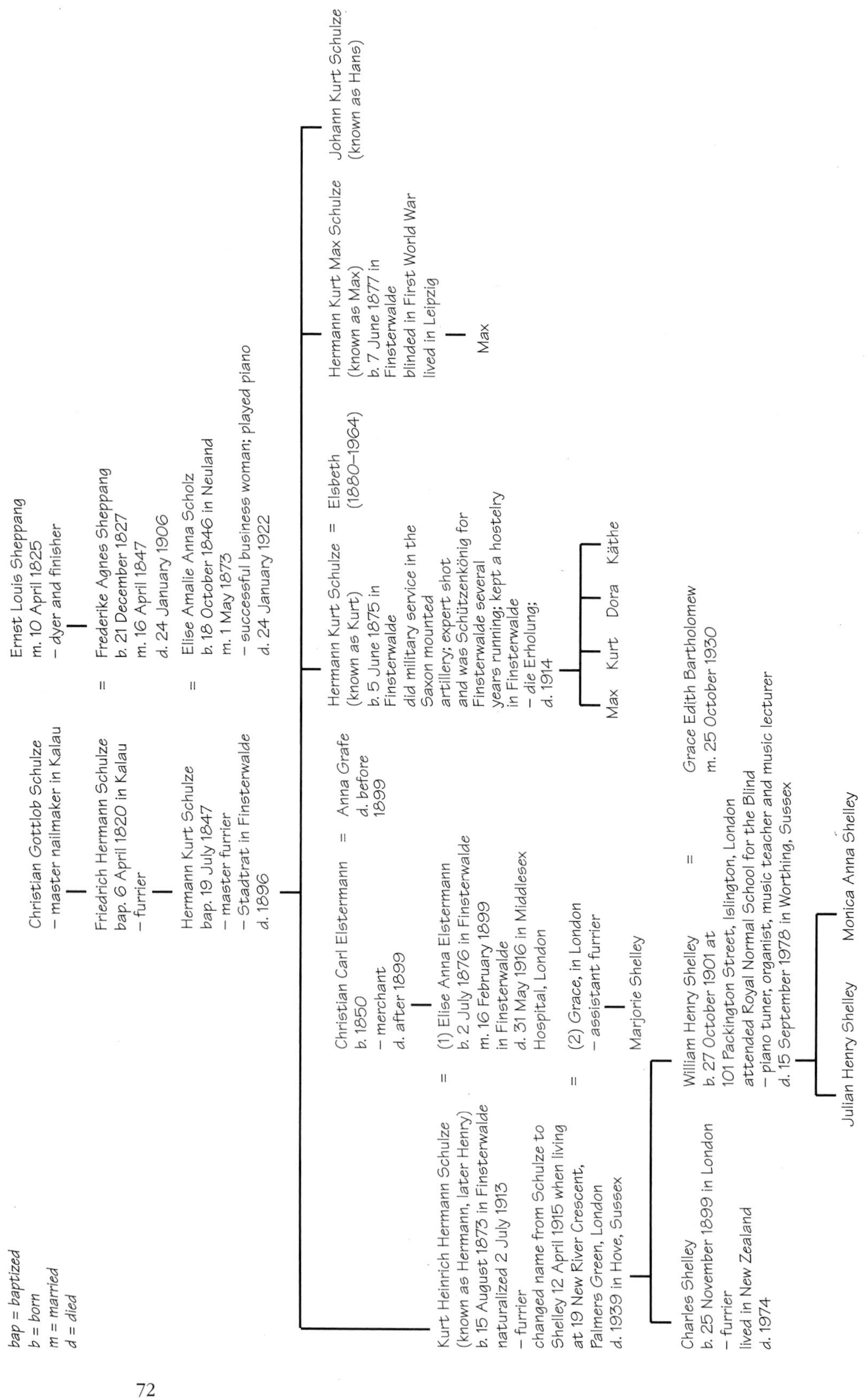

bap = baptized
b = born
m = married
d = died

Christian Gottlob Schulze
– master nailmaker in Kalau

Ernst Louis Sheppang
m. 10 April 1825
– dyer and finisher

Friedrich Hermann Schulze
bap. 6 April 1820 in Kalau
– furrier
=
Frederike Agnes Sheppang
b. 21 December 1827
m. 16 April 1847
d. 24 January 1906

Hermann Kurt Schulze
bap. 19 July 1847
– master furrier
– Stadtrat in Finsterwalde
d. 1896
=
Elise Amalie Anna Scholz
b. 18 October 1846 in Neuland
m. 1 May 1873
– successful business woman; played piano
d. 24 January 1922

Christian Carl Elstermann   =   Anna Grafe
b. 1850   d. before
– merchant   1899
d. after 1899

Hermann Kurt Schulze   =   Elsbeth
(known as Kurt)   (1880–1964)
b. 5 June 1875 in
Finsterwalde
did military service in the
Saxon mounted
artillery; expert shot
and was Schützenkönig for
Finsterwalde several
years running; kept a hostelry
in Finsterwalde
– die Erholung;
d. 1914

Max   Kurt   Dora   Käthe

Hermann Kurt Max Schulze
(known as Max)
b. 7 June 1877 in
Finsterwalde
blinded in First World War
lived in Leipzig

Max

Johann Kurt Schulze
(known as Hans)

Kurt Heinrich Hermann Schulze
(known as Hermann, later Henry)
b. 15 August 1873 in Finsterwalde
naturalized 2 July 1913
– furrier
changed name from Schulze to
Shelley 12 April 1915 when living
at 19 New River Crescent,
Palmers Green, London
d. 1939 in Hove, Sussex
= (1) Elise Anna Elstermann
b. 2 July 1876 in Finsterwalde
m. 16 February 1899
in Finsterwalde
d. 31 May 1916 in Middlesex
Hospital, London

= (2) Grace, in London
– assistant furrier

Marjorie Shelley

William Henry Shelley   =   Grace Edith Bartholomew
b. 27 October 1901 at   m. 25 October 1930
101 Packington Street, Islington, London
attended Royal Normal School for the Blind
– piano tuner, organist; music teacher and music lecturer
d. 15 September 1978 in Worthing, Sussex

Charles Shelley
b. 25 November 1899 in London
– furrier
lived in New Zealand
d. 1974

Julian Henry Shelley   Monica Anna Shelley

72

Figure 3.1 The Schulze–Shelley family tree covering the nineteenth and twentieth centuries (Source: compiled by Monica Shelley)

Figure 3.2   Photograph of Hermann Schulze and his fiancée, Elise Anna Elstermann, 1899
(Source: Schulze family, Finsterwalde)

Kurt Heinrich Hermann Schulze married Elise Anna Elstermann in February 1899 (Figure 3.2)
and moved to London where his eldest son, Charles, was born in 1899 and his second son,
William Henry, in 1901. Hermann Schulze set up in business as a wholesale furrier in east central
London in 1902 but he was declared a bankrupt in 1905. He was naturalized in 1913; in 1915 he
changed his name from Schulze to Shelley. His wife died of cancer in 1916, after which he moved
to Hove in Sussex where he died in 1939, having remarried (Figure 3.1).

_____ **EXERCISE 3.1** _____

What distinctive patterns can you discern in this family lineage? Make brief notes, using
information from Figure 3.1 and the basic facts stated above.

Comment p.220

1.3 WHY DID HERMANN SCHULZE MOVE?

First of all, the fact that my grandfather chose to emigrate was not in any way exceptional. As we have seen in Chapter 1 (section 4.2), estimates of the number of people who left Europe for overseas destinations in recent times are huge: over 50 million are recorded as having gone to the Americas and Australia between 1815 and 1930, of whom nearly 5 million were reckoned to have come from Germany (Baines, 1991, pp.7–8). What is less typical about Hermann Schulze was, of course, the short-distance nature of his emigration route, and the fact that he had moved to London at a time when the flood of emigrants out of Germany was past its peak. So why did he leave?

The only reason that has been passed down in the family is that he wanted to avoid doing national service in the German army, which, in the early 1900s, was compulsory, and that this was also why he did not return to Germany while he was still eligible. As with many family legends, there is probably some truth in this, but this one reason alone will almost certainly not represent the whole picture. Because Hermann's younger son, my father, would have nothing to do with him, Hermann has gone down in the family history as a thoroughly 'bad' person, and only the more disgraceful aspects of his character and behaviour are recalled. This is not, of course, to say that he was not a 'bad lot': but there were other factors, mainly economic, which could have influenced his decision.

1.4 THE GERMANY HE LEFT BEHIND

At the turn of the century Finsterwalde was, as now, a small town in a largely agricultural area – the relatively sparsely inhabited region between Leipzig and Halle to the west, Berlin to the north, Dresden to the south and the Oder–Neiße Rivers marking the border with Poland to the east (Figure 3.3). Before the Industrial Revolution, which took place later in Germany than in England, Finsterwalde was a major producer of textiles. But with the introduction of machines to replace handworkers, cultivation of tobacco became the main industrial activity. Following Germany's Industrial Revolution in the final decades of the nineteenth century, huge numbers of the population had moved from the country into large cities. In Berlin, for example, the largest city in Germany, less than a couple of hours by train from Finsterwalde, the population rose from 966,859 in 1875 to 1,587,794 in 1890 and 2,071,257 in 1910 – an increase of 114.2 per cent between 1875 and 1910 (Hohorst *et al.*, 1975, p.45). It has been stated that 'nowhere else in Europe did the transition from an economy based on agriculture to one dominated by industry occur with the same rapidity as in Germany' (Berghahn, 1987, p.1). At the same time, the overall population of Germany increased: it rose by 63 per cent between 1870 and 1913, from 41 to 67 million, which was a greater increase than anywhere else in Western Europe (Ritter and Kocka, 1977, p.34; Bade, 1984, p.83). This was attributed to the excess of births over deaths.

Around 1900, Imperial Germany was, as Berghahn has described it, 'a society which might be crudely divided into a traditional upper class, an increasingly differentiated middle class and an agricultural and industrial working class' (Berghahn, 1987, p.6). The Schulze family, self-employed furriers working in small units, belonged to that portion of the middle class which was finding it most difficult to keep up with the 'dynamics of a modern-industrialist capitalist system'

Figure 3.3 The regional setting of Finsterwalde, *c.*1883 (Source: Special-Karte von Deutschland und den benachbarten Ländern auf Grund der officiellen topographischen Karten bearbeitet von Ludwig Ravenstein, published by Bibliographisches Institut, Leipzig. Copyright, the Royal Geographical Society, London)

(Berghahn, 1987, p.8). Unemployment was on the increase and self-employment on the decrease (Bade, 1984, pp.152–3); trade, therefore, may well have been difficult for them, more especially as Hermann's father had died, relatively young, in 1896. Of Hermann's younger brothers, none is known to have carried on the family business in Finsterwalde. So, like the vast majority of German emigrants, it seems likely that Hermann Schultze's motives for leaving were mainly economic in nature (see Panayi, 1991, p.4).

In addition, there were various factors which might have made life in the Germany of the last decade of the nineteenth century seem inflexible and rigid. It might be argued that there were few opportunities for upward mobility, or a chance to try something that was different from the family profession. As the eldest son, Hermann also might have been put under particular pressure to follow in his father's footsteps. Strict codes of behaviour were still in force. Germany was an area intensely divided by regional loyalties at that time – the German Empire was made up of twenty-two principalities and three Hanseatic cities. While Prussia was the largest of these states, there were quite clearly defined regions even within Prussia. Most Germans saw them-selves not just as office workers or agricultural workers, but as *Hanoverian* office workers or perhaps as *Brandenburgian* agricultural workers. The vast majority of Germans were members of either the Protestant or Catholic churches and 'the local religious community continued to act as a focus which was able to exert a pressure on people's behaviour, especially in small towns and villages which lacked the greater anonymity of cities' (Berghahn, 1987, p.11). Kaiser Wilhelm II was not only Emperor of Germany – and thus had the right to conduct his country's foreign policy and appoint ministerial officials – but he was also the King of Prussia and in this capacity he was able to select the members of the Ministry of State and the Civil Service. So Hermann Schulze might have looked upon England as a place where he would be able to enjoy greater personal freedom than in a small Prussian town.

What sort of a person was Hermann Schulze? Since the only relatives who knew him are dead, we can only guess at the particular reasons why he left Finsterwalde and stayed away from it for the rest of his life. It has been suggested that particular kinds of people were more likely to select emigration, or have it selected for them; this often related to the need for a fresh start after some kind of disgrace (Jackson and Moch, 1989). Information about Hermann Schulze's life in England, plus his younger son's account of him, suggest that his family might have thought that Finsterwalde would have been better off without Hermann! Stories concerning his bankruptcy, relatively soon after setting up in business, the tales of his drinking problems, and his ill treatment of his mortally sick wife, have been passed down.

EXERCISE 3.2

After looking back at Chapter 1, section 3, prepare a short list of possible reasons for Hermann Schulze's emigration.

Comment p.220.

1.5 ENGLAND IN THE EARLY 1900s

It is only possible to theorize about why my grandfather chose to move to London, rather than to follow the hordes of his compatriots across the Atlantic (90 per cent of all German emigrants went to America; see Ritter and Kocka, 1977, p.35). A likely possibility, and one for which it might be possible to find evidence, is that links of some kind already existed between Hermann's father's fur business in Finsterwalde and London. Although this does not prove anything (since Schulze is an extremely common German name), a search of the London trade directories for the period reveals an Adolf Schulze operating as a furrier in London up till 1909.

How well did Hermann Schulze settle in his adopted country? Was the move successful in the long term? In common with many another migrant, his early years in his new country were not happy – neither for him nor for his family. After his bankruptcy in 1905, documents refer to him as a 'furrier's assistant' rather than 'furrier'. There was a crisis of some proportion in 1916, when his wife died of cancer in the Middlesex Hospital and he told his two sons to fend for themselves. Hermann had already decided to move down to Hove with the Englishwoman who was to become his second wife, and their child. Moreover, it was not all that pleasant for Germans living in England in the first two decades of this century. Panayi (1991) has summarized the anti-alien (and anti-German) mentality of the pre-war period as taking three basic forms. These were the general dislike of pauper immigrants (which led to the Aliens Act of 1905 and placed restrictions on entry); hostility towards rich Jews, particularly those of German origin; and, as a result of the Anglo-German diplomatic rivalry of the Edwardian years, a paranoia which gripped many people and persuaded them that all Germans in Britain worked for the Kaiser in preparation for an invasion. Although he was not Jewish, Hermann Schulze might well have encountered hostility because of his bankruptcy, his poverty after bankruptcy, and because of suspicions that he might have been involved in espionage.

It is interesting that, in adult life, both the sons of Hermann Schulze wanted to move on to other countries. Charles succeeded, and eventually arrived in New Zealand after the Second World War, where he enjoyed some prosperity as a furrier. William Henry, a musician, tried to find work abroad, but, perhaps wisely, he accepted the advice given him in 1927 by a patron, the chaplain at St George's Chapel, Windsor, who advised him not to try his luck in the colonies as 'you are not the only one seeking good appointments and a friend of mine tells me that the musical profession in the colonies is almost as overcrowded as it is at home, which I am afraid is not very encouraging ...' (letter from B.C.S. Everett to William Henry Shelley (my father), 19 October 1927). In consequence, William Henry settled in Sussex and made a living there with his music. His children and grandchildren went on to achieve a higher level of education and enjoy a better standard of living than his own father.

EXERCISE 3.3

In the context of what you now know about migration generally, how would you assess Hermann Schulze's success? Make a note of your response.

Comment p.221.

1.6   TAKING THE RESEARCH FURTHER

While much information has been gathered to illuminate the circumstances of Hermann Schulze's move from Germany to London, much work still remains to be done on the various factors underlying the decision to emigrate. Some key sources that might provide more information on Finsterwalde and about the Schulze family include the registers of the Finsterwalde Protestant Church, Prussian census records (available from 1831) and wills. Other important sources include local newspapers (both in Finsterwalde and in England), Finsterwalde civic records, the Hamburg emigration passenger lists, and official military records.

Specific German sources that could be useful if they exist for the Schulze family are: *Ortsippenbücher* (local family books), *Geschlechterbücher* (lineage books) and *Leichenpredig-ten* (funeral sermons). The examination of all these records will, of course, have to be undertaken in Germany.

There is very little possibility of gathering more direct oral evidence that relates to my grandfather's life, since my father and the rest of his generation are now all dead. More statistical information on migration, bankruptcy and the fur trade between Germany and England awaits further investigation to provide more clues as to the reasons behind his move.

What have I done with all this information so far? I have shown family trees to some younger members of my family – not all are interested! – and talked about the move from one country to another. Drawing on my own work, I have provided practical advice and guidance on sources in Germany to fellow members of the Anglo-German Family History Society. I have photographed the houses in which my grandfather lived and worked in London; that is, those dwellings that survived the bombs of the Second World War and the natural ravages of time. I have used rail maps of Germany to trace the emigration route taken by Hermann Schulze in 1899 – and the route followed by his wife and younger son when they revisited Finsterwalde in 1914. A planned visit to Germany will provide an opportunity to add to this archive of Schulze family material and chances to build up information about my grandmother's family, the Elstermanns. A letter sent in 1992 to the two Elstermanns listed in the current telephone book for Finsterwalde has produced further new direct links.

In general, the process of setting my family in a wider perspective has helped me to gain a deeper understanding of my own family background, as well as an appreciation of the way things were in Germany and England at the turn of the century. The same kind of procedure could benefit other family historians, especially those with immigrants in their families. The questions that I have attempted to answer might also be useful for others to investigate, as they can help people to link their own research into wider themes and scholarship.

2   'SWIRLS AND CURRENTS' OF MIGRATION: JEWISH EMIGRANTS FROM EASTERN EUROPE, 1881–1914

by Peter Braham

In an analysis of migration and British society, Holmes (1991) says that historians, unlike sociologists, have paid little attention to immigration: to who came to Britain and their subsequent experiences; while sociologists have concentrated too much on post-war Black and Asian immigration, failing to convey the extent to which immigration has been a continuing process in British history. However, the migration of Jews from Eastern Europe in the late nineteenth/early twentieth centuries is an exception to this neglect. This section, therefore, takes this example as an illustration of some current findings and also suggests further questions that could be explored and the kinds of sources that might be exploited.

Before proceeding, two other points made by Holmes should be mentioned. The first is that the historian has a duty to question the pervasive impression that Britain has been *tolerant* towards immigrants, an image also to be found among immigrant populations themselves. Second, enquiries into immigration must not be divorced from what Holmes calls 'the broader swirls and currents of society'; that is, from the wider context (Holmes, 1991, p.199). When we explore migration, the individual experience ought not to be divorced from that of the community or from the sort of wider questions that Holmes mentions.

2.1   JEWISH IMMIGRANTS – AND OTHERS: HISTORIC FORCES AND INDIVIDUAL DECISIONS

Let us approach our example in a different way from the last section – this time starting from more general trends before moving to individual examples (as you will see, however, the two aspects cannot be wholly separated).

In the period 1840–1914 there were three million Jewish international migrants, as well as hundreds of thousands of Jews who migrated to East European *Jewish* metropolises, such as Warsaw or Odessa, without crossing international boundaries (Gartner, 1960, pp.270–1). The location of Jews was thus profoundly altered: in one era most Jews lived in hamlets, villages or small towns; in the next era, in cities. The bulk of international Jewish migrants, some 850,000, went to the USA, as against 100,000 who settled in Britain, while lesser, though still substantial, numbers travelled to Canada, Argentina, South Africa, France, Germany and Palestine (Lipman, 1954, pp.86–7). England, nonetheless, played a notable role. First, every large city had an immigrant Jewish community – in some cases numbering tens of thousands (as in Leeds or Manchester), or, as in London, exceeded in size only by those of New York and Chicago. Second, England was a land of *trans*migration for Jewish emigrants en route to the USA: it was cheaper to travel from Hamburg to New York via London than to go direct! For some this transmigration merely meant disembarking at one British port before embarking at another (Krausz, 1964, p.4); for some it was still short-lived – for example, of the 1,364 inmates of the Poor Jews' Temporary Shelter in London's East End between June 1887 and May 1888, 270 proceeded on their way to America within a fortnight, most within a week (Fishman, 1988, pp.164–5); but for others, perhaps because of lack of means, plans to travel to the USA were never realized and they settled in England (or returned to their country of origin).

It is important to remember that this *Jewish* migration was merely one element of a much larger migration. From the mid-nineteenth century up to 1930 it has been estimated that some 62 million people – among them the Schulzes (whose story is told in section 1) – crossed international frontiers in what was the greatest voluntary migration in history (see Figure 1.6a,b in Chapter 1); many millions more migrated within the territories of specific nation states, yet, nevertheless, made a permanent crossing of the boundary between the rural and urban worlds.

Despite the parallels between Jewish and 'general' migration in this period, there are also significant differences. For example, among migrants to the USA in the early twentieth century we find that (a) Jewish migrants included substantially higher numbers of women and children, and (b) whatever the initial hardships, Jewish migrants were far less likely than others to return to their country of origin (Howe, 1976, p.58). It has also been said that *migration* holds a central place in Jewish history and in the conscious historical culture of Jewish migrants, which Gartner brings out in his study of Jewish immigration to England (Gartner, 1960). Emphasizing the role of the individual – 'both as an individual and as a member of an immigrant community' – he states that each of the Jews who left home in this period is 'the true subject in the history of migration': behind the historic 'causes', 'factors' or 'forces' was 'a family or a person who had to make an individual choice to move, and then carry it through to the ultimate destination'. For his sources, therefore, Gartner looks not just to the once flourishing Yiddish press or the written records of now defunct Jewish institutions, but equally to 'personal records, such as letters, diaries and even steamship tickets' (Gartner, 1960, pp.9–10, 15).

EXERCISE 3.4

What general factors do you think might help to account for this migration? Look back at Schema A in Chapter 2, section 4.2, p.56–7; see if you can add to it.

The causes of Jewish emigration from Russia and Poland in the period 1881–1914 are bound up with the history of these communities and with the disadvantaged situation of the Jews. Anti-Jewish policies were pursued by and on behalf of the Tsars and included punitive decrees concerning military service, the confinement of Jews to certain areas and their expulsion from others, and their exclusion from certain forms of education and occupation. Perhaps most harmful of all these policies were the limitations on domicile; almost all Jews had to reside in the so-called Pale of Settlement of Poland and western Russia, excluded from larger cities and border areas and from the land. They lived in proximity to their non-Jewish neighbours, yet could be said to occupy different worlds. So, though their routine dealings with local peasants might be friendly enough, underlying this was a degree of mutual fear and distrust. This antipathy, reflecting not simply religious and cultural differences but also a divide between an urban minority and the rural majority, sometimes culminated in anti-Jewish violence (*pogroms*), a phenomenon which the government, for its own reasons, at first failed to curb and later actively instigated.

Despite these adverse conditions, together with both increasing emigration and a particularly high death rate, the Jewish population of Russia and Poland grew from 1.6 million in 1820 to four million by 1880, a rise of 150 per cent (Fishman, 1975, pp.22, 25). The mass emigration of Jews from the Russian Empire after 1880 is, then, not simply an immediate response to deliberate oppression, but also a consequence of the inability of the artificially constrained Jewish economic structure to support such burgeoning numbers. Between April 1881 and June 1882 alone, some 225,000 Jewish *families* left Russia, the majority for the USA, but with a substantial minority coming to England, most of them to the East End of London (Fishman, 1975, p.30; Gainer, 1972, p.1).

This Jewish migration has its own specific history in the economic and social background of the Jewish migrants themselves, in the immediate reasons for their migration, and so on. But the distance between this and other migrations is not as great as it first appears. Seemingly intractable historical and structural forces turn out to be more complex than anticipated. Despite persecution, fewer Jews emigrated than remained, and some who had emigrated later returned to their home countries. On the other hand, would-be *inter*national emigrants were constrained by controls imposed by nation states at their borders: thus, some never emigrated and others did not reach their intended destination. In addition, these forces and constraints are interpreted, offset or evaded by *individual* decisions or actions. By examining the experiences of Jewish migrants in these contexts we learn something relevant to the experiences of migrants in general.

How do you think that general processes, such as demographic changes and alterations in economic conditions, might be related to the behaviour of individual migrants?

We might assume that potential migrants carefully weigh up the advantages and disadvantages of emigrating. Emigration – both Jewish and other – was certainly facilitated by improvements in communications: by the opening of railways from Russia to the West and by the establishment of regular, affordable transatlantic steamship services (competition had reduced the price of a steerage passage from Liverpool to New York from £12 in 1816 to £3 in 1846 – Lipman, 1990, pp.12–13; Williams, 1976, pp.144, 171, 327; see, also, Figure 1.7 in Chapter 1). Objective economic reality – the 'push' and 'pull' factors – is, however, not necessarily as important as the *perception* migrants have about opportunities in different places. The oppression and poverty that Jews experienced in Russia doubtless overshadowed concerns about their prospects abroad. Though few letters written back to Russia by Jewish immigrants about their conditions in England have come to light, personal letters – together with the cash remittances they often contained – must have played a significant part in persuading ambitious young men to emigrate: 'people began to leave our town, which is a small town and began sending over money and very often, and that made up my mind that I should go over there as well' (Gartner, 1960, p.29). In this sense, the decision to emigrate was, in the end, a personal one, 'a compound of emotions, calculations and individual circumstances' (Pollins, 1982, p.135).

Up to about 1880 the growth in the Jewish population of the United Kingdom was considerable, but no greater, proportionately, than that of the general population as measured by the censuses of 1811 and 1851. Lipman gives the Jewish population as 25,000 in 1815, 35,000 in 1851 and 60,000 in 1880, and the contribution of immigration to these figures as no more than 200 a year until 1850 or 1860 and almost 1,000 a year from 1860 to 1880, by which point at least a quarter, and perhaps more, of British Jews were of Russo-Polish origin (Lipman, 1961, p.70; 1990, p.13).

The Jewish community in Britain as it stood in 1880 could be described as consisting of a 'core' of middle-class merchants and shopkeepers of differentiated circumstances, plus, at contrasting ends of the economic spectrum, a number of financial and mercantile 'grandees' (from whom the institutions of established Anglo-Jewry drew their representatives) and a considerable number of artisans, tailors and the like (Finestein, 1961, p.107). Lipman describes this community, at least half of whom were born in Britain, as 'well organized in its communal life, emancipated politically and assimilated socially' (Lipman, 1959, p.84).

It was this community which was about to face an influx of co-religionists from Russia and Poland (and later from Romania), increasing the size of the Anglo-Jewish population, directly and through the high immigrant birth rate, by around 400 per cent in little more than 30 years (precise numbers are uncertain owing to the inadequacy of government statistics on immigration: thousands of immigrants en route to the USA were not classified as such only because when they arrived in England they did not possess a transatlantic ticket: Gainer, 1972, pp.9–10; see, also, Gartner, 1959). Even in the 1870s the modest growth in the number of immigrant Jews had caused alarm in Anglo-Jewish circles. By the 1880s, as immigration reached unprecedented heights, the Jewish establishment began to pay for advertisements in the European and Russian press to deter would-be immigrants from coming to England – ostensibly in the immigrants' own interests (the warnings typically mentioned the 'congested state of the English labour market'), but more probably reflecting native Jews' fears of being associated with such 'unpalatable co-religionists' (Fishman, 1975, p.65; 1988, pp.152–3). Such reactions tell us a great deal about the sense of security of the established Jewish community, but there is more to it than that. It was axiomatic to those campaigning against alien immigration that 'statistics on this subject are cooked ... [they] only had to go round that neighbourhood to see for themselves what was happening' (quoted in Gainer, 1972, p.13). Indeed, they could point to the concentration of Jewish immigrants in the East End of London, attracted there precisely because, as the largest established Jewish community in the country, it offered a degree of familiarity in a strange and perhaps hostile environment. More important than actual numbers, therefore, was their 'visibility' and the extent to which 'Jew' and 'immigrant' became interchangeable terms.

The dominant view within the Jewish community favoured keeping the gates of England open to all, but giving no encouragement to immigrants (Gartner, 1960, p.51). Eventually, however, the passage of time – and the realization that a policy predicated on the belief that the availability of aid would of itself encourage immigration, had done little to reduce the flow of immigrants *and* had worsened their circumstances after they arrived – caused a reappraisal of communal attitudes. It would thus be worthwhile to examine the way in which the communal welfare organizations, supported by well-established Jews, aided impecunious Jewish immigrants who arrived in Britain from the 1880s onwards. Communal bodies, such as the Poor Jews' Temporary Shelter and the Jewish Board of Guardians, amassed invaluable records about individual immigrants. For example, the Poor Jews' Temporary Shelter, whose representatives boarded incoming ships, interviewed migrants and attended to their accommodation, kept considerable records about their contacts – some 95 per cent of arriving Jewish immigrants (Lipman, 1959, p.88). And the Jewish Board of Guardians kept records of the name, address, age and place of origin of each applicant who approached them (Lipman, 1959, p.102).

In moving to England (or America), individual Jewish migrants immediately entered a world in which the East European exclusions and disadvantages no longer applied. Yet they also brought with them the dress, language and culture of the Jewish sphere in which they had existed. This heritage was not simply transplanted – but neither could it be quickly discarded. Some changes were relatively easy, particularly for younger immigrants: dress could be changed, fluency in English acquired and Yiddish spoken less. Other changes were more gradual, yet nonetheless profound. The synagogue, for example – the focus of self-contained Jewish life in Eastern Europe – no longer occupied such a dominant place in London. Secular institutions developed which both provided some continuity and helped to compensate for the dislocation of moving from a small Jewish town or village (*shtetl*) in Russia to a western city, a dislocation that was not simply physical, but involved separation from family and from established cultural patterns and moral values.

A fascinating illustration of this is contained in Burman's study of the contrasting perceptions of the economic role of Jewish women in Eastern Europe and in England. In the *shtetl*, the 'stated ideal' was for the man to study, while the woman took care, not merely of house and children, but also of breadwinning. In England, things changed dramatically: here the ideal seems to have been that Jewish women should cease work after marriage and that the husband's status now depended, not on learning, but on his ability to support wife and family (Burman, 1982, pp.31–2). Relying on first-hand information, Burman argues that reality was rather more complex than the ideals suggest: in Russia, economic adversity often had compelled both partners to be breadwinners, while in England many Jewish women worked after marriage. Nevertheless, these contrasting ideals played a part, interacting with the different social and status systems in the two Jewish communities and their relation to the wider society (Burman, 1982, pp.33–4). The economic role of women can be linked, in one case, to an emphasis on religious study as part of maintaining a distinctive culture in a climate of oppression and restriction, and, in the other, to the pressures on immigrant Jews to acculturate to middle-class norms in much freer circumstances (Burman, 1982, pp.27, 34, 36).

Gartner concludes his study as he began: it is the individual migrant who remains not only the true hero but also the real subject of any study of migration (Gartner, 1960, p.282). Central to this perspective are the three stages of the 'immigrant's odyssey': namely, the journey from home to point of embarkation, the voyage itself and the reception on arrival. The hazards included, at one end, bribing or evading Russian officials if leaving without a passport, and at the other, being cheated upon disembarkation by a host of 'sharks' and thieves anxious to steal their luggage, lead them to exorbitantly priced accommodation or sell them tickets to the wrong destination (Gartner, 1960, pp.31, 34, 36; see also Fishman, 1975, pp.35, 37).

2.2   THE EXPERIENCES OF TWO INDIVIDUALS IN THE CONTEXT OF MIGRATION RESEARCH

Given the value of individual accounts of migration and settlement, we can be grateful to Abramson for publishing the diary of his grandfather, Samuel, an emigrant from Russia to the USA in 1903 (Abramson, 1992). Equally useful is his extensive commentary and his discussion of the *value* and *meaning* of his grandfather's diary. Like Drake's usage of the letters of Joseph and Rebecca Hartley (see Volume 1, Chapter 2, section 3), Abramson shows how much can be extracted from quite short entries, and draws our attention to the degree of interpretation and research that may be involved, as well as to the importance of relating background information to the individual experiences and perceptions in the diary. Abramson also demonstrates how an individual's diary may be a *vital* (but not a *sufficient*) element in constructing a family history, and deepens our understanding of the often elusive relationship between 'individual' and 'general', family and community.

We can illustrate these points from a single extract from Samuel Abramson's diary, written many years after the events it describes, namely his birth, early life and arrival in the USA:

I was born on the 21st day of Cheshvan, in 1885. It was in a courtyard in the town of Kwartery, near Sislovitch, Grodne Province, in Russia.

I received my education in the cheders of the nearby towns of Sislovitz and Berestovitch. This type of education was common for the children in our area. Furthermore, I lacked for nothing as a child, because my grandfather Lieb (may he rest in peace) treated me very lovingly ... he was very good to me.

When I started learning Gemorah, I moved to Bialystok, where I 'ate days', like all the other boys. My Aunt Hodel, who lived there, was very good to me. However, after living in Bialystok for a while, I returned to my home.

I already knew some Polish and German, but felt the urge to know Russian, so I enrolled in the gymnasium. I learned to read and write Russian very fluently. Then I went to work in a nearby factory. It was extremely difficult, and after a year or so, I decided it was not for me, and returned home. I opened a little business – trading with the local landowner – and making a few dollars. Soon however, I received a steamship ticket for America, from my loving cousin Yechiel.

And so I left Europe, passed through Antwerp, and boarded the ship Fatherland for America. For 14 days I was seasick, suffering agonies. Finally, God helped, and I arrived in America – in the Golden Land.

(Abramson, 1992, p.17)

Abramson takes more than four pages to comment on this single extract. For example, he explains that:

1   Throughout his diary Samuel observes his birthday according to the Hebrew calendar, so its English date varies each year. (In 1885 the 21st of *Chesvan* corresponds to 30 or 31 October.) Was this perhaps one way in which Samuel straddled two cultures – 'although he lived in America, his internal "clock" was primarily Jewish' (see Abramson, 1992, p.18)?

2   'May he rest in peace' – a phrase used throughout the diary – reflects Jewish respect for the dead.

3   Kwartery is located 10 kilometres north of Sislovitch and 60 kilometres east of Bialystok, itself now in Poland, not Russia.

4   'Born in a courtyard' may be meant literally or it may refer to a large parcel of land owned by an absentee landlord employing a Jewish family to oversee the estate. [It is more likely in my view that this refers to the arrangement of houses *around* a courtyard, the normal practice in the *shtetl*.]

5   *Gemorah* is Yiddish for *Talmud*, containing discussion of legal texts (*Mishnah*) by Jewish scholars of the third to fifth centuries.

6   Bialystok, the town to which Samuel relocates, was then a major Jewish centre, containing 27,000 Jewish residents (64 per cent of the town's population at that time).

7   'Ate days' indicates that Samuel was one of the many Jewish children sent away to study whose families were unable to afford their room and board and therefore had to eat meals at a different home each day of the week. [In keeping with their obligation to support religious learning, Jewish householders would offer to feed as many students as their means allowed (Zborowski and Herzog, 1952, p.99).]

8   Samuel's inability to speak Russian may be because he lived in an area that had been part of Poland until 1815.

9   Samuel's decision to attend a gymnasium [i.e. a secular academic school instead of an orthodox Jewish *yeshivah*] may be the beginning of an 'inevitable chain of events' by which the Abramson family lost a strong religious tradition. When Samuel arrived in the USA he joined a conservative rather than an orthodox synagogue, and his son was involved with Reform Judaism; Abramson himself is an agnostic (Abramson, 1992, p.21).

10   Steamship tickets to America apparently had to be purchased with US currency; families able to afford them were generally well established in America. By the time Samuel emigrated in 1903 (when the steamship ticket from Antwerp to New York was $34), the procedures were more routine than in the 1880s when leaving Russia would have been much more hazardous.

This preliminary analysis of the raw data printed in the diary thus represents only the beginning of the research and not its conclusion. Abramson, himself, was confronted with the task of obtaining an accurate translation of the diary from Yiddish to English. He then had to obtain information about names and locales, and about the context within which his grandfather's migration took place, necessitating some description of the late nineteenth-century Russia in which Jews lived. Abramson also had to discover what he could about the tiny town where his grandfather was born and the larger towns in which he spent much of his life in Russia. Sources he consulted included:

1   Memorial Books – volumes compiled by survivors of the Holocaust to provide memories of particular towns and villages (see section 2.3 below).

2   Emigration records.

3   His grandfather's personal documents, such as his marriage certificate and family photographs.

4   A detailed map of nineteenth-century Russia.

Having obtained this information, Abramson could give a reasonably comprehensive description of Swislocz – or Sislovitch as Jews called it – the town near which his grandfather was born and in which much of his time in Russia was spent. Abramson describes the town's establishment and history; its layout and principal features; its commercial development; and the substantial number of Jews living in the town as measured by the censuses of 1847 and 1897, together with their chief occupations. He also comments generally on the situation of Jews in late nineteenth-century Russia, suggesting that the organization of the Jewish community – its customs and religion – contributed to Jewish well-being, but that Jews were over-taxed, oppressed and subjected to the anti-Jewish measure taken by the Russian state in the years after the assassination of Alexander II in 1881: 'it was against this backdrop that Samuel Abramson left Russia in 1903 … Perhaps Samuel concluded that it was now time to get out' (Abramson, 1992, p.9).

No *family* records revealed what life was like for the Abramsons in Sislovitch in the years before Samuel emigrated. The diary itself is silent on this – though we are told that his father's land had been confiscated. Abramson mentions various factors, which might have precipitated Samuel's emigration. One was that he would soon have been subject to the 25-year military service draft that applied specifically to Jews and which had been reintroduced in 1886 (see, also, section 1.3).

This also happens to be the reason that my own grandfather, Lewis Hyman (Figure 3.4), gave for emigrating from Russia in 1902. (In Russia his surname had been Surgan. It was changed to Hyman because of a misunderstanding so common at the point of entry. See, also, sections 1.2 and 1.5 and Exercise 3.1 answer.) So let me turn now to this second example. Because of his impending call-up in Russia, my grandfather could not obtain a passport for foreign travel (as distinct from an internal passport). Nevertheless, with the help of smugglers he was able to cross the Russian–German border at Edtkeuhnen (a well-known crossing point for Jewish migrants at that time) by hiding on the running board of an empty train returning to Germany at night. From there he travelled by train to the port of Bremen and then he took a steamship to London.

Although almost 70 years had passed when he recalled these events, my grandfather still had detailed memories of his life in Slutsk (one of the oldest cities in Russia, with Jewish inhabitants first recorded in 1583 and, according to the 1897 census, with a population of 10,264

Figure 3.4   Lewis Hyman, *c.*1908
(Source: Mrs Ray Braham)

Jews and 2,285 non-Jews). He also clearly remembered the house where his family lived on the main street. It had four rooms at the front, and a large room at the back containing a brick kitchen oven. It was destroyed by fire in 1899 when a large part of the town burnt down in about two hours, all the houses being of wood. His mother, as well as his father, had a shop. His mother sold groceries, sugar and sweets to the peasants, and his father sold 'the best kind of cakes', which had been baked at home, chiefly to Jewish customers. Neither shop was very large: his father's shop had only enough room for his father and a couple of shelves for the stock – the customers had to stand outside! (See the discussion of Burman's article in section 2.1.)

My grandfather recorded many other memories on tapes, made shortly before his death in 1972 and now stored at the Museum of Jewish Life, in London. Though his immediate family had often talked about capturing his experiences, the tapes were made at the instigation of a visiting American relative. In them he tells how he failed to reach his ultimate destination, how emigration split up his family, as well as of life in Russia. For example:

1   The results of the deaths, in childhood, of three of his brothers 'whose names were never mentioned in the family'. Because their births but not their deaths had been registered, as each reached 21, he was called up for military service. When each, in turn, failed to appear, a fine of 300 roubles (900 roubles in all) was levied on the family. As they could not raise such a sum, it was ordered that their furniture be auctioned instead.

2   On his arrival in London he was met by an older brother who had lived there for four years. A few months later this brother returned to Russia to do *his* military service. But, according to my grandfather, his real purpose was to be reunited with his parents: in my grandfather's words, he did not want 'to desert them forever – as I did'.

3   Like many Jewish migrants to England, others of my grandfather's immediate family had emigrated to the USA: for example, his brother, Chaim, a cabinet maker, who was much older than him, whose wedding he remembered, had gone to America in 1893 or 1894.

4   He made two attempts to emigrate onwards to the USA, both in 1906. On each occasion he was refused entry as he was suffering from trachoma. First, he got no further than Southampton, but on his second attempt he reached Quebec before he was turned back. Figure 3.5 shows a postcard he wrote from there to my grandmother (whom he married in 1908). The postcard bears the stamp of the Immigration Hospital and was written in Yiddish (but in Hebrew script). The translation (by Hana Pinner) is as follows:

> *Dear Yetta,*
>
> *Today, Tuesday, I have already seen the doctor. I shall have to stay in hospital for a few weeks. They will heal only one eye for me and therefore it will not take long. You can imagine how it felt in my heart when they told me that I cannot travel further before the eye is healed. Only now I calmed (myself) down a bit. A few weeks will go by and I shall be free. The hospital is like a prison. One is locked into a large stable and only permitted to go out into the yard. They count the people twice a day. Write me a reply soon and send me on the letter from home if you have received it.*
>
> *This is the suffering of man.*

5   Although his father had died in 1910, my grandfather remained in touch with relatives in Slutsk up to 1939 – letters were exchanged and he mentions sending cloth for a coat. But he has no knowledge of them after the Second World War. (If they had remained in Slutsk, this is not surprising because, according to an eyewitness, Slutsk itself was so utterly destroyed by the retreating Germans that even its *location* could not be readily identified: see Hindus, n.d., p.xv.)

Abramson argues that Russian-Jewish emigrants like his own grandfather paid a price for the undoubted gains that emigration had brought. His theory is that emigration 'does not necessarily obviate trauma and turmoil in the adopted homeland' (Abramson, 1992, p.175). By this he refers to the hardships in dealing with a new language, in lacking marketable skills, in facing prejudice and discrimination and in incurring family disintegration, all of which might postpone the hoped-for gains at the moment of emigration. Thus Abramson proposes a conception of Russian-Jewish emigration of the period in question as 'an investment that has a tremendous short-run downside risk, but a potential for long-term sustained growth' as adaptation to new circumstances took place (Abramson, 1992, pp.10, 175).

EXERCISE 3.5

1   Go back and consider, from the evidence I give, how far my grandfather's emigration illustrates Abramson's theory. (NB: to test this theory fully would mean discovering how well my grandfather's descendants had prospered.)

2   Apply the same exercise to any other example of emigration that is known to you.

Although it is clear from my grandfather's tapes that his family was by no means poverty stricken, life was still hard. By emigrating, Lewis Hyman avoided the military draft and had escaped the restrictions on Jews in Russia. On the other hand, his two attempts to reach the USA failed. Emigration also split up his family: at the end of his life my grandfather clearly regretted that his separation from his parents had been permanent. (There are many such expressions of regret in the memoirs of Russian-Jewish emigrants of this era. See, for example, Howe, 1976, pp.34–5.)

2.3   FOLLOWING UP THE CASE STUDIES: SOME SOURCES AND METHODS FOR FURTHER STUDIES

In constructing his hypothesis, Abramson was treating Samuel's diaries not merely as unique to Samuel, to *his* experiences and motivations, but also as a guide to wider issues of Russian-Jewish migration and settlement. It also, incidentally, proved an interesting question to apply to my own

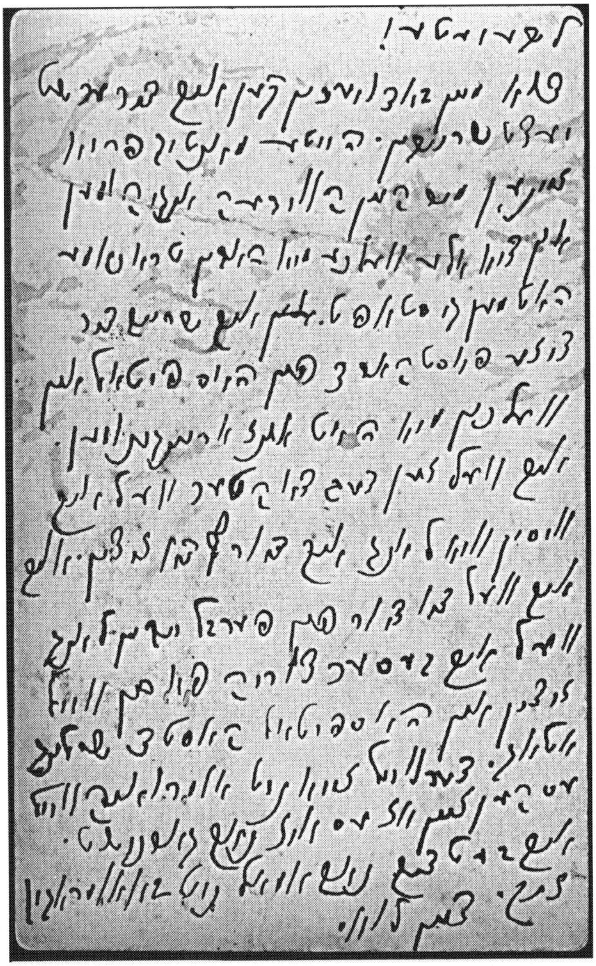

Figure 3.5 A postcard sent by Lewis Hyman in 1906 during his abortive attempt to settle in the USA (Source: Mrs Ray Braham)

family's experience of migration. This type of case study can be seen then, at one level, as providing an insight into a single individual and, at another, as portraying the social and historical world inhabited by that person (Runyan, 1982, cited in Abramson, 1992, p.189). It is worth reflecting on it further, too, because these basic approaches could, in principle, be applicable to research on other migrants – not just Jewish migrants or even just those from Eastern Europe.

Provided that close attention was given to its limitations, Abramson was content to treat his case study as 'evidence'. He had to consider, for example, his own possible lack of objectivity towards his grandfather's diaries and the extent to which the author of the diary intentionally distorted facts or – given that parts of the diary were retrospective – misremembered or wrote from hindsight. This reminds us of the importance of sources, and of the care needed in interpreting them.

EXERCISE 3.6

Apart from diaries, the main sources for recovering the individual and family history of migration include autobiographies and 'oral history' – sources you may be using yourself. Pause for a few moments to consider (a) the limitations of such sources, and (b) possible ways of replacing or supplementing such sources.

Abramson's starting point was a *diary*. This, in turn, led him to consult documentary sources, to construct a theory about emigration and, finally, to consider the status and value of case studies in general. Others have started without such a rich source, but have compensated for this initial disadvantage. Kurzweil, for example, constructed a questionnaire about each relative's immediate family and ancestors (Kurzweil, 1980, p.30). This could be used in the construction of the histories of families of immigrant origin (Jewish or non-Jewish) – as in Schema A below.

Schema A: Questions about emigration

1   Which towns did your family come from and where are these located? Did your family live in one town or did different branches live in different places? Did your own family move from one place to another?

2   Who were the immigrants – you, your parents, or your grandparents?

3   What was the specific reason for emigration?

4   What did they or do you know or remember of the journey?

5   In what port did the ship dock? What was the name of the ship? When did it arrive?

6   Describe life in your country of origin. In particular, do you have any childhood memories?

7   What contact continued with relatives who remained behind?

8   Was there any resistance to emigration on religious grounds?

9   Do you have your naturalization papers?

Source: based on Kurzweil (1980) pp.80–2

In addition to questions specifically for migrants, Kurzweil lists others relating to names of parents, mother's maiden name, brothers and sisters, occupations, documents, old photographs, family heirlooms, old letters written by family members, and so on (Kurzweil, 1980, pp.80–2).

As Kurzweil points out, in our enquiries we can uncover general history or examine details: 'we can see the crowd or we can examine individuals' (Kurzweil, 1980, p.154). For example, we can ask who travelled with whom? How old were they when they arrived? Where did they disembark and where did they live on arrival? Or we can ask about the frequency of steamship services, the cost of travel, the routes the steamships plied and the conditions that existed on board ship. We need to ask both kinds of question if we are to construct a rounded picture: placing a particular family history into the 'swirls and currents' of wider events, patterns and developments.

Besides the types of sources mentioned already, there may also be sources specific to the individuals or groups under study. In the case of Jewish immigrant history, there are problems in that much of the material is not in English and many of the original communities have been destroyed. One important source for reconstructing vanished communities is the series of several hundred Memorial (or *Yiskor*) Books published by Jewish societies known as *Landsmann-schaften*, formed by emigrants from a single community. These records vary from just a few lists of names and photographs, to several hundred pages of text containing historical articles on locations, with photographs and maps, which give a vivid idea of the size and layout of a particular community (see Figure 3.6), and may even be detailed enough to identify a particular family home; as well as photographs of individuals and the names of Holocaust victims. For example, the book commemorating the Jewish community of Volkovisk runs to 990 pages and

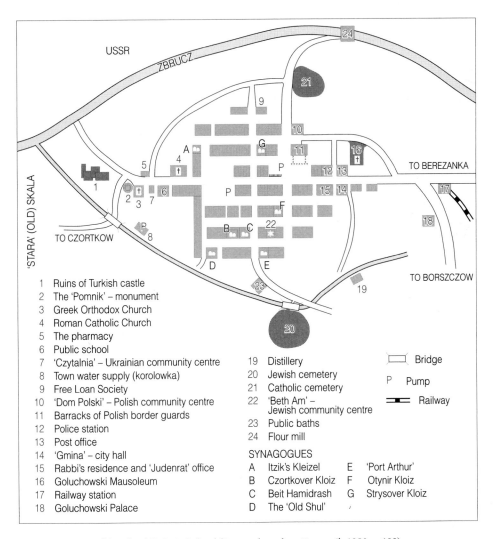

1	Ruins of Turkish castle		
2	The 'Pomnik' – monument		
3	Greek Orthodox Church		
4	Roman Catholic Church		
5	The pharmacy		
6	Public school		
7	'Czytalnia' – Ukrainian community centre	19	Distillery
8	Town water supply (korolowka)	20	Jewish cemetery
9	Free Loan Society	21	Catholic cemetery
10	'Dom Polski' – Polish community centre	22	'Beth Am' – Jewish community centre
11	Barracks of Polish border guards		
12	Police station	23	Public baths
13	Post office	24	Flour mill
14	'Gmina' – city hall		
15	Rabbi's residence and 'Judenrat' office		
16	Goluchowski Mausoleum		
17	Railway station		
18	Goluchowski Palace		

Bridge

P   Pump

Railway

SYNAGOGUES

A	Itzik's Kleizel	E	'Port Arthur'
B	Czortkover Kloiz	F	Otynir Kloiz
C	Beit Hamidrash	G	Strysover Kloiz
D	The 'Old Shul'		

Figure 3.6   Map of the *shtetl* Skala in Poland (Source: based on Kurzweil, 1980, p.193)

provides significant sociological and historical material, as well as details about individuals (Howe, 1976, p.190. See, also, Kurzweil, 1980, p.191; Gandy, 1982, pp.23–4).

EXERCISE 3.7

List (a) the main types of sources mentioned in this section, and (b) which of these (or others) you consider might be useful in investigating the experiences of immigrants other than those described here (e.g. a family, group or community in which you are interested).

Comment p.221.

2.4   WHAT HAPPENED TO THE IMMIGRANTS AFTER THEIR ARRIVAL?

We can consider East European Jewish emigrants both as a group and as individuals. Although we ought to be cautious about making sweeping generalizations when portraying *group* experience, we can say, at least, that the journey undertaken by these immigrants was not simply one of moving from one country to another, but also from one type of community to another. For them, this meant moving from a *confined* community to one which was *unconfined* – or at least where the forces that confined it were weaker or temporary. Pollins has captured the essential features of this transformation:

> *The greatest problem of all arose from the very freedom which Jews enjoyed in Britain. This centred on the desire to maintain the existence of a Jewish group, but freedom could easily result in defections from it. During the centuries of persecution the Jewish religion in Europe had survived through being bound together by the creation of elaborate rules and rituals. They provided a fence to protect Jews from external hostility. But as outside antagonism was modified it was inevitable that such ties would loosen and internal cohesion weaken.*

(Pollins, 1981, pp.4–5)

On the other hand, what was a problem for the group might, simultaneously, be an opportunity for the individual. In other words, as we saw in Chapter 1, section 3.4, for some the migration process involved a series of *intervening opportunities*, whilst for others these were seen as *intervening obstacles*. Consider, for example, the attitude of individual immigrants to the question of language. Although for some time the *Jewish Chronicle* produced a supplement in Yiddish (so that recent immigrants could follow events), in reality they were very ready, not merely to adopt English, but to abandon Yiddish altogether. Yiddish as a spoken language more or less died out within a generation (Kosmin *et al.*, 1976, p.26) – perhaps due also to a fanatical drive towards 'Anglicization' pursued by the élite of Anglo-Jewry mentioned by some commentators (e.g. Williams, 1985).

It would be wrong, however, just to picture individual advance and group fragmentation. In their analysis of the Sheffield Jewish community, Kosmin *et al.* (1976) describe Jewish ethnicity as a resource for Jews as a group *and* as individuals. In their view, this ethnicity was 'closely bound up with the whole Jewish historical experience as a minority group ... [and] to work successfully the group must be maintained, while at the same time it must provide the correct kind of support and solutions to the problems of individuals' (Kosmin *et al.*, 1976, p.27). (You will be able to read further about the Jewish immigrant experience in Chapter 8.)

_____ *EXERCISE 3.8* _____

Do you notice any parallels between the processes here and those of other incoming groups? Look back at Chapter 1, section 3, and Chapter 2, section 3; see also section 3 of this chapter.

2.5   CONCLUSION 1: WHAT FURTHER QUESTIONS ARISE ABOUT JEWISH MIGRATION ...?

I have mentioned three different aspects of Jewish migration from Eastern Europe in this era: (1) it was part of a much larger migration; (2) its scale and intensity were considerable; and (3) though many Jews emigrated, more did not.

How can we explain that one-third of Jews emigrated, but two-thirds remained behind?

Each aspect suggests something different. At a general level there were poverty, lack of opportunity and adverse economic developments, as well as the coming of efficient means of transport to lands of greater opportunity. In these circumstances emigration was only to be expected.

However, because Jews were faced with special disadvantages, Jewish emigration was particularly heavy. For example, between 1881 and 1889 Jewish emigration to the USA was ten times that of the 1870s (reflecting *pogroms* and discriminatory legislation) and between 1903 and 1907 it was 64 times (reflecting, *inter alia*, renewed *pogroms*) (Kuznets, 1975, p.43). In the period 1881–1914 as a whole about one-third of Jews left their homelands; between 1899 and 1914 an average of 15.6 per thousand Jews left Russia *each year*, a rate matched only by that of Irish emigration in the mid-nineteenth century (Hersch, 1931, cited in Howe, 1976, p.63; Chapter 2, section 4; Chapter 7, section 2).

This Jewish migration is, understandably, often portrayed as inevitable, as 'a spontaneous and collective impulse, perhaps even a decision by a people that had come to recognize the need for new modes and possibilities' (Howe, 1976, p.26). One emigrant wrote in his memoirs: 'It is impossible ... that a Jew should regret leaving Russia' (quoted in Howe, 1976, p.27). But if only a minority of Jews emigrated, we need to consider why some emigrated and others did not. There is, of course, ample evidence about their hardship, poverty and persecution. Nevertheless, several factors may explain why the *majority* stayed. Many were no doubt gripped by a feeling of inertia; some may have been dissuaded by the cost of travel or dubious about the economic opportunities abroad; the very precariousness of the *shtetl* may have promoted a sense of cohesion and community in the face of a hostile world; and for many the practice of religious orthodoxy, central to *shtetl* life, offered a degree of continuity and certainty – indeed, there was strong resistance to emigration from orthodox Jews who depicted life in America and England as sinful and corrupting.

We need to know more about who emigrated, who returned after emigration (for a general treatment see King, 1986; Jackson and Moch, 1989), who remained where they were and, in each case, what motivated them. Though most of those who emigrated from Eastern Europe are, as in the case of my grandfather, now dead, their experiences are not necessarily lost. Valuable material is waiting to be discovered (for a systematic listing of Jewish institutions, sources and references, see Kushner, 1991; see, also, *Shemot* – the journal of the Jewish Genealogical Society of Great Britain – and Chapter 8 below). Its value will not be realized, however, unless it is placed within the wider context of the 'swirls and currents' of migration.

2.6   CONCLUSION 2: … AND ABOUT OTHERS?

Just as the individual cases of Samuel Abramson and Lewis Hyman needed to be both retained *and* put in wider context, so the kinds of questions and sources used to explore their experiences can also be exploited to consider the experiences of immigrants from other backgrounds. Some of the processes may be similar, some different – the contrasts themselves being perhaps part of your findings – but here, too, you need to explore both the value of individual records and the complexity of those wider 'swirls and currents'.

3   STUDYING THE 'NEW' BRITISH: SOME QUESTIONS TO INVESTIGATE

by Ruth Finnegan

This section gives some background, possible sources and methods, and suggestions for research on the 'new' British: a shorthand way of referring to those coming to Britain in the present century and now part of the resident population. The examples here are mainly from the period after the Second World War, and about Britain, but you will also recognize themes from earlier chapters, and similar questions could be raised for other migrants.

3.1   STARTING FROM ILLUSTRATIVE CASES

Let us start with a few examples before considering possible patterns and contrasts.

One entrant to Britain in 1956 was 'Mr H.', a young man from Cyprus:

> He had married two years earlier and had a baby son. His village was close to the district town of Larnaca where he had been able to get intermittent labouring work, mainly in the construction industry. His elder brother, who had left for Britain several years earlier, urged him to join him; so having saved enough for his own and part of his wife's passage, he left the island to find a job in London, leaving his wife and child with her parents in the neighbouring village. His brother's plan for him to obtain work in a tailoring business did not work out, but he soon found work instead in the kitchen of a major West End hotel. Part of his wage he sent back to help support his wife and child at home, while from the rest he gradually saved up the extra money needed for his wife's passage to London. Eventually, about five months after his departure he was able to send for her and the baby, to join him in the single room he had rented above a shop in Camden town.

(Oakley, 1979, p.19)

We see here not just a chunk of one man's life, but also characteristic ways in which thousands of Cypriots came to Britain after the war. Mr H. was not just an isolated individual. His travels were linked both with the 'push' factors in his local economic and political situation and with the typical developmental cycle of the Cypriot family. Many migrants were young men just starting to set up their own families. Like them, Mr H. travelled ahead to find a job and housing, then he saved enough money to send for his family. He also relied on Cypriot traditions of personal support through both close family relatives and more distant kinship and patronage (the classic process of chain migration).

By 1966 about 100,000 Cypriots had settled in Britain, including first-generation children born here. Like many migrant groups, they were clustered rather than dispersed throughout the country. About three-quarters were in Greater London, mainly in boroughs north of the centre, making up what, in 1979 (but not necessarily now?), could be described as a 'cohesive and well-organized Cypriot community' (Oakley, 1979, p.34). This had diversified from earlier interests in the restaurant trade into a variety of craft businesses, and was supported by a network of churches, political groups and other associations. People also kept up their kinship links with those still in Cyprus. Indeed, in 1961 'as many who had brothers in Britain also had brothers in Cyprus' (Oakley, 1979, pp.22–3) – it was unusual for *all* the siblings to emigrate. There was thus a constant flow of information through both letters and visits.

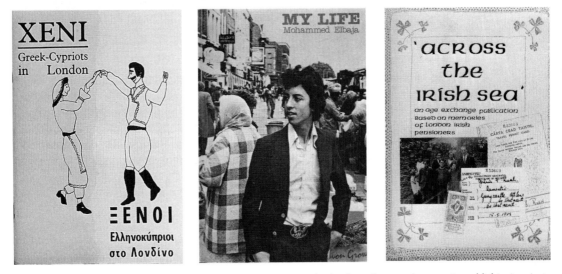

Figure 3.7 Remembering and recording immigrant experiences: a selection from the many 'community publishing' projects drawing largely on oral reminiscence (see Bornat, 1992) (Sources: top left: source of photograph unknown; top right: Tim Smith/Guzelian/Bradford Heritage Recording Unit; bottom left: Ethnic Communities Oral History Project; bottom centre: source of photograph unknown; bottom right: Alex Schweitzer/Age Exchange Theatre Trust)

Different, but also partly similar, were the post-war settlers from Jamaica. Again, it was common for one parent to come ahead, if only because it cost too much for the whole family to emigrate together. This was usually, but not always, the father: indeed, often the children were only sent for after *both* parents had saved enough. Women as well as men worked to this end, the men often in the transport industry, in engineering or labouring, the women in nursing, services or clothing. Many Jamaicans (like other West Indian immigrants) became home owners, perhaps partly because discrimination made renting harder. Again, there were continuing links with the original country: families in Jamaica regularly included relatives abroad – not just in Britain – because emigration was part of established Jamaican culture (Thomas-Hope, 1980; Foner, 1977). Migration was thus part of the normal life course, with the hope among first-generation migrants that they would, one day, return to Jamaica. It would be interesting to explore how far this 'myth of return' continued in the next generation. Was it overtaken by assimilation within the local culture, or perhaps by the potent symbol of 'Black culture'? Did this work out differently in different families or localities? (Some key aspects of chain migration are reviewed in Chapter 1, section 3.5). Jamaican settlers were scattered rather than clustered in small neighbourhoods. In the first generation anyway, this meant greater isolation for nuclear family households and fewer kin nearby for family support – one reason perhaps, together with women's wage-earning status in Britain, for more sharing of domestic and leisure activities between husband and wife than in Jamaica.

It is not just Jamaicans but, probably, many other first-generation immigrants who experience fragmented families: that is, the absence of the nearby extended family networks on which they could call in their original homes. Nielson's conclusions on Muslim immigrants from Asia might well be applied and tested out more widely:

> Migration has resulted in a partial fragmentation of traditional family structure … There are usually no grandparents, but often one or more adults – brothers, sisters, cousins – in addition to the nucleus of a married couple and their children. Among Pakistanis, 40 per cent of households consisted of three or more adults in the 1981 census, as compared with 23 per cent for the whole population. The pattern of chain migration has often brought several parts of an extended family to Britain. But patterns of employment have tended to disperse them among different locations, and the physical limitations of traditional British domestic architecture has tended further to disperse them into several households.

(Nielson, 1984, p.7)

This illustrates again the common pattern (summarized in Schema B below) for younger men to come first, living on their own or in shared bachelor accommodation or hostels, only later joined by their families. Caroline Adams' oral history of migration and settlement among the Bangladeshi (Sylheti) population of Tower Hamlets, in London, provides another example. She explores both personal motivations and the general migration process: the move from earlier single-men settlement to family-based population, and the recruitment of the next generation (Adams, 1991; Eade, 1990).

Schema B: Some common migration stages – or are they?

1 Individual pioneers.

2 Densely packed, all-male households in inner city areas.

3 Large-scale entry of wives and children and a move to less crowded housing.

---

4   Move away from the more insalubrious ghettoes and emergence of a British-educated second generation.

(For further elaboration see Ballard and Ballard, 1977, pp.21–2; also Chapter 7, section 1, below.)

But there are counter examples too. Among the most striking are the Sikhs from East Africa who came to Britain in the 1960s (Bhachu, 1984). They are twice-removed migrants, already experienced in settling abroad, for in the early twentieth century their forebears had moved from India to East Africa to work on the railways. So, in contrast to many other immigrants, they arrived as well-established full family units. They were already property owners with capital and qualifications, the women educated and in jobs; nor did they settle in ghetto-like clusters. And though there was a strong *community* sense of responsibility to other East African Sikhs, wider kinship links were less marked (they tended to live in nuclear rather than extended family households). Finally, although they kept up some contacts in both East Africa and India, they differed from Jamaican settlers in having little or no potential 'myths of return'.

EXERCISE 3.9
---

1   Looking through the four short examples in this sub-section, list at least three possible headings you could use to highlight similarities and/or differences between them.

2   Re-read Mr H.'s story on p.92. Underline key phrases that illustrate (a) the migration process in general, and (b) the specific form followed by Cypriot immigrants in the 1950s.

Comment p.222.

3.2   THEMES AND QUESTIONS

Each family or individual has, of course, their own circumstances, their own ways of exploiting, following or altering the prevailing constraints and opportunities. Still, it is also interesting to explore how far individual cases do fit with more general patterns: a focus for further investigation.

Our four short examples have already illuminated a remarkable number of concepts, patterns and contrasts. But further variants may be relevant to your own particular interests. Here, then, are some other categories and questions to consider.

The processes of coming and settling   These could involve one (sometimes more) of the following:

1   Sudden and involuntary events: war, famine, drastic political change (for refugees generally, see Bramwell, 1988; for a case study, Edholm *et al.*, 1983).

2   Sustained long-term trends. Notice how the chain migration process applies as well to recent immigrants from India, Pakistan or the West Indies, as to internal nineteenth-century migrants who, likewise, 'moved along kinship channels into slots prepared for them by kin … advice and assistance flowed along these channels in both directions' (Anderson, 1971, p.160, on Preston, Lancashire).

Such channels are sometimes 'more like a spider's web than the conventional bipolar model of migration' (Eades, 1987, p.8); or involve 'transcontinental families' with members in several continents (Kelly, in Clarke *et al.*, 1990, p.251 ff.). People keep links with their area of origin through marriage contracts, cultural visits, ritual links, or flows of news or gifts, even when committed to their present residence.

3   Short-term movements: for example, a cycle of coming and going between two places; return migration; movement originally *intended* as temporary. Sometimes Britain is just one staging point, with some or all of the family moving on elsewhere (in the next generation perhaps).

Does this last category recall any patterns in Chapter 1, section 4 or Chapter 2, section 4? Or any examples of which you have personal knowledge?

Change and continuity?   There are many interesting questions under this heading. How important are original cultural influences such as attitudes to education, family, gender divisions, marriage patterns (e.g. the Muslim encouragement – unlike the Hindu or Sikh – of cousin marriage, see Ballard, 1990); values; the role of religion? Have these changed in successive generations?

One much-discussed question is how far ties are maintained with the original place of origin, or with co-immigrants from the same origins. These may be relatively few from the outset; in other cases they remain extensive. Sometimes they fade over the years. Life in what may be perceived as an alien, even hostile, environment sometimes *strengthens* rather than weakens previous allegiances, or may *create* new ethnic identities (a phenomenon not confined to recent immigrants – think back to the Welsh chapels in Chapter 2, section 3, and look out for similar themes among, say, Irish or Jewish immigrants).

It may not be a question of some simple 'retention' or 'rejection' of traditional values, or even 'assimilation' as against 'segregation' – though these are reasonable starting concepts. Rather, there may be a *selective* following of particular cultural traits (and changing ones at that) to exploit changing opportunities, both in Britain and in the original home area. The culture of origin may be significant only for certain limited purposes (recreation, say) with little sense of solidarity with other immigrants, whether of the first or second generation. This possibility, too, is worth investigating – 'ethnic' solidarity cannot just be *assumed* to exist.

Influences are not just one-way. The changing character of local areas can also be studied. Earlier concentrations of immigrants from parts of Africa or China, for example:

> ... *led to cultural changes in certain seaport towns [while] today parts of Southall have assumed a strong Asian ambience. In all such areas patterns from the immigrants' past have been recreated; shops, foodstores, restaurants, clubs, credit organizations, stiebels and mosques.*
>
> (Holmes, 1982, p.192)

Do any of these themes link with the concepts discussed in Chapter 1 – especially the migration theories discussed in sections 3 and 4?

It is striking how many of the same ideas surface again and again: chain migration, push-and-pull factors, the relevance of both cultural institutions and family links in migration, generational change. You may also have noticed that, while this volume opened with the conventional distinction between migration, immigration and emigration, we are now raising themes that embrace migration much more generally.

In the light of these themes, what contribution might you make? The cases summarized so far are from published research. But among recent immigrants there is also a great deal of knowledge in people's own memories, some recorded on tape in recent oral history projects, some in local publications such as those in Figure 3.7 (p.93) (also Bornat, 1992). You may have been involved in such projects already or may now be starting to make your own recordings. If so, consider exploring one of the questions below.

QUESTIONS FOR RESEARCH

1   Compare and contrast the experiences of a particular group of twentieth-century immigrants with those of at least two other examples of recent immigrants (e.g. from section 3.1 above or others that you have read about). Relate your findings either to one of the themes discussed in section 3.2 above or to a question from section 3.3 below.

We suggest exploiting audio sources (advice on techniques is given below), and focusing on a small area or a small set of people rather than attempting to generalize across an immigrant group as a whole. In listening to tapes recorded by others (or, indeed, recorded by yourself), look out especially for comments on:

o   the context of arrival (with whom? why?);

o   jobs and making a living;

o   education;

o   housing;

o   roles of women and/or of men (changing?);

o   relationships with members of own family or kin;

o   relationships with other immigrants;

o   relationships with the established local population;

o   questions of identity;

o   the next generation(s);

o   any other experiences that seem to have been particularly important to the individual migrant.

2   In 1989 Jonathon Green published a collection of transcriptions from 103 taped interviews with first-generation immigrants to Britain. He began with the tentative theory that certain experiences are common to all immigrants. His eventual conclusion, however, was that the racial intolerance in British society meant *different* experiences for black and for white immigrants:

> *To be poor, and worse than that, black, too, is to lay oneself open to the least enviable of contemporary fates ... For the white immigrants, often politically rather than economically motivated, circumstances have been very different.*

(Green, 1990, p.9)

What evidence can you find from people's experiences in specific localities for either Green's first theory or his final conclusion? If it is not possible to reach *general* conclusions, does your own evidence throw any new light on such diversities?

How do you locate relevant audio sources? You have various options:

o   Contacting a local sound archive accessible to you (perhaps through Weerasinghe's *Directory*, 1989).

o   Consulting the journal *Oral History* about current work in your own area (see Figure 3.8).

o   Using recordings made by yourself or by your contacts (e.g. in a local school or reminiscence project).

o   Consulting the informative article on audio sources by Perks (1992).

You do need to reflect critically on the strength and limitations of oral and audio material as sources for research purposes. They are often idiosyncratic and personal, and dependent on the selectivity of memory. But that is also their strength. And, as has often been observed, they can be more effective vehicles for personal experience than more formal and official sources.

Listening to audio is time-consuming. So, for an initial exercise try just one short recording (say, 30 minutes; you can always go on to more later). If written transcripts are available these can be added to and extended – writing is *much* quicker to skim – but listen as well. Further advice and guidance on audio sources are available in Volume 4, Chapter 6, section 5.

JOURNAL OF THE ORAL HISTORY SOCIETY

• NORTH YORKSHIRE
YORK

Open Minds is a new publication which seeks to link older people's life stories with the issue of multi-disciplinary educational opportunities. The book includes a series of interviews with eight York people aged seventy or over, making the point that: 'older people hold a great deal of information, can be a source of inspiration to others and should be involved in the planning and delivery of services focused on their learning needs'.

The book has been edited by Peter Phillips, who has added a useful introduction and his own reflections about the experiences of the men and women who share their lives with the reader. He invites us to consider key issues from the point of view of the old person – about aspects of discrimination, about the availability, accessibility and appropriateness of educational opportunities, about meeting the need to move from familiar surroundings, about learning to live with a changed role and, perhaps crucially, about the low expectations held by the interviewee and their acceptance of their situations.

Open Minds is available, price £3.50 plus 50p p&p from Open Minds, York CVS, 10 Priory Street, York YO1 1EZ. For more information about the project contact Peter Phillips, 64 Dale Street, York YO2 1AE, tel 0904 655182.

• WEST MIDLANDS
WALSALL

Walsall Local History News is the bi-monthly newsletter from Walsall Local History Centre. Apart from news of the town's Leather Centre Museum, Local Studies and Conservation News, a recent issue includes news of oral history activities:

'Three local schools, Edgar Stammers, Harden Junior and Manor Farm Community are working together on the "Goscote Valley Project". The aim of this is to study the history of the area in its many aspects and record memories of life there, past and present. It will draw upon the talents and abilities of all pupils in all age ranges. Each child will have the opportunity to contribute towards an exhibition of the project in Walsall Central Library'.

The newsletter is published by Walsall Local History Centre, Essex Street, Walsall WS1 7AS, tel 0922 721305/6.

Figure 3.8 Current British work in oral history: extracts from typical entries in the journal *Oral History*, an excellent source of information about on-going work in oral history (Source: *Oral History*, 20, 2, Autumn 1992, pp.1, 10–11)

3.3   WHAT OTHER QUESTIONS AND THEORIES ARE SCHOLARS CURRENTLY RAISING?

Movement across frontiers is nothing new, and so most of the theories and questions in earlier sections can equally be applied to recent migrants. However, certain additional points from recent publications do need to be mentioned here.

A challenging overview of British historical studies of immigration by Colin Holmes (1991) points out the many openings for further research. He provides a handy summary of the main forms of immigration to Britain: the Irish ('the largest single immigrant minority living in Britain during the last hundred years': Holmes, 1991, p.192); continental Europeans, including not only east Europeans but also the less-studied Germans, Belgians and Italians; and immigrants from further afield such as those from the West Indies, South Asia and China (for some idea of the variety of immigrants to Britain, see Figure 3.9). Equally important, he points to major gaps in our knowledge where we need, as he puts it , 'to recover more':

1   The history of European groups (including Belgian refugees during the First World War, or the Hungarians after the 1956 uprising).

2   The pre-1945 history of minority groups, including those from outside Europe.

3   The history of immigrant minorities *throughout* Britain and Ireland (i.e. not just in England).

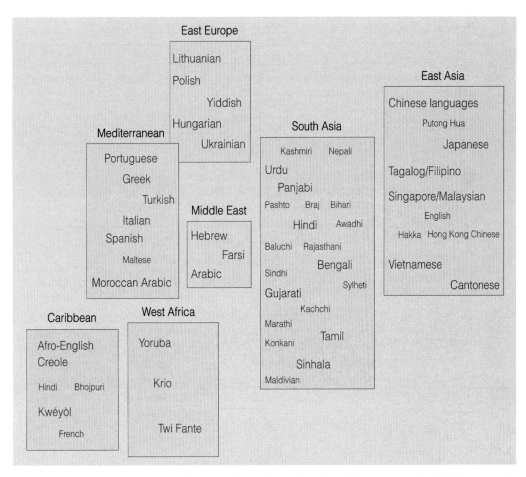

Figure 3.9   Some languages spoken in the British Isles, excluding those long indigenous to the British Isles and north-western European languages (based on Alladina and Edwards, 1991, vol. 2, p.13)

4 The history of immigrant groups outside London (though work is still needed there); for example, in Bradford, Liverpool and Manchester.

5 The history of immigration 'warts and all': not just celebratory studies of integration, but also detailed analyses, where applicable, of hostility and conflict.

These gaps do not apply just to recent immigration. They also highlight two particularly relevant points: first, the intrinsic importance of studies of this kind – sometimes wrongly regarded as peripheral in traditional historical scholarship; and, second, the need for research on the detailed *patterns* and *processes* of migration and of settlement at local level, as well as on the experience of particular families or groups. (For references to further work see the useful review in Holmes, 1991 – not a full coverage, however, of work by historical geographers; recommended further reading at the end of this chapter, especially Gilbert, 1990, and Robinson, 1992; and relevant references in Chapters 7 and 8 below).

Further questions arise from considering migration in the context of European dimensions (see Jackson and Moch, 1989). An emerging consensus in migration studies is to reject older simplified pictures of 'modernization' as the basis for understanding migration: for example, the view that migration to the towns was a sign of 'modernity', that rural–urban movements were an integral part of the radical change from a 'traditional' rural state to a modern industrialized urban society, characterized by alienation and the rise of social problems. The contrary argument is that migration in fact goes back much further into the past – scarcely something new and alien – and has always taken varied and complex forms. The corollary is that generalized concepts like 'industrialization' or 'modernization' need to be challenged as blanket explanations – or at least we should supplement them by detailed studies of just how all the various trends summed up in such ideas actually worked out in specific instances.

Following through this argument, Jackson and Moch (1989) present us with a useful 'research agenda' of topics that will repay further study and investigation (Schema C below).

Schema C: A research agenda of migration themes

1 Migrant selectivity: migration was not total but *selective* in nature, related to such variables as age, gender, landholding status, education, income and perhaps individual psychology. How did these apply in particular cases?

2 Motivation: how important were subjective perceptions, gained perhaps from other migrants, as against 'objective economic reality'? What were the roles played by established migration networks, or by family (not just individual) decisions?

3 The *flows* of moves: that is, not just gross numbers but the nature of the actual patterns within the various moves, including return migration and multiple moves.

4 The impact on the places that people had left, and on their destinations.

5 Consequences of migration for the individual mover. Detailed studies of these are important, as against simplified 'pessimistic' or 'optimistic' generalizations.

Many descriptive studies of migration remain to be undertaken. There are many opportunities and openings for researchers with interests in specific cases to relate them to questions such as those listed above in Schema C. Such studies can help to uncover the essential human quality and the complexities of the migration process; they can also reveal the role of common people – all too often obscured by academic controversies and generalizations.

———————————————————— *QUESTIONS FOR RESEARCH* ————————————————————

Here are some examples of possible small-scale studies:

1   An analysis of one family history in depth (more than just lists of names and dates), relating it to its wider context and to one or more of the questions raised above, for example:

(a)   multiple moves over two or more generations or within a single generation (see questions raised in Jackson and Moch, 1989; also in Chapter 2, section 3);

(b)   the consequences for individual movers and/or later generations (see also the long-term investment theory suggested in Abramson, 1992; and sections 1.5 and 2.2 above);

(c)   motivation, perception and experience, before or after migrating;

(d)   the roles played by the family: is migration primarily a process relating to *families* rather than individuals (as suggested in Jackson and Moch, 1989, p.30; Elliott, 1990, p.68; Schürer, 1991; see also Chapter 2, section 1)?

(e)   changes over the generations in, for example, the structure of the family; division of labour by gender; employment; links with overseas relatives' aspirations and values.

2   A study of a particular network or 'spider's web' among recent migrants. How far this network was localized might form part of the study (some elements might indeed be local, others regional, national, or even international). You could relate this to issues and themes raised above, also to questions as to the extent of a self-conscious sense of 'identity', 'ethnicity' or 'community' (there is more on this in Chapter 9, section 1).

Your methods and sources will depend on practical and personal considerations. Some sources overlap with those discussed in earlier chapters (see the answer to Exercise 2.7). For post-war immigrants, taping memories through oral enquiry could also be a major source, supplemented, perhaps, by existing audio sources (see advice on p.97 above). These sources are invaluable for expressing subjective experience – an approach that is fully consonant with the emphasis on experiential dimensions in recent migration studies; similarly with personal sources such as letters, diaries or autobiographies (see Volume 4, Chapter 4, section 8). You may yourself have family letters (treasured, for example, in some West Indian families) or, eventually, even if not immediately, access to family records overseas, say, in India. Buildings, photographs, locally available records and surveys (also considered in Volume 4) are all of relevance in understanding behavioural aspects of migration.

Many localities and groupings have not been properly investigated, and these can serve as testing grounds in which to examine established patterns and questions or to elucidate new ones. It is in studies of this kind, with their specificity and their complexity, that: 'Ordinary citizens of the past [can] be endowed with their role as active agents of change in the urban–industrial world we have gained' (Jackson and Moch, 1989, p.33).

4   REVIEW AND CONCLUSION

The three perspectives in sections 1 to 3 of this chapter are, in themselves, both different in type yet, from a methods point of view, they are also complementary. We started with Hermann Schulze and his family tree; section 2 presented the migration histories, amongst others, of Samuel Abramson, Lewis Hyman and Jewish emigration, generally, from Eastern Europe. Section 3 explored methods of researching the migration experiences of the 'new' British.

In all these investigations our understanding of individual and group movements has been taken much further than it would have been just in the construction of a family tree. In a very real sense, the researchers, who started off by acting locally, have ended up by thinking globally. Our knowledge has been expanded; our understanding of specific events has gained considerable enrichment; and we have been led forward into questions as to the origins, make-up and the nature of communities.

_____ *EXERCISE 3.10* _____

1 Glance back through the case studies in Chapters 2 and 3 and list four questions, comparisons or concepts that struck *you* as interesting in themselves or worth following up in research.

2 Adapt one of Exercises 2.7 or 2.8 at the end of Chapter 2 to take account of the case studies discussed in Chapter 3.

Comment p.222.

REFERENCES AND FURTHER READING

Note: entries marked with an asterisk are suggestions for further reading.

Abramson, P.R. (1992) *A case for case studies,* Newbury Park, CA, and London, Sage.*

Adams, C. (1991) 'Across seven seas and thirteen rivers', *Oral History,* 19, 1, pp.29–35.

Age Exchange Theatre Trust (1989) *Across the Irish Sea,* London, Age Exchange.

Alladina, S. and Edwards, V. (eds) (1991) *Multilingualism in the British Isles,* 2 vols, Harlow, Longman.

Anderson, M. (1971) *Family structure in nineteenth century Lancashire,* Cambridge, Cambridge University Press.

Bade, K.J. (1984) *Auswanderer, Wanderarbeiter, Gastarbeiter,* Ostfildern, Scripta Mercaturae Verlag.

Baines, D. (1991) *Emigration from Europe, 1815–1930,* Basingstoke, Macmillan Education.

Ballard, R. (1987) 'The political economy of migration: Pakistan, Britain, and the Middle East', in Eades (1987).*

Ballard, R. (1990) 'Migration and kinship: the differential effect of marriage rules on the processes of Punjabi migration to Britain', in Clarke *et al.* (1990).

Ballard, R. and Ballard, C. (1977) 'The Sikhs: the development of south Asian settlements in Britain', in Watson (1977).

Baxter, A. (1986) *In search of your European roots,* Baltimore, MD, Genealogical Publishing Co. Inc.

Berghahn, V.R. (1987) *Modern Germany: society, economy and politics in the twentieth century,* 2nd edn, Cambridge, Cambridge University Press.

Bhachu, P. (1984) 'East African Sikhs in Britain: experienced settlers with traditionalistic values', *Immigrants and Minorities,* 3, 3, pp.276–96.

Bornat, J. (1992) 'The communities of community publishing', *Oral History*, 20, 2, pp.23–31.

Bradford Heritage Recording Unit (1987) *Destination Bradford: a century of immigration*, Bradford, Bradford Libraries and Information Service.

Bramwell, A.C. (ed.) (1988) *Refugees in the age of total war*, London, Unwin Hyman.

Burman, R. (1982) 'The Jewish woman as breadwinner: the changing value of women's work in a Manchester immigrant community', *Oral History*, 10, 2, pp.27–39.*

Camp, A. (1987) *My ancestor was a migrant*, London, Society of Genealogists.*

Clarke, C., Peach, C. and Vertovec, S. (eds) (1990) *South Asians overseas: migration and ethnicity*, Cambridge, Cambridge University Press.

Currer-Briggs, N. (1982) *Worldwide family history*, London, Routledge and Kegan Paul.*

Desai, A.V. (1968) *Real wages in Germany*, Oxford, Clarendon Press.*

Drake, M. (ed.) (1994) *Time, family and community: perspectives on family and community history*, Oxford, Blackwell in association with The Open University (Course Reader).

Eade, J. (1990) 'Bangladeshi community organisation and leadership in Tower Hamlets, East London', in Clarke *et al.* (1990).

Eades, J. (1987) 'Anthropologists and migrants: changing models and realities', in Eades, J. (ed.) *Migrants, workers, and the social order*, ASA Monographs 26, London, Tavistock.*

Edholm, F., Roberts, H. and Sayer, J. (1983) *Vietnamese refugees in Britain*, London, Commission for Racial Equality.

Elbaja, M. (1978) *My life*, 2nd edn, London, The English Centre.

Elliott, B. (1990) 'Biography, family history and the analysis of social change', in Kendrick, S., Straw, P. and McCrone, D. (eds) *Interpreting the past, understanding the present*, Basingstoke and London, Macmillan (for the British Sociological Association). Reprinted in Drake (1994).

Evans, R.J. (1986) *The German peasantry: conflict and community in rural society from the eighteenth to the twentieth centuries*, London, Croom Helm.*

Finestein, I. (1961) 'The new community 1880–1918', in Lipman, V. (ed.) *Three centuries of Anglo-Jewish history*, Jewish Historical Society of England.

Fishman, W. (1975) *East End Jewish radicals, 1875–1914*, London, Duckworth.*

Fishman, W. (1988) *East End 1888*, London, Duckworth.*

Foner, N. (1977) 'The Jamaicans: cultural and social change among migrants in Britain', in Watson (1977).

Gainer, B. (1972) *The alien invasion: the origins of the Aliens Act of 1905*, London, Heinemann.

Gandy, M. (ed.) (1982) *My ancestor was Jewish*, London, Society of Genealogists.

Gartner, L. (1959) 'Notes on the statistics of Jewish immigration to England, 1870–1914', *Jewish Social Studies*, 21, pp.97–102.

Gartner, L. (1960) *The Jewish immigrant in England, 1870–1914*, London, George Allen and Unwin.*

Gilbert, V. (1990) 'Current bibliography of immigrants and minorities: monographs, periodicals, articles and theses, 1985–1987. Part 1: Great Britain', *Immigrants and Minorities*, 9, 2, pp.195–220.*

Green, J. (1990) *Them: voices from the immigrant community in contemporary Britain,* London, Secker and Warburg.

Hammersmith and Fulham Ethnic Communities Oral History Project (1990) *XENI: Greek-Cypriots in London,* London, Hammersmith and Fulham Ethnic Communities Oral History Project.

Hammersmith and Fulham Ethnic Communities Oral History Project (1992) *The motherland calls: African Caribbean experiences,* 2nd edn, London, Hammersmith and Fulham Ethnic Communities Oral History Project.

Hersch, L. (1931) 'International migration of the Jews' in *International Migrations,* 2.

Hindus, M. (n.d.) *Slutzk after World War II (as seen by an eye witness),* in The American 'Slutzk Yizkor Book Committee', *Slutzk Yizkor Book,* pp.xv–xvii.

Hohorst, G., Kocka, J. and Ritter, G.A. (1975) *Arbeitsbuch: Materialen zur Statistik des Kaiser-reichs 1870–1914,* Munich, Verlag C.H. Beck.

Holmes, C. (1982) 'The impact of immigration on British society 1870–1980', in Barker, T. and Drake, M. (eds) *Population and society in Britain 1850–1980,* Batsford, London.

Holmes, C. (1991) 'Historians and immigration', in Pooley and Whyte (1991). Reprinted in Drake (1994).*

Howe, I. (1976) *World of our fathers: the journey of East European Jews to America and the life they made there,* New York, Touchstone/Simon and Schuster.*

Jackson, J.H. and Moch, P.L. (1989) 'Migration and the social history of modern Europe', *Historical Methods,* 22, 1, pp.27–36. Reprinted in Drake (1994).*

Khan, V.S. (ed.) (1979) *Minority families in Britain: support and stress,* London, Macmillan.*

King, R. (ed.) (1986) *Return migration and regional economic problems,* London, Croom Helm.

Kocka, J. (1975) *Unternehmer in der Deutschen Industrialisierung,* Göttingen.*

Kocka, J. (ed.) (1987) *Bürger und Bürgerlichkeit im 19 Jahrhundert,* Göttingen.*

Kosmin, B., Baner, M. and Grizzard, N. (1976) *Steel City Jews,* London, Research Unit, Board of Deputies of British Jews.

Krausz, E. (1964) *Leeds Jewry,* Cambridge, W. Heffer and Sons for the Jewish Historical Society of England.

Kurzweil, A. (1980) *From generation to generation: how to trace your Jewish genealogy and personal history,* New York, Schocken Books.

Kushner, T. (1991) 'Directory of Jewish historical and heritage resources in the United Kingdom', *Immigrants and minorities,* 10, pp.212–29.

Kuznets, S. (1975) 'Immigration of Russian Jews to the United States', *Perspectives in American History,* ix, pp.35–124.

Lipman, V. (1954) *Social History of the Jews in England, 1850–1950,* London, Watts.

Lipman, V. (1959) *A century of social service, 1859–1959: the Jewish Board of Guardians,* London, Routledge and Kegan Paul.

Lipman, V. (1961) 'The age of emancipation, 1815–1880', in Lipman, V. (ed.) *Three centuries of Anglo-Jewish history*, Jewish Historical Society.

Lipman, V. (1990) *A history of the Jews in Britain since 1858*, Leicester, Leicester University Press.

Nielson, J.S. (1984) *Muslim immigration and settlement in Britain,* Birmingham, Selly Oak Colleges.

Oakley, R. (1979) 'The Cypriot migration to Britain', in Khan (1979).

Panayi, P. (1991) *The enemy in our midst: Germans in Britain during the First World War,* Oxford, Berg.

Perks, R. (1992) 'Oral history resource list 1. Oral history and sound archive resources for history in the national curriculum', *Oral History,* 20, 1, pp.70–4.

Pollins, H. (1981) *A history of the Jewish working men's club and institute, 1874–1912*, Oxford, Ruskin College Library Occasional Publication, 2.

Pollins, H. (1982) *An economic history of the Jews in England,* Rutherford, NJ, Fairleigh Dickinson University Press; London, Associated University Presses.

Pooley, C.G. and Whyte, I.D. (eds) (1991) *Migrants, emigrants and immigrants: a social history of migration,* London, Routledge.

Ritter, G.A. and Kocka, J. (1977) *Deutsche Sozialgeschichte:Dokumente und Skizzen Band II 1870–1914,* Munich, Verlag C.H. Beck.

Robinson, V. (1992) 'The internal migration of Britain's ethnic population', in Champion, T. and Fielding, T. (eds) (1992) *Migration processes and patterns,* vol. 1, London, Belhaven Press.[*]

Runyan, W. (1982) *Life histories and psychobiography,* New York, Oxford University Press.

Schürer, K. (1991) 'The role of the family in the process of migration', in Pooley and Whyte (1991).

Thomas-Hope, E. (1980) 'Hopes and reality in the West Indian migration to Britain', *Oral History,* 8, 1, pp.35–42.

Watson, J.L. (ed.) (1977) *Between two cultures: migrants and minorities in Britain,* Oxford, Blackwell.[*]

Weerasinghe, L. (ed.) (1989) *Directory of recorded sound resources in the United Kingdom,* London, British Library, National Sound Archive.

Williams, B. (1976) *The making of Manchester Jewry, 1740–1875,* Manchester, Manchester University Press.[*]

Williams, B. (1985) 'The anti-semitism of tolerance: middle-class Manchester and the Jews', in Kidd, A. and Roberts, K. (eds) *City, class and culture,* Manchester, Manchester University Press.

Zborowski, M. and Herzog, E. (1952) *Life is with people: the culture of the shtetl,* New York, Schocken Books.

CHAPTER 4

USING QUANTITATIVE AND CARTOGRAPHIC TECHNIQUES: TWO EXAMPLES

by W.T.R. Pryce

Numbers, and the ebb and flow of migrants to this or that destination, lie at the heart of migration research. Therefore, statistical techniques remain of central importance and, because migration is inherently spatial, so does the use of sketch maps and interpretative diagrams. In this chapter, two useful approaches that can be adapted for investigations elsewhere are demonstrated. Both are based on the birthplaces as recorded in the CEBs, which, because only the differences between places of birth and enumeration are evident, are known as *life-time migration data*. The first study considers the *mechanisms of movement* into a single, expanding urban centre, Preston in Lancashire; the second deals with the *regional patterns of movements* into and within north-east Wales.

The focus is on techniques and methods – particularly ways of data capture from samples, the laying out of information in tabular form, the use of matrices, and cartographic techniques for the presentation and interpretation of results. Clearly, all this material builds on the approaches discussed earlier in Chapter 1.

1 TESTING TWO COMPETING HYPOTHESES: THE CASE OF PRESTON, LANCASHIRE, IN 1851

From Ravenstein and others (Chapter 1, section 3) we know that in the nineteenth century migration from rural communities to industrial towns was usually short distance in nature. But what *mechanisms* underlay these movements?

The 1851 census revealed that Preston had a resident population of 69,500. One-third of the adults in the town were employed directly in the cotton mills: indirectly, many more were dependent upon them. A magnet for migrants, 70 per cent of the population (children included) had been born elsewhere. In order to explore migration to this growing centre, Anderson (1971) adopted, as his research hypotheses, two potentially conflicting statements:

1 Migration takes the form of a wave-like motion, with migrants moving from the countryside to neighbouring small towns, before later moving on to larger centres like Preston in 1851 (Ravenstein, 1885; Redford, 1926). (See Figure 1.3 in Chapter 1, section 3.1.)

2 Towns stimulated population growth in their immediate rural hinterlands and some of this population ('surplus' to local employment needs) was 'siphoned off' by them (Deane and Cole, 1967).

To test these two hypotheses Anderson drew a 10 per cent *systematic sample* of *households* from the CEBs of Preston and its surrounding parishes. The birthplace of everyone in his samples was identified and plotted on a large-scale map. This showed migration distances from Preston as a series of concentric rings. (For sampling and for techniques to standardize the migrant flows to take account of the areas, see Volume 4, Chapter 8, section 6.)

Anderson's calculations confirmed that most movements were short distance and that the volume of movements tended to decline with increased distance from the town. To explore his finding in more detail, next he drew further samples from the CEBs within a 30-mile radius of Preston. In parishes to the south-east there was no clear directional pattern, and long-distance migrants were few in number. But north-west of the town, calculations of the migration balances, parish by parish, revealed that as many as 60 per cent of migrants to Preston had been replaced by migrants from further afield. This *step migration with replacement* is the underlying process that determined the wave-like motion identified by Ravenstein.

By comparing the birthplaces of the eldest co-residing child with that of his or her father, Anderson was also able to demonstrate the extent of *simple step migration* (i.e. when temporary halts are made in the course of the movement) (Table 4.1). Counting only the eldest child is a practical way of avoiding the inevitable bias that otherwise would arise due to differences of family size.

Table 4.1 Birthplaces of eldest co-residing children in Preston's migrant families, 1851

Father born at	Birthplace of eldest co-residing child (per cent of all birthplaces)			
	Father's birthplace (%)	Intermediate location (%)	Preston (%)	Actual numbers of eldest children
0–4.9 miles	14	26	60	99
5–9.9 miles	15	23	62	174
10–19.9 miles	17	24	60	80
20–29.9 miles	7	36	57	67
30 miles and over	5	36	58	91
Total	**12**	**28**	**60**	**511**

Source: based on Anderson (1971) Table V, p.24

Of the 511 children analysed, 28 per cent were found to have been born at an intermediate location between Preston and the birthplace of the father, 60 per cent in Preston itself, and 12 per cent in the birthplace of their father (Table 4.1).

Such an analysis catches only part of the movements: some children born at intermediate locations might have died or left home; other couples might have moved to an intermediate location after their first child had been born; some couples had decided to move late in life, when the woman could no longer bear children. Table 4.1 also shows that step migration was positively correlated with distance – that is, of those who had moved 30 miles and over, 36 per cent had a child born at an intermediate site, as against 26 per cent of those who had moved 4.9 miles or less.

Nevertheless, in the differences between parishes to the south-east and those to the north-west of Preston, Anderson had found evidence that supported both his research hypotheses.

QUESTIONS FOR RESEARCH

1 The two specific migration hypotheses explored by Anderson need to be verified and tested on other towns that were emergent regional centres – an appropriate theme for a local research project.

2 Anderson's research involved large numbers of people. But worthwhile investigations can be undertaken on much smaller numbers – say, up to 50 householders (with their co-residing children). To sharpen the focus, these can be selected by specific criteria (e.g. skilled craft workers, professionals, etc.).

3   Here are three typical questions that could be explored:

(i)   To what extent did the migration *distances* vary between specific occupations and levels of skill in a small locality or, say, at two contrasting locations?

(ii) To what extent did the *mechanisms* of movement (e.g. simple step migration or step migration with replacement) differ by occupation?

(iii) What changes occurred in these patterns of movement over time – say, between 1851 and 1891?

(For further details on the CEBs, see Volume 4, Chapter 3, section 2; for the measurement of standardized distances, see Volume 4, Chapter 8, section 7; on research strategies, see Volume 1, Chapter 2, section 2; Volume 4, Chapter 1, section 2; also, Collins and Pryce, 1993.)

2   SEX RATIOS, INTRA-REGIONAL FLOWS AND CARTOGRAPHIC ANALYSIS: NORTH-EAST WALES IN 1851

The research on which this section draws was concerned with the impact of migration on language areas during the industrialization of north-east Wales (Pryce 1975, 1978). The population of this region grew from *c*.59,000 in 1750 to 133,750 by 1851 when new industrial townships had emerged (Figure 4.1). Here we focus on methods of analysing the complex ebb and flow of migration *within a region* rather than on just the movements to and from a single centre like Preston.

Figure 4.1   The developing rural coalfield around the town of Mold *c*.1860, with the Clwydian Hills beyond. The tower of the parish church can be seen (right centre). A three-carriage steam train (left centre) is seen approaching Mold station, opened in 1849. The landscape is dotted with industrial buildings and colliery winding gear (Source: lithograph print published by Pring and Price, Mold. National Library of Wales)

2.1   SEX RATIOS: A USEFUL MIGRATION SURROGATE

Before 1841 the census did not report on place of birth. In consequence, researchers need to seek other indicators of migration, such as significant local differences in the ratio of men to women compared with the overall national ratio. The approach is based on Ravenstein's ideas regarding the sex-differentiated nature of some forms of migration (see Chapter 1, section 3.1, Schema C, Law 6) which can be applied to regional circumstances within north-east Wales as follows:

1   Colliery districts made substantial, continuing demands for male labour: therefore the census recorded more men than women in these locations.

2   Where the demand for domestic servants was substantial (e.g. in upper-class residential districts), there would be a 'surplus' of women.

3   Young women were much more likely than young men to move in search of employment (especially in domestic and personal service). Therefore, farming communities showed a 'surplus' of men.

To explore these three linked ideas, the ratio of men to women was calculated from the census reports. Where the local sex ratio differed from that of England and Wales by more than two standard deviations, it can be assumed that differential migration had taken place (Figure 4.2). (For calculating the sex ratio and standard deviations see Volume 4, Chapter 8.)

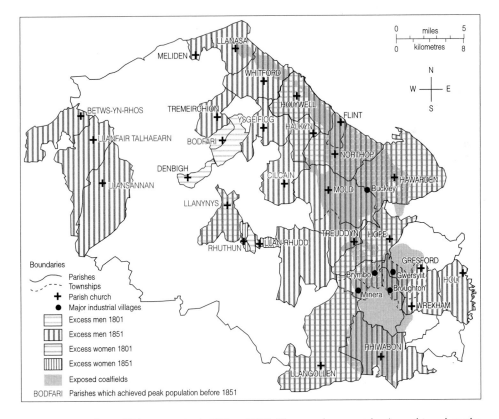

Figure 4.2   North-east Wales: sex ratios in 1801 and 1851. The map shows parishes/townships where the local sex ratio differed from that of England and Wales as a whole by more than two standard deviations (Source: based on Pryce, 1975, pp.85, 86)

———————————————————— *EXERCISE 4.1* ————————————————————

Examine Figure 4.2 closely and then consider the following:

1 What methods are used to distinguish 'surplus' men and women?

2 What cartographic technique has been used to separate out significant differences in 1851 from those in 1801?

3 List additional features on the map that help in interpretation.

Comment p.222.

___

Figure 4.2 shows that men were significantly more numerous (in the statistical sense) in all those parishes with labour-intensive mining and heavy industries. Whereas the older colliery districts had a 'surplus' of men in 1801, by 1851 this was true also of the inland districts where new mines had been opened around Mold, Rhiwabon and Wrexham. In the rural west, and in the depressed lead mining communities of central Flintshire (Cilcain, Halkyn, Ysgeifiog), where the population was in decline, the selective out-migration of women had left a 'surplus' of men. Conversely, in the towns of Wrexham (1801), Rhuthun (1801 and 1851) and Denbigh (1801) significantly more women than men were enumerated, reflecting the dominance of service employment. A 'surplus' of women also occurred in the cotton mill town of Holywell (1801). It should be emphasized that the evidence of these sex ratio differences is indicative rather than conclusive. In the absence of direct information, here we are relying on indirect (or surrogate) measures: these call for careful interpretation and, wherever possible, support from other sources.

———————————————— **QUESTION FOR RESEARCH** ————————————————

Examine, using data from a specific CEB and tests for significant differences between proportions, the sex ratios within particular age cohorts, occupational or social class groupings. (For methods of calculation, see Volume 4, Chapter 8; for the classification of occupations, see Volume 4, Chapter 3, section 2.1.1, and Armstrong, 1972.)

Depending on the size of the area/population under investigation, this could turn out to be a very substantial and demanding project. At the outset, special attention needs to be focused on the scope of the research. The findings should throw light on aspects of work, social status, and social and geographical mobility (see Volume 3, Chapters 1–5).

2.2 SAMPLING TECHNIQUES AND THE STUDY OF MIGRATION

In 1851 the CEBs covering north-east Wales contained entries for 28,693 households with a total population of over 133,000. Faced with such large numbers, the lone researcher must resort to sampling. The census authorities used the household as the basic social unit for collecting data. Therefore, convenience, rather than strict scientific accuracy, leads us to choose the household as our *sampling unit.* The total number of households (28,693) makes up our *sampling frame.* One option would be a *random sample* of households (see Volume 4, Chapter 8, section 6; Henry, 1990) but it is easier, and acceptable in scientific terms, to draw a *systematic sample.* The final question, then, is how many of these 28,693 households to include in the sample?

DECISIONS ON SAMPLE SIZE: A ROLE FOR PILOT STUDIES

Conventionally, one draws a 5, 10 or 20 per cent systematic sample, depending upon the assumed variability (diversity) of the locality under investigation. For example, is the employment dominated by one industry or is there a wide spread of different occupations? Were most inhabitants born in Wales? How many English or, for example, Irish people were enumerated? In the research on north-east Wales, it was decided to conduct three small pilot studies involving 5, 10 and 20 per cent samples of households in the district of Hope (located on the eastern border, see Figure 4.2). The three samples were then compared with all households enumerated in the Hope district to see if they were representative. These so-called 'goodness of fit' tests involved the application of the Chi-square statistical test on occupations, age structures and birthplaces (see Startup and Whittaker, 1982; Ebdon, 1985; Bryman and Cramer, 1990: all provide guidance on methods of calculation).

After considering the results from these pilot studies it was decided to take a 10 per cent sample of households in the thirteen larger areas, increasing the sample fraction to 20 per cent for the six smaller localities where less than 1,000 households had been enumerated.

To limit bias in the selection of households, it was decided to adopt the method known as *systematic sampling with a random start*. Thus, when a 10 per cent sample was drawn, ten bits of paper were numbered 1–10 and placed in a hat. One was drawn out and that household was the first chosen, followed by every tenth afterwards. Because of the likelihood of involuntary migration, institutional 'households' (e.g. workhouses, prisons, hospitals, army barracks, boarding schools, etc.) can be ignored.

_____ **EXERCISE 4.2** _____

For a 20 per cent sample, no. 3 has been drawn from the hat. Give the numbers of the next seven household schedules to be drawn from the CEB.

Answer p.223.

POINT ESTIMATES AND SAMPLING ERRORS

After the samples have been analysed, we can – for ease of comparison – convert these numbers into percentages: that is, such-and-such a per cent came from this or that place. But, *because we are dealing with samples*, these are estimates of the situation in the total population – hence known as *point estimates*.

By calculating the *standard error* of the sample (see Volume 4, Chapter 8, section 4, Table 8.3) (also called, in some statistical textbooks, the *sample error*), we can show how close our estimate is likely to be to the actual proportions of migrants in the total population. The larger the number of individuals in the sample, the smaller is the range of 'error' due to sampling procedures. Thus, it is the size of the sample itself – *not* the proportion of the total population included in the sample – that is crucial (Figure 4.3).

_____ **EXERCISE 4.3** _____

Figure 4.3 shows the percentage (estimated) of in-migrants to specific locations within north-east Wales, 1851, based on 10 or 20 per cent samples of households in each area.

1   How many persons were included in the samples drawn for the Denbigh, Holywell and Llanrhaeadr registration sub-districts?

2   What percentage of the population in Llanarmon and in St Asaph recorded birthplaces in the neighbouring areas?

3   What point estimates and standard (or sample) errors are shown for Holywell and for Llanrhaeadr?

4   What do these values mean?

5   What relationship can you identify between the range of the standard (or sample) errors and the numbers included in each sample?

Answers and comments p.223.

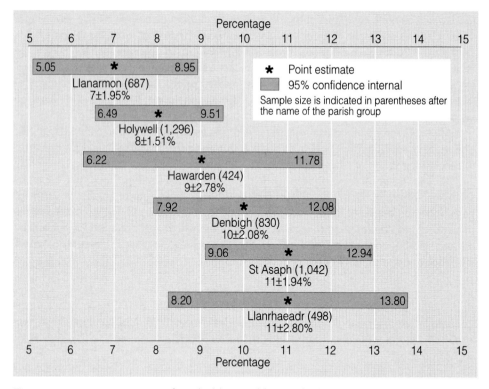

Figure 4.3   Point estimates, range of standard (or sample) errors (at the 95 per cent confidence level) for proportions of the population born in neighbouring areas of north-east Wales, 1851 (Source: Pryce, 1982, p.82)

To make comparisons as to the likely numbers of migrants in the samples from different areas, the figures need to be *grossed up*. This is done by multiplying the numbers in each of the sample by the sample fraction used. Thus, if we have drawn a one-in-ten (10 per cent) sample, the sample is multiplied by ten; if a one in five (20 per cent), by five, and so on.

2.3   MAPPING MIGRATION FLOWS

Before we can map the migration flows, our birthplace data need to be laid out in the form of a *data matrix* – a convenient way for arranging and storing all the information. So that the findings could be linked to other data on births, marriages and deaths (not included here), *registration subdistricts,* rather than ecclesiastical parishes, were adopted for the nineteen territorial divisions within north-east Wales and for analysing movements within the region (Figure 4.4). As we are interested in mapping both *gross* and *net* migration flows, two data matrices need to be prepared (Tables 4.2 and 4.3 on pp.114 and 115).

In Table 4.2 the nineteen registration sub-districts are arranged in a 19 x 19 matrix, with the sending areas (birthplaces) occupying the columns (numbered 2–20 across the top) and the receiving areas (places of census enumeration) occupying the rows (1–19 on the left side of the matrix). To avoid ambiguity, the identification number for each area (e.g. Abergele = 1; Llanrhaeadr = 13) appears in both the columns and the rows. Next, the point estimates have been grossed up according to the sample fraction used (see above). It is these grossed-up figures that are entered into the appropriate cells of the matrix.

Since our interest is in migration between neighbouring areas, many of the cells in the matrix will be left empty. Because we are *not* interested in movements *within* each area we place a dot where the columns and the rows intersect (e.g. column 2 and row 1 = Abergele; column 3 and row 2 = Cyffylliog), the complete sequence of dots forming the diagonal across the matrix. Next, a

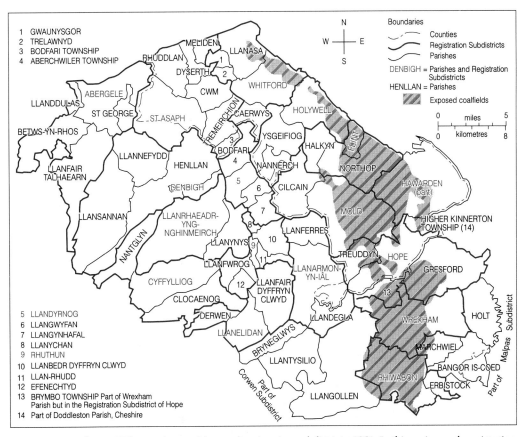

Figure 4.4   North-east Wales: ancient parishes and registration subdistricts, 1851. In this region each registration subdistrict comprised between just one (e.g. Wrexham) and up to six (e.g. St Asaph) ecclesiastical parishes. The names of the parishes in each subdistrict can be obtained from the 1851 published census reports. The boundaries of the ancient parishes (not always the same as the boundaries of the later *civil* parishes) can be obtained from either (1) Ordnance Survey (two miles = one inch) *Index to the first edition six-inch maps (county maps)* 1856–93, or (2) Ordnance Survey (one inch) First Edition *Index to the tithe survey* 1813–65. The latter was a special printing of the one-inch OS map First Edition to show boundaries of townships and parishes. For further details, including index maps showing the sheet numbers covering specific areas, you should consult Harley (1964)

cross is placed in the co-ordinate where any two areas do not share a common boundary (this information has been obtained from Figure 4.4). For example, in the case of Abergele (area no. 1) this excludes all other registration subdistricts except Denbigh (no. 3) and St Asaph (no. 17). Finally, we fill all the remaining cells with our grossed-up point estimates. Our completed matrix tells us, for example, that Rhiwabon (no. 15) *received* 170 persons born in Holt (no. 7), 280 from Llangollen (no. 11) and 370 from Wrexham (no. 19). On the other hand, the Rhiwabon area (no. 15) *sent* 110 to Holt (no. 7), 50 to Llangollen (no. 11) and 430 to Wrexham (no. 19).

Table 4.2 thus records both in- and out-movements area by area (i.e. *gross migration*), and from this we can calculate how far each locality was a 'gainer' or a 'loser' (i.e. *net migration)*. Thus, for example, there were 370 migrants in Abergele (no. 1) from Denbigh (no. 3) and 280 in Denbigh from Abergele. Therefore, Abergele recorded a net balance of +90 migrants; Denbigh a net loss of –90 migrants. Table 4.3 shows these balances for each pair of contiguous areas. By summing these, the overall net gains or losses from surrounding areas can be worked out (Table 4.3, columns 21 and 22). Now that all the internal migration flows have been calculated using these two matrices (Tables 4.2 and 4.3), all the information can be summarized and presented as simple flow-line maps (methods of preparation are covered in Mills and Pryce, 1993). What do these now tell us? (Figure 4.5a,b on p.116).

Table 4.2 North-east Wales, 1851: gross migration flows between adjacent areas

Sending areas (birthplaces in neighbouring registration subdistricts)

(1) Registration subdistricts	(2) 1 Abergele	(3) 2 Cyffyliog	(4) 3 Denbigh	(5) 4 Flint	(6) 5 Hawarden	(7) 6 Holywell	(8) 7 Holt	(9) 8 Hope	(10) 9 Llanarmon	(11) 10 Llandyrnog	(12) 11 Llangollen	(13) 12 Llanelidan	(14) 13 Llanrhaeadr	(15) 14 Mold	(16) 15 Rhiwabon	(17) 16 Rhuthun	(18) 17 St Asaph	(19) 18 Whitford	(20) 19 Wrexham
1 Abergele	•	X	[370]	X	X	X	X	X	X	X	X	X	X	X	X	X	240	X	X
2 Cyffyliog	X	•	70	X	X	X	X	X	X	X	X	55	45	X	X	35	X	X	X
3 Denbigh	[280]	130	•	X	X	X	X	X	X	140	X	X	240	X	X	X	150	X	X
4 Flint	X	X	X	•	150	300	X	X	X	X	X	X	X	400	X	X	X	X	X
5 Hawarden	X	X	X	190	•	X	X	190	X	X	X	X	X	250	X	X	X	X	X
6 Holywell	X	X	X	730	X	•	X	X	X	160	X	X	X	340	X	X	X	820	X
7 Holt	X	X	X	X	X	X	•	75	X	X	X	X	X	X	[110]	X	X	X	230
8 Hope	X	X	X	X	130	X	40	•	190	X	X	X	X	290	X	X	X	X	610
9 Llanarmon	X	X	X	X	X	X	X	90	•	X	X	X	X	200	X	95	X	X	55
10 Llandyrnog	X	X	100	X	X	X	X	X	X	•	X	X	X	10	X	100	X	X	X
11 Llangollen	X	X	X	X	X	X	X	X	X	X	•	55	X	X	[50]	X	X	X	20
12 Llanelidan	X	70	X	X	X	X	X	X	65	X	35	•	X	X	X	140	X	X	X
13 Llanrhaeadr	X	250	265	X	X	X	X	X	250	80	X	X	•	X	X	50	X	X	X
14 Mold	X	X	X	290	260	130	X	210	X	X	X	X	155	•	X	110	X	X	X
15 Rhiwabon	X	X	X	X	X	X	[170]	X	90	X	[280]	X	X	X	•	X	X	X	[370]
16 Rhuthun	X	230	X	X	X	X	X	X	X	X	X	160	50	40	X	•	25	X	X
17 St Asaph	610	X	580	X	X	X	X	X	X	350	X	X	X	X	X	X	•	700	X
18 Whitford	X	X	X	X	X	240	X	X	X	X	X	X	X	X	X	X	410	•	X
19 Wrexham	X	X	X	X	X	X	370	590	80	X	150	X	X	X	[430]	X	X	X	•

Receiving areas (place of enumeration)

Note: columns 2–20 indicate the origins of people who are enumerated in the parish groups listed in column 1. The symbol 'X' is used to identify areas which are not contiguous, and the symbol '•' is used for the same-name co-ordinates. Numbers in boxes are discussed in the text.

Source: based on Pryce (1982) p.84

Table 4.3 North-east Wales, 1851: net migration flows between adjacent areas

Columns (2)–(20) = Sending areas (birthplaces); columns (21)–(22) = Net migration balances. Rows = Receiving areas (place of enumeration).

Registration subdistricts (1)	1 Abergele (2)	2 Cyffyliog (3)	3 Denbigh (4)	4 Flint (5)	5 Hawarden (6)	6 Holywell (7)	7 Holt (8)	8 Hope (9)	9 Llanarmon (10)	10 Llandyrnog (11)	11 Llangollen (12)	12 Llanelidan (13)	13 Llanrhaeadr (14)	14 Mold (15)	15 Rhiwabon (16)	16 Rhuthun (17)	17 St Asaph (18)	18 Whitford (19)	19 Wrexham (20)	In-migration (21)	Out-migration (22)
1 Abergele	•		[+90]														-370			+90	-370
2 Cyffyliog		•	-60										-205			-195				0	-475
3 Denbigh	[-90]	+60	•							+40			-25				-430			+100	-545
4 Flint				•	-40	-430								+110						+110	-470
5 Hawarden				+40	•			+60						-10						+100	-10
6 Holywell				+430		•		+35		+85				+210				+580		+1,305	0
7 Holt							•												-140	+35	-200
8 Hope					-60		-35	•	+100		+25	+105		+80	-60	+5			+20	+200	-95
9 Llanarmon								-100	•				+75	-50		+40			-55	+135	-205
10 Llandyrnog			-40			-85				•				-70			-325	-55		+115	-575
11 Llangollen									-25		•	+125			-230				-130	+125	-385
12 Llanelidan		+15							-105		-125	•				-50				+15	-280
13 Llanrhaeadr		+205	+25							-75			•			-180				+230	-255
14 Mold				-110	+10	-210		-80	+50	+70				•		+70				+200	-400
15 Rhiwabon							+60				+230				•				-60	+290	-60
16 Rhuthun		+195							-5	-40		+50	+180	-70		•				+425	-115
17 St Asaph	+370		+430							+325							•	+290		+1,415	0
18 Whitford						-580				+55							-290	•		+55	-870
19 Wrexham							+140	-20	+25		+130				+60				•	+355	-20

Note: in columns 2–20, '+' = net in-migration, and '–' = net out-migration for each of the parish groups listed in column 1; '•' = same-name co-ordinates. Numbers in boxes are discussed in the text.

Source: based on Pryce (1982) p.85

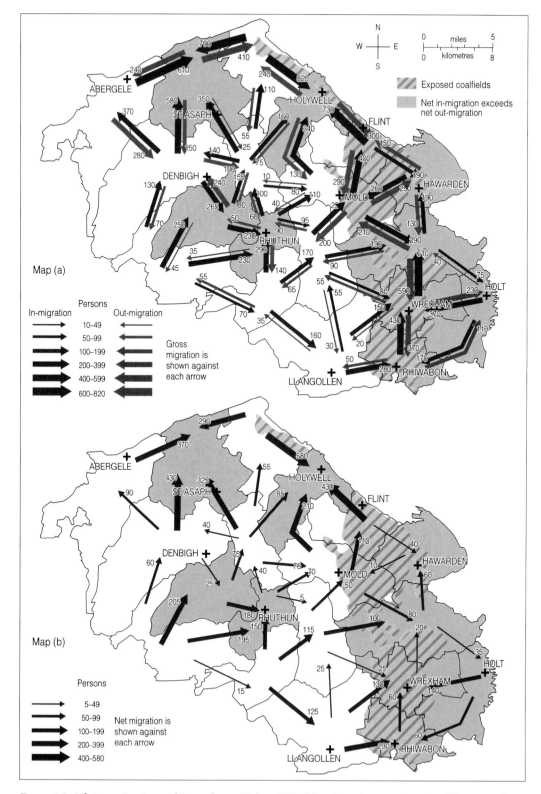

Figure 4.5 Lifetime migration within north-east Wales, 1851: (a) estimated gross migration; (b) estimated net migration, between adjacent registration subdistricts (Source: Pryce, 1975, p.97)

In the rural west the movements tended overwhelmingly to be in one direction: from upland moorland communities to the richer lowlands around the market towns of Denbigh and Rhuthun. In turn, these flows were related to a marked tendency for migrants to move northwards towards the coast and eastwards across the Clwydian Hills to the towns of Mold, Holywell and Flint on industrial Deeside. A second major flow, evidently arising in these same upland communities, was channelled in another direction, down the Dee valley towards Llangollen, eventually reaching the Wrexham–Rhiwabon coalfield. Hence, Figure 4.5 provides strong evidence of the nature and extent of the rural exodus: a draining of people away from the upland communities to the growing industrial townships in the east and towards the incipient seaside resorts on the northern coast.

As the increased thicknesses of the arrows indicate, *gross* migration flows (Figure 4.5a) were considerable within the coalfield communities, and along the northern coastline – clear evidence of Ravenstein's 'counter currents' (Chapter 1, section 3.1, Schema C, Law 4).

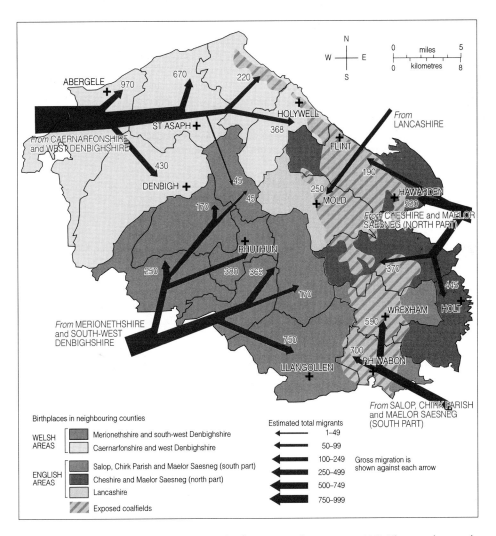

Figure 4.6   Lifetime migration to north-east Wales from surrounding counties, 1851. The map shows only the first-ranking birthplaces in each area (Source: Pryce, 1982, p.86)

117

The *net migration balances* in Figure 4.5(b) represent a finer tuning of the dominant trends. Clearly, *step migration with replacement* (Chapter 1, section 3.1, Figure 1.3) was the underlying mechanism: parishes around the small market town of Rhuthun functioned as collecting centres, as staging posts before migrants moved off to seek opportunities elsewhere. Equally significant is that, despite the substantial flows of migrants between neighbouring areas within the coalfield (Figure 4.5a, again), this did not result in much *net* migration between these areas (Figure 4.5b).

Our understanding of the overall regional situation is more complete when migration into north-east Wales from outside the region is analysed (Figure 4.6). Much of this was short-distance and tended to reinforce linguistic and cultural differences: migrants from English-speaking origins settled in the east, Welsh-speakers in the west; and the major migration streams met in the developing townships of the coalfield, engendering bilingual communities.

This closely integrated network (or system) of migratory flows that had developed within the region of north-east Wales by 1851 is, in some respects, comparable to the internal shifting of people in nineteenth-century Leicester described in Chapter 2, section 2.1. It is worth reminding ourselves that our models and mechanisms, our statistical and cartographic manipulations relate to the actual movements of men, women and children! For many, the sudden change from a dominantly rural way of life to that of the bustling, hot, noisy iron foundry, lead mine, colliery or textile mill hardly could have been less than traumatic. But for many there was an added hurdle. The newly arrived migrant from upland Wales was coming into a dominantly English-speaking milieu, a language with which he or she often would have had but little previous contact (Pryce, 1975, 1978). Not surprisingly, the distinctively Welsh-speaking migrants from the west and the distinctively English-speaking migrants from the east settled initially, and where possible, in communities where their own language was the dominant language and where mutual support was likely to be forthcoming. The responses of migrants to changes of cultural milieu and the selective nature of residence and settlement are key themes awaiting further exploration elsewhere.

3   REGIONAL STUDIES AND PROJECT WORK

Techniques for analysing migration flows and ebbs within a regional framework have tended to be neglected in much published work. Regional studies do provide a context that gives added meaning to smaller-scale enquiries involving individual families or local communities. Moreover, because it embraces a broader range of circumstances, the regional dimension may throw up interesting migration research hypotheses that can be applied to individual families or local communities – as, for example, in the case of north-east Wales, the implied links between industrial development and language change. Moreover, a knowledge of migration trends within a larger area may indicate something as to the opportunities open to potential migrants, revealing, therefore, something, also, as to the significance of the choices made by individuals. Research that is more restricted in scope might well miss these important behavioural considerations.

But, having extolled the added dimensions that such studies can bring, we do need to remind ourselves that work on a regional scale is demanding in terms of time and resources; and it calls for much foresight and practical acumen – particularly in the planning stages.

4   CONCLUSION

This chapter has shown how quantitative information and cartographic techniques can be applied to small-scale projects in migration research. (For further information on statistical techniques, see Volume 4, Chapter 8; also Startup and Whittaker, 1982; Ebdon, 1985; Siegel, 1988; Henry, 1990; and on computer-aided statistics, Bryman and Cramer, 1990; or Ebdon, 1985. On the presentation of data in map form, see Volume 4, Chapter 11, section 2; Mills and Pryce, 1993; also Davies, 1973; Keats, 1989; Matthews and Foster, 1989; and, in particular, Monkhouse and Wilkinson, 1978.) Whether the topic of enquiry concerns movements to a single regional centre, such as Preston, or shifts of population within a whole regional complex, as in north-east Wales, these approaches provide new insights. Although needing to be thought out carefully so that they are appropriate to specific lines of enquiry, all these methods are merely another means for the pursuit of investigations – not an end in themselves. Once the general migration patterns have been established, we need to draw on further independent information for the purposes of data enrichment – probably evidence that will be of a qualitative nature, reflecting the historical context as well as experiential and behavioural considerations.

At this particular juncture you will also find it useful to look back, briefly, over the whole of Part 1 of this volume. Chapters 1 to 4 have been concerned primarily with movements over territorial space and through time; and with all the implied dimensions of migration activities – including their effects on sending areas, on receiving communities and on the migrants themselves. Clearly, the specific considerations of regional *location* and *place* are of much importance. What kind of place do we live in now? Where did 'they' live in the past? Are notions of 'place' and 'community' interchangeable in family and community history? Chapters 5 and 6, which follow, deal with the geographies of towns, villages, urban communities and their regional settings. It is to these particular considerations, and the useful frameworks they provide, that we now turn.

REFERENCES AND FURTHER READING

Note: entries marked with an asterisk are suggestions for further reading.

Anderson, M. (1971) 'Urban migration in nineteenth century Lancashire: some insights into two competing hypotheses', *Annales de Démographie Historique*, pp.13–26.

Armstrong, W.A. (1972) 'The use of information about occupation', in Wrigley, E.A. (ed.) *Nineteenth-century society: essays in the use of quantitative methods for the study of social data,* Cambridge, Cambridge University Press.[*]

Braham, P. (ed.) (1993) *Using the past: audio-cassettes on sources and methods for family and community historians,* Milton Keynes, The Open University.[*]

Bryman, A. and Cramer, D. (1990) *Quantitative data analysis for social scientists,* London, Routledge.

Collins, B. and Pryce, W.T.R. (1993) 'Census returns in England, Ireland, Scotland and Wales', audio-cassette 2A in Braham (1993).

Davies, P. (1973) *Science in geography series: data description and presentation,* Oxford, Oxford University Press.

Deane, P. and Cole, W.A. (1967) *British economic growth, 1688–1959,* Cambridge, Cambridge University Press.

Ebdon, D. (1985) *Statistics in geography: a practical approach,* 2nd edn (reprinted 1992), Oxford, Blackwell.*

Harley, J.B. (1964) *The historian's guide to Ordnance Survey maps,* London, National Council for Social Service, for The Standing Conference for Local History.

Henry, G.T. (1990) *Practical sampling,* London, Sage.*

Keats, J.S. (1989) *Cartographic design and production,* London, Longman Technical and Scientific Books.

Matthews, H. and Foster, I. (1989) *Geographical data: sources, presentation and analysis,* Oxford, Oxford University Press.

Mills, D.R. and Pryce, W.T.R. (1993) 'The preparation and use of maps', audio-cassette 3A in Braham (1993).

Monkhouse, F.J. and Wilkinson, H.R. (1978) *Maps and diagrams: their compilation and construction,* 3rd edn, London, Methuen.

Pryce, W.T.R. (1975) 'Patterns of migration and the evolution of culture areas: cultural and linguistic frontiers in northeast Wales, 1750 and 1851', *Transactions, Institute of British Geographers,* 65, pp.79–107.*

Pryce, W.T.R. (1978) 'Welsh and English in Wales 1750–1971: a spatial analysis based on the linguistic affiliation of parochial communities', *Bulletin, Board of Celtic Studies,* 28, pp.1–36.

Pryce, W.T.R. (1982) 'Migration in pre-industrial and industrial societies', in The Open University, *D301 Historical sources and the social scientist,* Units 9–10 *Patterns and processes of internal migration,* Milton Keynes, The Open University.

Ravenstein, E.G. (1885) 'The laws of migration', *Journal of the Royal Statistical Society,* 48, pp.167–227.

Redford, A. (1926) *Labour migration in England 1800–1850,* Manchester, Manchester University Press. (The second edition, revised by W.H. Chaloner, was published in 1964.)*

Siegel, S. (1988) *Nonparametric statistics for the behavioral sciences,* 2nd edn (revised by N.J. Castellan), New York, McGraw Hill.

Startup, R. and Whittaker, E.T. (1982) *Introducing social statistics,* London, Allen and Unwin.

PART II

PLACE AND COMMUNITY

❖ ❖ ❖

CHAPTER 5

TOWNS AND THEIR REGIONAL SETTINGS

by W.T.R. Pryce

As we have seen, people move – but they also stay. They live in communities, in *places*. So places and their interrelationships are the concern of family and community historians.

This chapter focuses on one influential approach to the study of place, known as 'central place theory'. Not only has this theory had a crucial influence within geographical research, but – equally important for our purposes here – it constitutes, also, an exceptionally useful stimulus for those who wish to produce studies of changes over time as to the relative importance of towns. This approach provides opportunities to link research on a specific locality with more general theory.

Central place theory may at first sight appear to be concerned primarily with *towns:* a topic, of course, of some importance. But, as you will see, central place theory can provide a framework for research, not just on towns, but on many different kinds of localities and their relationships.

1   TOWNS, THEIR HINTERLANDS AND CENTRAL PLACE THEORY

In the past the territorial relationships between town and countryside tended to be somewhat different to those of our times. This does not mean, however, that present-day theories cannot be useful for organizing our knowledge and for the interpretation of local conditions in a wider framework. In other words, we should not just seek specifically unique explanations of local circumstances: that is, *ideographic* explanations. Universal (or *nomothetic*) generalizations can present local specific circumstances in a substantial new light.

1.1   WHAT IS A 'TOWN'?

What constitutes a town? To some, this question may appear to be mere rhetoric for the answer is self-evident. Towns *are* towns: they exist and their existence is widely recognized. Don't all of us do much of our shopping 'in town'? But, of course, there are towns, *and towns*! When is a settlement a town? When is it a village? When is it a city?

Clearly, we start with the idea that towns are settlements (close clusterings of houses and buildings) where large numbers of people live and work, and with high densities of population within their built-up areas. As Carter states, to a considerable degree 'what a town does, or did in the past, determines its location and controls its growth' (Carter, 1981, p.7). Moreover, towns fit 'naturally' into the series of graded ranks – that is, in an *urban hierarchy*. At the lower end this starts with the isolated house or building, set in the countryside. It incorporates, as we move up the hierarchy, hamlets, small and large villages, subtowns, market towns, regional centres and provincial cities, conurbations (occurring when urban centres coalesce through sustained territorial expansion) and major capital cities, culminating in metropolitan (or world class) cities (see Carter, 1983, pp.96–113; Jones, 1990).

Schema A: Some indicators of urban status in a historical context

1 Large population, concentrated at high densities within the settlement.

2 Legal identity derived from charters and laws that endow the settlement with separate and enhanced status, based, usually, on special trading privileges.

3 Presence of physical built-up structures and intensive use of space.

4 An economic structure that means that the settlement becomes a centre for distinctive functions.

5 A clear relationship with the surrounding countryside or trading zone (hinterland).

6 Strong links with neighbouring towns that enjoy higher or lower status in functional terms.

In this book we are concerned primarily with local and community studies – that is, with the smaller centres, including market towns. Many centres became recognized as towns because they possessed a clear, distinct legal identity as enshrined in official charters and market rights. But we need to remember that some centres turned out to be much less successful as central places than others. Market charters were obtained by very small settlements, many of which never developed any importance. This demonstrates that there are two varying factors in the identification of towns: the criteria of definition and the ultimate success or otherwise of a centre in historical terms. For these reasons, in addition to the possession of market-place functions, other indicators have been included in Schema A. Towns not only serve, through their market activities, the needs of their own inhabitants, but, also, they develop close links with the surrounding areas.

Over time, changing emphases have made it virtually impossible to define a town simply, and in terms of any one of the criteria in Schema A. *Taken in isolation*, large population size is not necessarily an appropriate indicator of full urban status; neither is the holding of legal or burghal rights *unless the markets continue on a regular basis* (Patten, 1978, pp.23–7). Moreover, Scottish towns have their own distinctive features (Adams, 1978), and in Ireland some urban centres started off as agencies of early colonialism and plantation (Butlin, 1977; Royle, 1993). Similarly, there was no early long-term indigenous urban tradition in Wales. The idea of towns as a protected community of settlers, somewhat exclusive in origin and culture, came with the English colonizers. In consequence, the older towns of Wales originated as 'alien' settlements transplanted into a distinctive culture area which have 'been both modified and modifier' (Carter, 1965, p.352).

1.2   CHRISTALLER AND CENTRAL PLACE THEORY

Thus, towns first came into being to serve the communities and the surrounding countryside whose various demands could be met only at a central place. Therefore, whatever its size and importance, no town is an isolated island of economic and social activities set in the countryside. These ideas were first articulated by Walter Christaller (1933) who was fascinated by the apparent regularities of spacing between towns in his native southern Germany. Christaller's concepts have proved of fundamental importance in urban studies. These seek to explain: (1) the importance of a town in the context of its surrounding hinterland; and (2) the relationship of a specific town to other centres of greater or lesser regional importance.

Christaller's ideas were based on the primary economic laws of demand and supply as they are assumed to operate at specific locations. Reduced to the basic essentials, he developed general models of the *theoretical landscape* as determined by:

o   *Population thresholds*: the numbers of people/consumers needed to make the provision of a particular service viable as a business.

o   The *range of a good or service*: the maximum distance that people are prepared to travel to purchase a good or service.

From these basics Christaller developed the notion that the numbers, sizes and distribution of towns can be explained by the 'principles of ordering'. *Low order centres* (i.e. those providing for everyday needs, e.g. a bakery) have low population thresholds and, therefore, a relatively small local catchment area or hinterland; and there are large numbers of them. *High order centres*, providing costly services (e.g. university textbooks, high fashion clothing), need large hinterlands to generate sufficient demand for their relatively specialized goods and services; and there are fewer of these. Between these two extremes come a large number of centres with intermediate functions – the so-called *middle order centres* (Schema B).

Schema B: Essential assumptions and features of Christaller's central place models

1   The basic 'landscape' in which these centres are assumed to exist is an *isotropic surface* – that is, an evenly distributed population spread across a flat landscape with no hills, valleys or interrupting physical features or, as Christaller put it, 'an unbounded uniform plain'. The population is assumed to be homogeneous in every respect: 'taste', preferences, demands for products and services, and in terms of their purchasing power. Moreover, to complete the concept of the theoretical 'landscape', all consumers are assumed to be equidistant from each other.

2   Demands for goods and services are met by the system of service points. These are termed *central places*.

3   Each central place carries a cluster of retail and service facilities referred to, collectively, as 'goods', further categorized into *orders* according to their relative abundance in the system. Thus, 'high order goods' are of a specialized nature and, therefore, are not generally available; 'low order goods' are available virtually everywhere, at all times and they enjoy ubiquitous distribution.

4   Whether or not these goods and services are offered in a particular centre is determined by the demands from potential customers in the surrounding areas that comprise the urban hinterland or market catchment area. Christaller referred to these as the *complementary areas*. Progressively higher orders of goods and services will have progressively larger complementary areas (or trade hinterlands).

5   Central places with large populations are able to satisfy most demands for goods and services; medium-sized centres provide only middle *as well as* low order goods and services; small centres, with restricted numbers of potential customers, are able to offer *only* low order goods and services.

6   The *functional status* of an urban centre relates, therefore, to its importance in a regional context. Christaller used the term *centrality* to describe the degree to which a settlement served the surrounding areas in competition with other centres. Further, urban centres within a particular region or country can be ranked in terms of their relative functional status, giving rise to a *hierarchy of urban centres.*

Source: devised by W.T.R. Pryce, based on Lewis (1977) pp.51–2

In Figure 5.1 we see the *theoretical* 'landscape' that results when five different functional levels are recognized in the urban hierarchy. Towards the bottom of the hierarchy come the lower order centres (in Figure 5.1, the D centres) with their relatively restricted hinterlands. Each is dependent on the 'complementary regions' of six, much smaller E centres. In turn, the hinterlands of six D centres are needed to support each C centre.

In reality, of course, hinterlands of adjacent towns in the urban hierarchy overlap. However, Christaller postulated that, *in theoretical terms*, at any one level in this hierarchy hinterland boundaries would pack together to form hexagons around each centre; and the trade areas of the lower order centres are conceived as 'nesting' within the hinterlands of higher order centres (see Carter, 1981, pp.64–7; Herbert and Thomas, 1990).

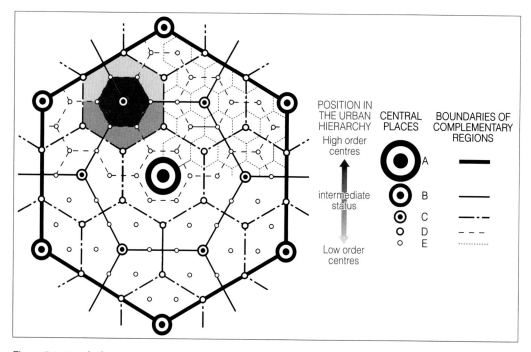

Figure 5.1   Interlocking complementary regions for five grades of centre (K = 3 landscape, the letter K standing for the mathematical constant involved). The complementary region of each higher order centre is partitioned into the equivalent of three complementary regions of the next lowest order. The complementary region of one C-grade centre in the top left has been shaded to show that it contains the equivalent of three complementary regions of the next lower order (i.e. D-grade centres) (Source: based on Lewis, 1977, p.55)

Although central place theory can be criticized – for example, for its assumptions about the K = 3 relationship between town and hinterland – it does offer a number of useful templates for research purposes, which are substantially independent of date and regional location. Many of these ideas can be adopted as exploratory hypotheses for research projects in family and community history.

EXERCISE 5.1

Which *seven* of the following are appropriate to the definition of a town as a functional entity? Tick your selection:

(a) physical built-up area

(b) the only locations for craft workers

(c) low rents

(d) possession of a market

(e) military barracks

(f) specialized trading functions

(g) large houses

(h) large concentration of population

(i) good route centre

(j) places of political unrest

(k) services provided for surrounding communities

(l) social structure dominated by landed interests

(m) corporate legal status

(n) attractive residential centres for the wealthy

Answer p.223.

EXERCISE 5.2

Allocate each of the central place terms listed below to one of the following three categories: (1) low centrality; (2) high centrality; (3) not relevant.

Expensive goods, low status, isotropic surface, everyday needs, market town, yeomen, cheap goods, scarcity, small catchment area, high demand, hexagonal shape, low population threshold, goods and services of 'high range/order'.

Answer p.223.

---

2 MARKET TOWNS AND REGIONAL CENTRES

2.1 MARKET AREAS AND TOWN DISTRIBUTION

There is considerable evidence that the possession of an official market was a valid indicator of urban status before the Industrial Revolution (see Schema A, p.122). Many towns, which later became important as regional centres in their own right, started off as market places (Figure 5.2).

The more successful grew into entrepôts; places of exchange; meeting places for traders; centres attracting the established professions, dealers, drovers, middlemen, wholesale factors

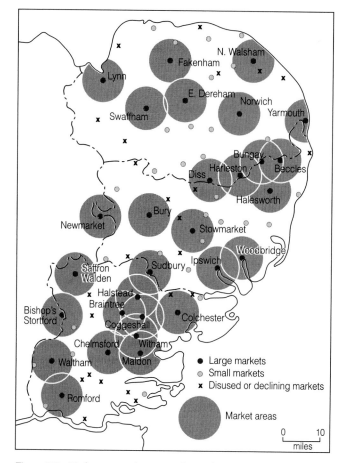

Figure 5.2 Market centres in East Anglia, early nineteenth century. Each of the larger markets has been given an arbitrary market area with a radius of six miles, the usual outer limit before the advent of modern transportation (Source: Dickinson, 1934, Figure 6, p.179)

and wayfaring traders of all kinds. The business facilities that developed included inns, coaching taverns and an expanding communications network. By the later nineteenth century, some of the early market centres had begun to emerge as regional and local shopping centres, and as centres for newspaper publication, and retail distribution. The emergence of the 'newer' professions – land surveyors, land and property valuers, printers and publishers, accountants, architects, engineers, bankers and insurance brokers – meant that, as central place functions were extended to meet local needs, towns were able to extend their grip over the communities around them. Ultimately, it is from these origins that the major regional capitals of the early twentieth century have emerged:

> *... over the last three or four centuries there can be no doubt that the ... town has fulfilled a crucial function in the development of regional self-consciousness ... . It was there that both 'county' and 'country' met. These regional capitals, in other words, were not only the natural focus of the county community; they were also the natural focus of the countryside or 'pays' surrounding them; and it was the influence of both county and country that shaped their distinctive economy and society.*

(Everitt, 1979, pp.89–90)

This full flowering of the relationship between town and hinterland has been of considerable importance in the continuing processes of urbanization and in the development of regional consciousness: without an urban focus of some kind, a truly regional culture can hardly ever have come into existence.

3   INTERACTIONS AND LINKAGES

Therefore, the links between a town and its hinterland are of considerable importance. As we saw in Chapter 1, section 3.1, towns have been migration magnets. The constant flows of people to them, not just the comings and goings to market, have contributed directly to their growth. Also the ties between countryside and town were cemented closer and closer through those direct links arising from the discharge of service functions, and communication networks involving the flow of ideas, messages and new life styles, as well as movements of raw materials and finished goods. All these developments reflected the inherent 'centrality' of urban centres and further emphasized the increased interdependency of town and countryside.

3.1   EMERGENCE OF ROAD SYSTEMS

Before the railway age, trackways and roads provided the principal means of overland communication. So difficult and costly was it to maintain these links that, wherever possible, water routes were sought out as the cheapest form of transport. This helps to explain, for example, the concentration of market centres in eastern Scotland (Adams, 1978, p.50).

From medieval times onwards, the long-distance overland road system gradually evolved, linking together regional centres and providing a network of interconnected routes. From the mid-nineteenth century, as the turnpike roads extended throughout much of southern England, north into Scotland and west into Wales, we see the beginnings of a fully fledged transport system. The piecemeal manner in which these routes focused on certain centres confirmed the evolving relationships between emergent towns and their hinterlands within the various regions (Pawson, 1977, pp.31, 41–6; Turnbull, 1977; Thrift, 1990).

In addition to the longer-distance routes, in every locality there had also evolved a local network. The significance of this has been summarized as follows:

> The purpose of the village carrier ... was to unite a market town with the villages of its hinterland, with the local area dependent upon it, and not town with town. He was almost invariably a villager himself usually operating on quite a humble scale, setting out in the morning and returning home at night, and running a comparatively light vehicle – a cart or van rather than a wagon.

> (Everitt, 1979, pp.179–80)

Recently published studies continue to remind us that too much emphasis may have been placed, perhaps, on the apparent separateness of life between the countryside and in towns. 'Rural life in Britain', it has been pointed out, 'had never been separate from the towns and, as the nineteenth-century urbanization developed, the inter-connectedness of countryside and town became stronger and more obvious' (Lawton and Pooley, 1992, p.158). Initially, as has been mentioned, the turnpike roads acted as means of town–country integration; but soon the development of major through-routes by railway companies, as well as by road, was to bring further integration. By 1890 most villages had become linked into complex and increasingly comprehensive transportation networks.

_____ *QUESTION FOR RESEARCH* _____

Bus routes and traffic flows have been used extensively by urban geographers to work out the regional importance of urban centres as well as to delimit spheres of urban influence (see section 4.2 below). Relatively few studies have been completed for the early nineteenth century using details concerning the routes operated by carriers and stage coaches.

Advertisements in contemporary newspapers and entries in trade directories (see Volume 4, Chapter 4, section 1) are sources from which much useful statistical information can be extracted on specific routes, frequency of journeys, distances, and the nature of the services operated. Further suggestions are presented below.

_____

3.2   DEVELOPMENT OF RAILWAYS

Starting in the 1790s, networks of canals, navigable rivers and their short feeder tram routes were developed, mainly for bulk transport. But, in reality, these transport systems were somewhat incomplete and never offered any direct and significant opportunities for the enhancement of the links between town and country. Rather, it was the rapid development of railways following the period of high speculative investment during the 1840s – the so-called 'railway mania' – that was largely responsible for the transport revolution between 1840 and 1852. Although the backbones of the railway network had been completed by 1860, construction – but often still of a speculative nature – continued for another 50 years. By 1914, the rail network of mainland Britain extended over some 20,000 miles, serving virtually every community and extending into remote parts of rural Wales and the Scottish Highlands; in Ireland, too, it extended deep into the countryside (Figure 5.3). By 1910, virtually any part of England or Wales could be reached within a six-hour

(a) Circa 1840   (b) Circa 1900

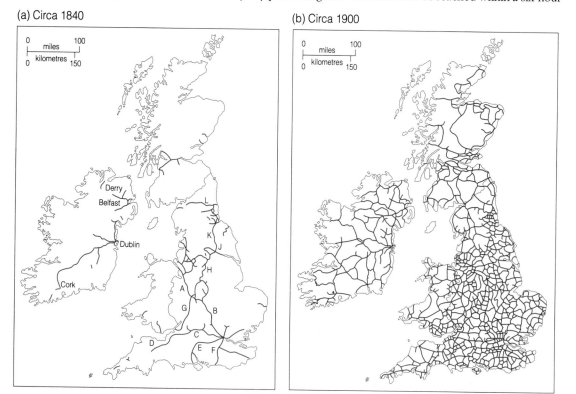

Figure 5.3 Railway networks: (a) *c.*1840; (b) *c.*1900. A = Grand Junction; B = London and Birmingham; C = Great Western; D = Bristol and Exeter; E = London and Southampton; F = London and Brighton; G = Birmingham and Gloucester; H = North Midland; J = Hull and Selby; K = Great North of England; L = Newcastle and Carlisle (Sources: based on Langton and Morris, 1986, Figures 9.10 and 9.13, p.89; Proudfoot, 1993, p.245)

(a) Stage-coach travel, 1820s

(b) Railway travel, August 1910

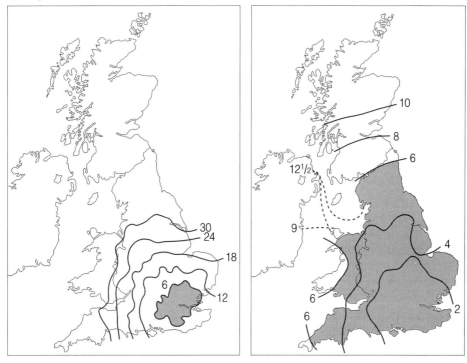

Figure 5.4 Travel times (hours) from London, 1820s and 1910 (Source: Langton and Morris, 1986, Figures 9.14 and 9.16, p.90)

journey by train from London. In contrast, back in the 1820s, even after a six-hour, somewhat uncomfortable ride in a stage coach, travellers would still not have cleared many of the small towns around London, which, by this date, had emerged as the highest order centre in the country (Figure 5.4).

Despite this transport revolution, because they were capable of adaptation, many relict features survived. Thus, whilst the railways substantially replaced the longer-distance road carrier services, small-scale *local* carriers continued to exist in most districts, carrying goods and passengers from the local rail head to the villages, hamlets, farms and industries within the hinterland of many a country town. These remained as vital links between a market town and countryside.

3.3   LOCAL BUS SERVICES AND MOTOR VEHICLES

The First World War brought further profound changes to life in the countries and regions of the British Isles, not least in transport systems. Despite the development of the internal combustion engine in the later nineteenth century, it was not until the 1920s that motor lorries, buses and private cars – in part, developed for military needs during the Great War – began to displace horse-drawn vehicles. Whilst the railways continued to provide the chief means for long-distance transport, after the First World War it was the bus that competed with the railway companies in the provision of local services (Hibbs, 1989, pp.69–107). The motor-driven bus, with its much greater flexibility to ply different routes, rapidly became the favoured means of public transport: and at much lower operating costs than railways. Although there were considerable regional differences, the greatest expansion of bus services came after 1918 (Green, 1951).

By 1939, the network of scheduled bus services embraced virtually every village and hamlet in England and Wales, and all but the most sparsely populated and remote parts of Scotland and Ireland (Hibbs, 1989, p.264 ff.). After the period of direct challenge to *local* railway services, eventually it was the country bus that emerged in the early 1930s to fulfil complementary roles, acting as a passenger feeder to branch-line railways (Figure 5.5). From the 1920s to the mid-1950s, bus networks focused on every town, large and small, to such an extent that, as we shall see in section 4.1, they came to reflect spheres of urban influence and the overall importance of a particular town within its region.

Eventually, it was the increased popularity of the private motor car, particularly in country areas, that took passengers away from the country bus. In 1911 there were less than two private cars in regular use for every 1,000 inhabitants in mainland Britain. A decade later, the numbers had grown to 5.7 per 1,000. But private vehicle registration increased rapidly, reaching, after the material and fuel shortages of the war-time conditions of the 1940s, 48.7 per 1,000 population in 1951, 116.6 per 1,000 in 1961, doubling to 223.5 per 1,000 in 1971. Although the official statistics are confusing (because, sometimes, taxis are included), it is clear that the period of significant growth up to 1931 was followed by the steady decline of local buses that continued through to the 1980s. Despite the blip on the graph in the 1950s, similar trends have been recorded in Ireland (Figure 5.6).

Figure 5.5 Country connections in western England, 1930s. A branch-line train, drawn by the Great Western Railway 2–6–2 Prairie Tank Locomotive No. 5572, pauses at an imaginary country station. Passengers transfer to the connecting local Bedford WLB bus *c*.1935 (built mainly for owner drivers). The chauffeur awaits with 'the family's' car (Source: Breckon, 1986, pp.68–9)

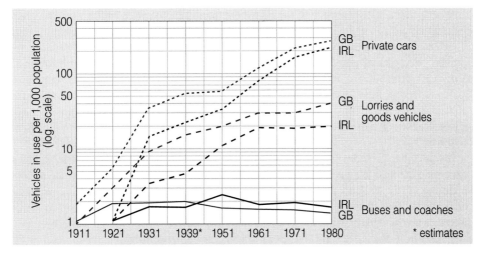

Figure 5.6 Motor vehicles, 1911–80. GB = Great Britain (England, Wales and Scotland); IRL = Ireland (Northern Ireland and the Republic of Ireland). The figures for buses and coaches in GB 1911–39, and those for public service vehicles in Northern Ireland, include taxis (Source: devised by W.T.R. Pryce, based on Mitchell, 1988, pp.9–14, 557–60)

4 URBAN HINTERLANDS AND SPHERES OF INFLUENCE

Families in past times tended to live much of their lives within the framework of their own local communities. Nevertheless, many day-to-day aspects were shaped by urban influences – in the countryside as well as in towns and villages. This section focuses on problems of defining town hinterlands and spheres of urban influence and their changes over time – that is, some of the practical ways in which Christaller's 'complementary regions' (no. 5 in Schema A; no. 4 in Schema B; also Figure 5.1) can be identified at specific dates in the past. The focus here is on practical 'do-it-yourself' approaches, on how to use data sources and diagrammatic maps to explain relevant themes. Remember, as far as spatial and territorial relations are concerned, a carefully prepared map – even a simple sketch map – conveys much more than does just the written word standing alone (see Mills and Pryce, 1993)!

4.1 HINTERLANDS BASED ON A SINGLE INDICATOR

CARRIERS AS RECORDED IN DIRECTORIES

Local directories first began to appear in the closing decades of the eighteenth century. Despite some shortcomings, they remain invaluable as sources for the study of specific towns (for further comments on directories, see Volume 4, Chapter 4, section 1). Moreover, this information is available for specific dates and, usually, repeated over many decades. Everitt (1979), for example, drew on directories to delimit the trade hinterland of Maidstone, Kent, in the later nineteenth century. In 1881, Maidstone (then with a population of 30,000), despite its importance as the administrative capital of the county of Kent, was still poorly served by railways. For this reason, a considerable network of local and long-distance carrier routes to neighbouring centres continued to serve northern Kent whilst elsewhere branch railway lines had captured much of the local traffic.

To analyse the directory information, Everitt plotted all routes and noted, especially, the numbers of intermediate halts on the scheduled journeys from Maidstone to such towns as Ashford, Hastings and Tunbridge Wells. His final map is simple, neat and effective (Figure 5.7). By means of proportional squares, he shows the relative importance of other towns in relation to Maidstone, including those with their own markets. In the early 1880s some 370 carriers operated services each week but only 24 of these climbed the steep slopes of the escarpment northeast of the town.

Everitt's map provides new information for testing a number of Christaller-type hypotheses concerning the links between town and country: (1) the territorial extent of the trade area of Maidstone; (2) the frequency of intermediate halts, indicating the relative status of other urban centres within the sphere of influence of the town; (3) the effects of distance – the 'friction' of distance – revealed in the ways in which the numbers of intermediate halts decline, progressively, away from Maidstone; and (4) aspects of competition between towns (the routes used by carriers were more numerous in the Weald, to the south of Maidstone, than to the east and north of the town where, in terms of central place functions, Maidstone was in direct competition with other centres). An alternative method of showing this same information is to use flow-line techniques indicative of the numbers of journeys (see Figure 5.10, p.135).

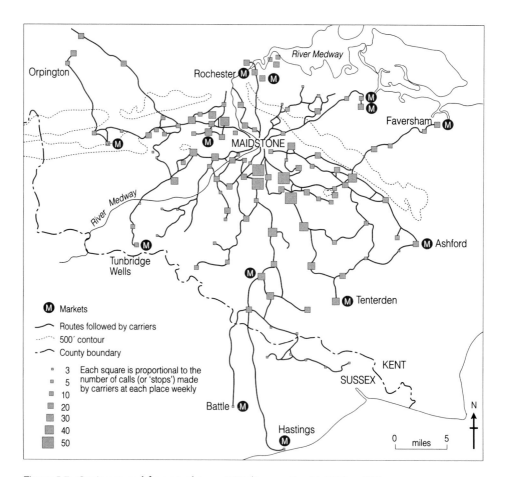

Figure 5.7 Carriers to and from Maidstone, 1882 (Source: Everitt, 1979, p.199)

POOR LAW ADMINISTRATION AND METHODIST PREACHING CIRCUITS

Some researchers have found that administrative areas did, in fact, reflect central place functions at specific dates in the past. Thus, following the recommendations of the Royal Commissioners on the Poor Law (1834), parishes and townships were grouped to form coherent units for administrative purposes. The Commissioners pointed out that these new 'unions' were to be formed 'by taking a market town as a centre and comprehending those surrounding parishes whose inhabitants are accustomed to resort to the same market' (Carter, 1983, p.93). Poor Law Unions, therefore, have been used by geographers to delimit urban spheres of influence (Carter, 1983, p.93; see, also, Carter, 1955, 1956).

Another fascinating approach comes from research on Methodist preaching circuits as indicators of urban spheres of influence (Greaves, 1968). By 1871, 1,389 Methodist chapels served virtually every centre of population in Yorkshire. Preachers visited each chapel in turn and the circuit had become the means by which the administrative and religious life of Methodism was organized. Each circuit, of which there were 50 in Yorkshire by 1830, was based on a key chapel, usually located in a town formally recognized as the 'circuit head' or 'circuit town' (Greaves, 1968, pp.232, 255, 263).

'Efficiency of movement' within the circuit system was in the interests both of administrative economies and pastoral oversight. The evangelistic zeal of preachers and Methodist officials constituted the 'energy' flowing through the circuits. The preaching circuits had been designed so that, on theoretical grounds, minimum energy input would achieve the maximum effectiveness in the promotion of the Christian religion, with greatest savings and efficiencies. It is clear that the circuit system came to reflect local variations in the population and urban geographies of nineteenth-century Yorkshire (Greaves, 1968, pp.225, 231).

Greaves argued that these arrangements were in the interests both of economy (in administering the circuit) and effective pastoral oversight. In the early nineteenth century, for example, Methodist officials became concerned about the expenses incurred by preachers on the Driffield circuit, and it was decided, at a local preachers' meeting in 1841, that no more than 2s. 6d. could be paid to a local preacher for journeys up to six miles! Moreover, Methodists felt that this could not be paid during the three summer months! Constraints such as these meant that, whilst serving as many societies as was possible, individual circuits had to be kept compact and travelling costs kept to the minimum.

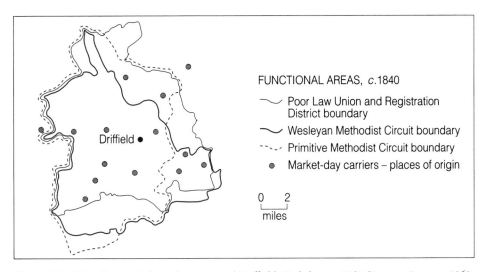

FUNCTIONAL AREAS, *c.*1840

⌣ Poor Law Union and Registration District boundary

⌣ Wesleyan Methodist Circuit boundary

----- Primitive Methodist Circuit boundary

● Market-day carriers – places of origin

Figure 5.8   Methodist circuit boundaries around Driffield, Yorkshire, *c.*1840 (Source: Greaves, 1968, Figure 41)

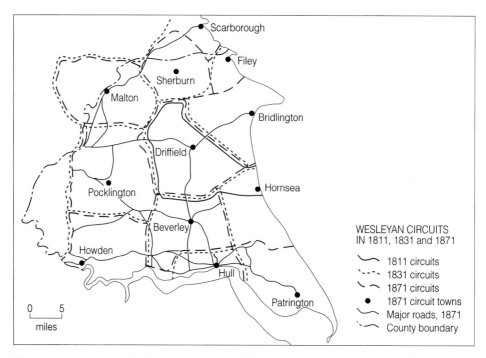

Figure 5.9   Wesleyan Methodist circuits in East Yorkshire, 1811–71 (Source: Greaves, 1968, Figure 42)

As Figure 5.8 shows, the Driffield circuit boundaries, although worked out through independent criteria, fitted very closely to the extent of the local Poor Law Union, reflecting the market hinterland of the town. In other words, the circuit areas resulted from cost minimization along the same lines as the 'economic' arguments advanced by Christaller himself for defining urban centrality (section 1.2 above). Moreover, when seen in their regional context, circuit areas tended to be hexagonal in shape, as postulated by Christaller, allowing the greatest amount of 'packing together' into an area consistent with minimal movement (Figure 5.9). As one urban expert has remarked, 'Perhaps this *is* one geographical model that was made in heaven' (Jones, 1981)!

LOCAL BUS SERVICES

As mentioned earlier (section 3.3), local buses operated from virtually every market town from the early 1920s to the late 1950s. These are of special interest for research on changing relationships between town and countryside. Detailed timetables were published, some of which may still survive in company archives, local record offices or amongst the records of the former Regional Traffic Commissioners. Where available these can be used to explore a number of hypotheses related to central place themes – such as the rise of competition between adjacent centres, or the ways in which local communities were interconnected (for a review of these approaches see Carter, 1981, pp.86, 90–3).

One interesting example is the research, conducted by Green, on local bus services. As he pointed out: '... in providing a new form of transport the bus services were creating a demand, and perhaps altering the natural spheres of influence of towns' (Green, 1950, p.65). Eventually, this led to the 'encouragement' of major centres which grew in population and influence at the expense of the smaller towns (Green, 1950; see, also, Curruthers, 1957) – fitting Christaller's tenet that it was competition between towns that led to successful centres becoming dominant foci within the regional urban hierarchy (section 1.2 above).

To explore these issues, Green extracted the following information from bus timetables:

o   *Local regular routes*: that is, approved stage services (because the objective was to delimit the contiguous areas lying within an urban hinterland); express and long-distance bus services were excluded.

o   Only the *market day services* were counted.

o   Urban centres were identified as those places from which *at least one local service* started.

o   Only *winter services* were counted (to avoid distortions due to seasonal holiday traffic).

Figure 5.10(a,b), based on bus services operating out of Reading and Newbury, Berkshire, illustrates how Green converted the timetable information into cartographic form. The frequency of bus services on specific routes is shown by proportion lines (flow lines); urban hinterlands are indicated by joining together all those places where services from each town met (the dotted line) (Figure 5.10a). Shading indicates areas where services from Reading and from Newbury over-lapped (Figure 5.10b). Note, in particular, how the outer limits of these bus-service areas are independent of county boundaries.

To verify his results, Green collected additional information on the location of cinemas and of towns where local newspapers were published. He found that, in 1947–48, only twelve (mainly in rural Wales) of the 700 bus centres in England and Wales did not have a local cinema and he remarked 'such a high degree of correlation indicates the great significance which the cinema has now attained in rural as well as urban life' (Green, 1950, p.69). We need to remember, of course, that Green was writing before the rise of popular television.

Thus, information from bus timetables – sources that, in themselves, are ordinary and ephemeral – can be analysed, within the context of central place theory, to provide findings that have wider significance. The cartographic approaches and the methods of analysis devised by Green and his contemporaries can be applied to other sources: for example, services operated by carriers (as recorded in directories), passenger rail timetables or message flows over the public telephone system (see, for example, Davies and Lewis, 1970, pp.22–45; Clark, 1973).

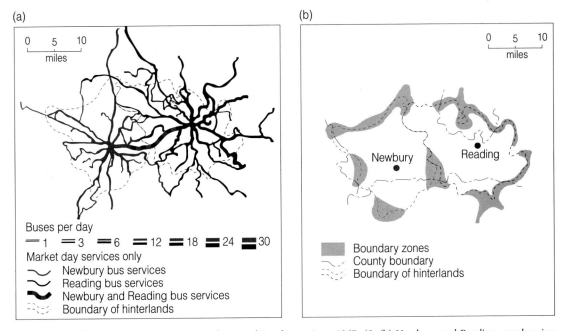

Figure 5.10   (a) Bus services based on Newbury and Reading, winter 1947–48; (b) Newbury and Reading: overlapping hinterlands (based on local bus services), 1947–48 (Source: Green, 1950, p.67)

4.2   HINTERLANDS BASED ON MULTIPLE INDICATORS

Each of the sources discussed in the previous section has been largely created by the pre-existing 'centrality' of the urban centre concerned. In some research it might be more appropriate to draw on a larger number of indicators.

CARMARTHEN AND HAVERFORDWEST IN THE MID-TWENTIETH CENTURY

Despite the neatness of Christaller's idealized urban 'landscape' (Figure 5.1, p.124 again), hinterland boundaries cannot be defined sharply as hexagons; nor, for example, as precisely as the watershed between one river basin and the next; nor as clearly as the boundaries, say, between one administrative unit and the next. In the real world, the territorial influence of a town gradually merges into that of neighbouring centres. Geographers refer to such intermediate areas as the 'zone of transition'. Even from Green's researches, this is evident in the overlaps between neighbouring towns (Figure 5.10b).

Depending on local and regional circumstances, there are wide differences as to the nature and extent of these transitional zones. Carter (1965), for example, used five different criteria to delimit spheres of influence of market towns in south-west Wales as they existed in the mid-1950s. His final results indicate that, whilst the towns of Carmarthen and Haverfordwest dominated their immediate hinterlands, the outer boundaries of their respective hinterlands overlapped considerably (Figure 5.11).

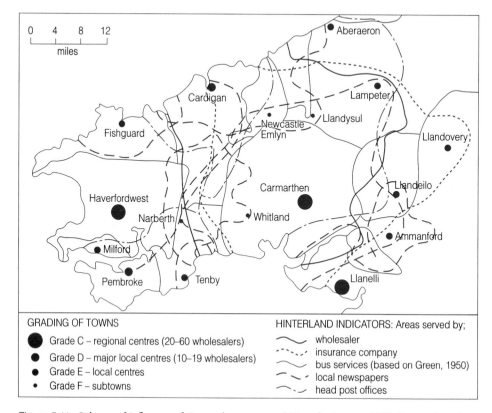

Figure 5.11 Spheres of influence of Carmarthen town and Haverfordwest, *c.*1955 (Source: based on Carter, 1965, Figure 18, pp.108, 118)

136

LEICESTERSHIRE TOWNS IN THE MID-NINETEENTH CENTURY

The development of communications meant that, by the early nineteenth century, more and more service functions came to be centralized in towns whose sites and locations endowed them with good accessibility.

Movements of local carriers, access to rail transport, local bus services, the areas served by town-based wholesalers and shops, as well as local newspaper circulation areas, are examples of the criteria used for the designation of town hinterlands. But all these approaches focus on hinterland definition from the viewpoint of the central place itself: a townsperson's vision as to the sphere of influence. Alternatively, it is possible to base hinterland definition on indicators linked directly to the behaviour of the consumers living in the countryside. This was the approach adopted by Odell (1957). First, using information from directories, local newspapers

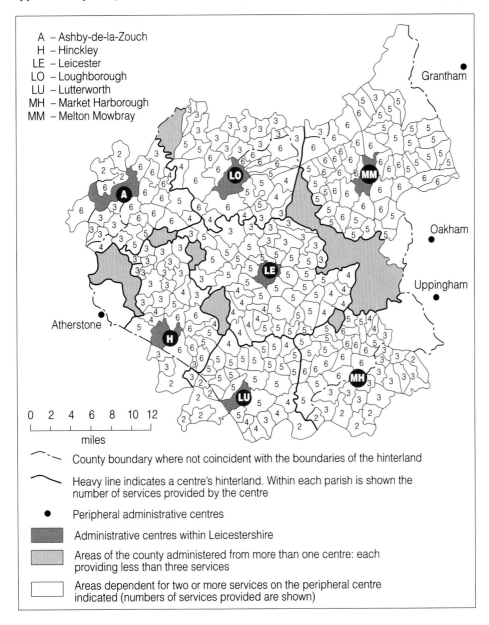

Figure 5.12   Urban hinterlands in Leicestershire, *c*.1851 (Source: Odell, 1957, Figure 8, p.40)

and other sources, he looked closely at each parish/township and noted the specific market town listed as providing each of up to six administrative services to that particular community (unfortunately, perhaps through editorial cuts, the particular services are not specified in his published report). Some parishes received all services from just one centre; elsewhere, services were provided locally by a number of competing nearby towns.

To work out the urban hinterlands, Odell started off with (1) a base map showing all parish boundaries; and (2) a list of the services provided in each parish, town by town. Hinterland boundaries were then inserted by clustering together all those parishes that depended on one particular nearby market town for the provision of at least three services (Figure 5.12).

The results show that market town hinterlands covered similar distances, the boundaries occurring midway between neighbouring centres. Some parishes situated near to the county's administrative border (those with only two services provided locally) looked towards centres outside Leicestershire. Within the county there were considerable variations in the numbers of functions performed by any one centre. Melton Mowbray, for example, provided all six services for about half the parishes within its immediate hinterland, and five for most of the other communities. This indicates a close and, as Odell puts it, a 'total relationship' between town and countryside. Elsewhere, as the map shows, there were many 'marginal areas' and no dominant loyalties to any one centre. These resulted from the particular regional location of a town within the county as well as from the fact that some local officials insisted on the observation of 'rigid artificial divisions' – that is, staying with Leicestershire for some of their public services when it may have been more efficient to go to the neighbouring county (Odell, 1957, p.4).

_____ *EXERCISE 5.3* _____

Town growth has had, and continues to have, considerable impact on life in the countryside. 'Urbanism' remains a somewhat intangible influence and its measurement poses a number of methodological challenges. Just as occupation and life style are regarded as valid indicators of social status/class, the impact of a town on the surrounding rural communities can be revealed, as we have seen, through the use of carefully chosen surrogate indicators.

Select one town and one village known to you. For each, list not more than five indicators that could be used to measure local spheres of influence specifically for the periods (1) between 1801 and 1851, and (2) between 1921 and 1951.

Comment p.223.

---

5   TOWNS IN THE WALES–ENGLAND BORDERLANDS, 1828–1965

As we saw in section 1.2 above, the *functional status* of a town is dependent on the number and the range of services discharged for the surrounding areas (Schema B, pp.123–4). Thus, all urban centres within a region can be listed in rank order according to the ranges of the goods and services provided. In this section we draw on central place theory and trade directories to work out details of urban hierarchies and changes within them over time.

Which town was more important than others in past times? How did one particular town relate to neighbouring centres over several decades? What sorts of change occurred over time? Since, even in the countryside, the lives of previous generations were lived within the orbit of urban influences, such questions are of considerable significance in our understanding of life in past times.

Such questions have been explored for 21 towns in the middle borderlands between Wales and England – a tract of countryside extending from Shrewsbury in the north to Hereford in the south (Lewis, 1975). Lewis explained the scientific need to take care in defining the study area:

This rural area, which contains an array of central places from regional shopping centres down to service villages, was considered to be a functioning system. There is little need to stress the importance of giving close attention to the definition of the field area [i.e. the area for detailed study] in central place analysis for numerous workers have noted that, unless the centres under study are interdependent in a functioning system, the derived results will relate to a meaningless abstraction.

(Lewis, 1975, p.49; emphasis added)

Many of the source data used by Lewis were extracted from local directories, published at various dates from *c.*1830 onwards, in order to explore:

o   *Functional relationships* between different towns.

o   *Relative status* of individual towns in the context of all towns within the study area.

o   *Changes* in these relationships over time.

Conducted in the mid-1960s, Lewis updated his research to 1965 by collecting further information in each of the 21 centres. His field surveys recorded details of the numbers of shops and services – data comparable with those that had been recorded and published for more than a century in the directories. In order to offer meaningful comparisons over time, Lewis calculated the *Functional Index Percentage Values* for each town at five specific dates: 1828 (or 1831), 1850, 1868, 1891 (or 1895) and 1964–65. These values provided the *standardized* measures as to the 'centrality' (i.e. functional importance) of each town in relation to other centres within the area under study. (The procedures for calculating these indices are given Volume 4, Chapter 8, section 8.)

To complete the analysis, Lewis ranked the seventeen main centres according to their Functional Index Percentage Values (Figure 5.13). Whilst the major centres, Shrewsbury and Hereford, maintained their prominence at the top of the regional urban hierarchy throughout the period 1828 to 1965, all the others recorded functional shifts over time, especially after the 1890s. The larger centres increased their regional importance and developed a progressive dominance over the smaller towns – mainly through, as we have seen in section 3, improvements in transport systems and increased access. As is evident in Figure 5.13, the smaller towns either recorded somewhat erratic trends over time or a sustained but continuous decline in status.

The value of these approaches is that they rely on standard, widely available data sources. Moreover, these techniques provide a *generalized measure of centrality* from information that appeared, originally, to be unique and specific in character and not capable of providing data for comparisons with changes elsewhere. Nevertheless, one small reservation needs to be kept in mind. The indices assume a closed regional system when, in reality, as we saw in mid-nineteenth century Leicestershire (section 4.2 above), the functional status of settlements located in the peripheries of the study region may have been affected by larger centres outside.

Having charted the main trends, Lewis (1975) goes on to discuss the circumstances under which these functional divergencies occurred. His research concludes with a review of changes in local craft industries (especially woollen textiles), new developments such as the rise of spa towns, and the impact that all these innovations were to have on regional structures. Here, however, as researchers in family and community history, our immediate interests focus, not so much on Lewis's own particular conclusions, but rather on his approaches and on the analytical tools that he used. These offer considerable potential for new lines of enquiry in other regions and at other locations.

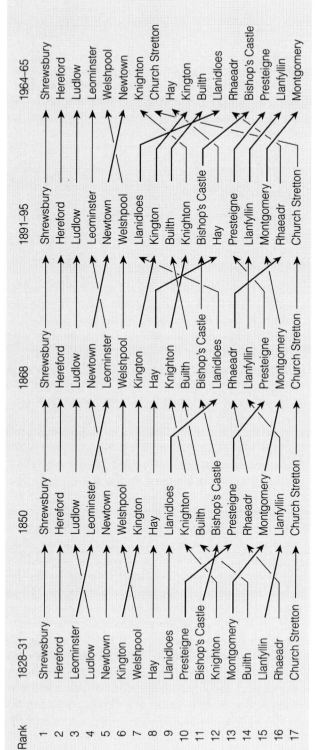

Figure 5.13   Towns of the middle Welsh borderland: rank order changes, 1828 (or 1831) to 1964–65 (Source: Lewis, 1975, Figure 4, p.59)

6 CONCLUSION

This chapter has reviewed a range of ideas, approaches and techniques that are useful in the study of town and countryside and the changes over time. The theoretical context, present throughout our discussions, applies as much to the study of society in the past as it does to our own world. It will be clear from the issues discussed that in central place theory geographers have developed a whole range of powerful research concepts and techniques. As we have seen, these fundamental theoretical ideas are capable of application to much local research. The practical aspects of these appoaches take us away from what may have started off, initially, as a prime concern with individuals, and individual families, towards the study of villages, hamlets and market towns, regional cities and urban hinterlands, towards community and society, and the specific contexts in which our ancestors lived in times past.

REFERENCES AND FURTHER READING

Note: entries marked with an asterisk are suggestions for further reading.

Adams, I.H. (1978) *The making of urban Scotland*, London, Croom Helm.

Breckon, D. (1986) *Don Breckon's Great Western Railway*, Newton Abbot, David and Charles.

Butlin, R.A. (ed.) (1977) *The development of the Irish town*, London, Croom Helm.

Carter, H. (1955) 'Urban grades and spheres of influence in southwest Wales: an historical consideration', *Scottish Geographical Magazine*, 71, pp.45–58.

Carter, H. (1956) 'The urban hierarchy and historical geography; a consideration with reference to north east Wales', *Geographical Studies*, 3, pp.85–101. Reprinted, with an updating supplementary note, in Baker, A.R.H., Hamshere, J.D and Langton, J. (eds) (1970) *Geographical interpretations of historical sources: readings in historical geography*, Newton Abbot, David and Charles.

Carter, H. (1965) *The towns of Wales: a study in urban geography.* Cardiff, University of Wales Press.

Carter, H. (1981) *The study of urban geography*, 3rd edn, London, Edward Arnold.*

Carter, H. (1983) *An introduction to urban historical geography*, London, Edward Arnold.*

Christaller, W. (1933) (trans. C.W. Bask, 1966) *Central places in southern Germany*, Englewood Cliffs, NJ, Prentice Hall.

Clark, D. (1973) 'Urban linkage and regional structure in Wales: an analysis of change, 1958–68', *Transactions, Institute of British Geographers*, 58, pp.41–58.

Curruthers, I. (1957) 'A classification of service centres in England and Wales', *Geographical Journal*, 123, pp.371–85.

Davies, W.K.D. and Lewis, C.R. (1970) 'Regional structures in Wales: two studies of connectivity', in Carter, H. and Davies, W.K.D. (eds) *Urban essays: studies in the geography of Wales*, London, Longman.

Dickinson, R.E. (1934) 'The markets and market areas of East Anglia', *Economic Geography*, 10, pp.172–82.

Everitt, A. (1979) 'Country, county and town: patterns of regional evolution in England', *Transactions of the Royal Historical Society*, Fifth Series, 29, pp.79–108.

Graham, B.J. and Proudfoot, L.J. (eds) (1993) *An historical geography of Ireland*, London, Academic Press.

Greaves, B. (1968) *Methodism in Yorkshire 1740–1851*, unpublished PhD thesis, University of Liverpool.

Green, F.H.W. (1950) 'Urban hinterlands in England and Wales: an analysis of 'bus services', *Geographical Journal*, 116, pp.64–88.

Green, F.H.W. (1951) 'Bus services in the British Isles', *Geographical Review*, 41, pp.645–55.

Herbert, D.T. and Thomas, C. (1990) *Cities in space: city as place*, London, David Fulton Publishers.*

Hibbs, J. (1989) *The history of British bus services*, 2nd revised edn, Newton Abbot and London, David and Charles.

Johnston, R.J., Gregory, D. and Smith, D.M. (eds) (1986) *The dictionary of human geography*, 2nd edn, Oxford, Blackwell.*

Jones, E. (1981) Personal letter to the author from Professor Emrys Jones, London School of Economics.

Jones, E. (1990) *Metropolis: the world's great cities*, Oxford, Oxford University Press.

Langton, J. and Morris R.J. (eds) (1986) *Atlas of industrializing Britain*, London, Methuen.

Lawton, R. and Pooley, C.G. (1992) *Britain 1740–1950: an historical geography*, London, Edward Arnold.

Lewis, C.R. (1975) 'The analysis of changes in urban states: a case study in Mid-Wales and the middle Welsh borderland', *Transactions, Institute of British Geographers*, 64, pp.49–65.

Lewis, R. (1977) 'Central place analysis', in 'Spatial analysis', Unit 10 of *D204 Fundamentals of human geography*, Milton Keynes, The Open University.

Mills, D.R. and Pryce, W.T.R. (1993) 'Preparation and use of maps', audio-cassette 3A in Braham, P. (ed.) *Using the past: audio-cassettes on sources and methods for family and community historians*, Milton Keynes, The Open University.

Mitchell, B.R. (1988) *British historical statistics*, Cambridge, Cambridge University Press.

Odell, P.R. (1957) 'Urban spheres of influence in Leicestershire in the mid-nineteenth century', *Geographical Studies*, 2, pp.30–45.

Patten, J. (1978) *English towns, 1500–1700*, Folkestone, Dawson/Archon Books.

Pawson, E. (1977) *Transport and economy: the turnpike roads of eighteenth century Britain*, London, Academic Press.

Proudfoot, L.J. (1993) 'Spatial transformation and social agency: property, society and improve-ment, *c.*1700 to *c.*1900', in Graham and Proudfoot (eds) (1993).

Royle, S.A. (1993) 'Industrialization, urbanization and urban society in post-famine Ireland, *c.*1850–1921', in Graham and Proudfoot (eds) (1993).

Thrift, N. (1990) 'Transport and communications 1730–1914', in Dodgshon, R.A. and Butlin, R.A. *An historical geography of England and Wales*, 2nd edn, London, Academic Press.

Turnbull, G.L. (1977) 'Provincial road carrying in England in the eighteenth century', *Journal of Transport History*, 4, pp.17–39.

CHAPTER 6

TOWNS AND VILLAGES: SOCIAL DIVISIONS AND SPATIAL PATTERNS

by Harold Carter and Roy Lewis

Families exist within communities, and communities in physical settlements, be they towns, villages, hamlets or even a network of single dispersed farms. It follows that the environment constituted by settlements is crucial to the study of families and communities. That environment underwent radical change – revolution is not too strong a word – during the nineteenth century and has continued to do so during the twentieth century, the critical point being the growth in the dominance of urban areas. Thus, the urban population of England and Wales increased eightfold between 1800 and 1900, whilst the proportion living in towns rose from a third in 1801 to over three-quarters in 1901. In 1801, London was the only city with a population of over 100,000; by the end of the century there were 33 cities with populations over that figure (Law, 1967). So dominant was urban growth that, by 1861, rural parts were showing actual losses and a phase of rural depopulation had set in.

Paradoxically, in contrast to massive urban growth, more recent events have seen the great cities losing population and the countryside experiencing increases. This had begun even by the end of the nineteenth century, with the start of out-migration from the central areas of towns and cities to the suburbs, and was to become the dominant process of change during much of the twentieth century. Therefore, although total population has not increased, towns have grown outwards physically as people have sought to move, while, at the same time, the average size of households has decreased.

This chapter highlights some key themes in the development of towns and villages since the early nineteenth century. Here we aim to provide reviews of appropriate concepts and issues as well as a framework for specific projects in family and community history.

1 SOCIAL AND ETHNIC DIVISIONS

The amassing of large numbers of people, often of diverse origins, at high density in urban areas produces inevitable consequences. An urbanized society results in a competitive system which in turn generates a complex stratification deriving partly from the economic rewards of skilled tasks, both manual and professional, and partly from the esteem in which such tasks are held (Wirth, 1938). The nineteenth century saw a significant elaboration of this class system. Each group sought to establish its own identity, and to distance itself from the group below and emulate the one above. One way in which this could be done was by the selection of residential location. Hence the towns of Britain became segregated, in terms of status and prestige, on the basis of social class.

A further element of segregation which developed from this heterogeneity of large towns and cities related to immigrant populations who were set apart from the indigenous people by, for example, skin colour, language or religion. Two factors have kept immigrants together within cities. The first is that, initially, they generally lacked those urban skills that gave opportunities for advancement. Thus, in the early nineteenth century, immigrants from Ireland were mainly rural people with no experience of living in large industrial cities. The second factor is that, in a new and hostile environment, immigrants find security in association. Thus, during the nineteenth century, ethnicity and social class became the bases on which large towns and cities were segregated.

These national and local changes in the distribution of the population were a direct consequence of (1) the factory system, for the basic imperative to assemble labour was the progenitor of urbanization; and (2) increased mobility. For much of the nineteenth century, movement was predominantly by foot, even over long distances. In terms of urban localities, this gave rise to what has been called 'the walking city'. Hence the imperative of concentration. But that constraint was progressively broken by 1901. Starting with the horse-drawn omnibus in the mid-nineteenth century, the transport revolution in urban areas initially involved a move to the streetcar or tram, dominant after 1880. This was followed by the suburban railway, both steam and electric. Finally, came the motor car and, with the building of roads and the so-called urban motorways or freeways, the emphasis was switched from the vehicle to the 'path' on which it moved (see Chapter 5, section 3).

The increase in mobility had a major impact upon the countryside and upon rural settlement. As we have seen in Chapter 5, the early part of the nineteenth century was still one of relative isolation in which shop goods were made available by coastal shipping, and carriers to market by horse and cart. The changes in transport were to transform local movement. The village as central place with general store, post office, pub and smithy/garage was strengthened during the nineteenth century with rises in real incomes, but it was also progressively opened up to urban influence through transport improvements. The major changes, however, were to come later with the development of commuter services and the motor car, for these brought the possibility of rural living to urban-based workers. The consequence was that new residential estates were grafted on to rural villages. The countryside was faced with two processes working in conjunction. The first was depopulation: as the employment opportunities and urban jobs beckoned, so that there was a drift away of the traditional rural dweller. This resulted in decreased demand (partly also a consequence of easier access to towns) which led to a loss of rural services and the continued fight to maintain schools, cottage hospitals, post offices and the range of services which had been developed by previous generations. The second process was an invasion by suburbanites, a new and alien element. Beyond the reach of the larger towns, no new incomers settled permanently until the counter-urbanization processes of the last quarter of the twentieth century.

_____ **_EXERCISE 6.1_** _____

Note down briefly why you think attention has been drawn specifically to class, ethnicity and mobility in these opening sections.

Comment p.224.

_____

2 THE VILLAGE: ITS NATURE, ROLE AND FUNCTION

Settlements in rural areas underwent major modification during the nineteenth and twentieth centuries. That modification is often expressed in terms of community development, but it is extraordinarily difficult to define a community (G.J. Lewis, 1979, pp.28–44). The definition offered by Reiss can be put forward as an initial basis: 'A community arises through sharing territorial space for residence and sustenance, and functions to meet common needs generated in sharing this space by establishing characteristic forms of social action' (Reiss, 1959, p.118). The theme of 'community studies' became widely popular after the Second World War, especially during the late 1950s when Reiss was writing. However, the difficulty of finding a precise definition for a nebulous concept was shown by the considerable criticism such definitions received, as, for example, in Stacey's paper 'The myth of community studies' (Stacey, 1969). Stacey's main objection to Reiss's definition was to the necessity of 'territorial space' since not all interactions within it contributed to community, nor did all interrelations have a necessary spatial definition. She proposed the alternative term of 'local social system', but this has never been fully adopted and the imprecise, though widely used, term 'community' remains (for further discussion of the term, see Chapter 9, section 1; also the example in Phillips, 1986).

The concept of the community has been introduced since, in any examination of the village over time, the question immediately arises as to the extent to which the nature of a 'community' has changed. In addition, associated with this are questions as to how the role and the function of the village have altered. These issues can be explored in the context of two studies that are in contrast – both in time and in regional location.

2.1 THE RURAL COMMUNITY IN BRITAIN

The pioneering work on rural communities in the British Isles was carried out in the west of Ireland just before the outbreak of the Second World War (Arensberg, 1939; Arensberg and Kimball, 1940), but the first British study, based on participant observation in the early 1940s, was *Life in a Welsh countryside* by Alwyn D. Rees (1950), a study of the Welsh parish, Llanfihangel yng Nghwynfa, in the rural uplands of central Wales.

The nature of that community is best illustrated by Rees's chapters on family, kindred and neighbours. The family was the fundamental social unit, and the basic unit of production was the family farm. The significance of family and farm was epitomized by the fact that 'an unmarried son is never referred to … [other than] … by his christian name or one of its diminutives followed by the name of his father's farm. Even though he is an elderly bachelor farming a holding inherited from his parents, he is still John Ty Uchaf (John from Upper House Farm), or Wil y Wern (Wil from Aldergrove)' (Rees, 1950, p.64). Rees concludes, 'although the old tribal society has long since passed away, something of its spirit lives on in the cohesion and paternalism of the present-day family' (Rees, 1950, p.72).

In addition to the significance of the family, however, intermarriage, constrained by immobility, had meant that a wide network of kinship characterized the parish (Figure 6.1): 'Almost two-thirds of the families of Llanfihangel contain members who are related in the first degree to at least one other family, and one-third contain members who are related in this way to at least two other families' (Rees, 1950, p.74). A dense, if superficially invisible, reticule of kin linkages is spread across the parish. According to Rees, the resultant solidarity had 'an organic quality: what happens to the individual member is felt by the whole group. To offend one member is to arouse the hostility of a formidable section of the community' (Rees, 1950, p.80).

The third element in what Rees calls 'this intricate social network' is neighbourliness: 'By friendliness towards his neighbours the countryman overcomes the isolation imposed upon him by his environment' (Rees, 1950, p.91). The critical part was co-operation in farm working, especially at the time of threshing and of sheep dipping and shearing, and, to a smaller extent, in the hay and corn harvests. These all built up a set of mutual obligations which reinforced the cohesion of the community.

Finally, it must be noted that the parish consisted largely of separate farms with only three small hamlets, one with two shops, the post office and an inn, as well as a school. The other two had only one shop and a school. Although the basic shop goods were provided, as well as the

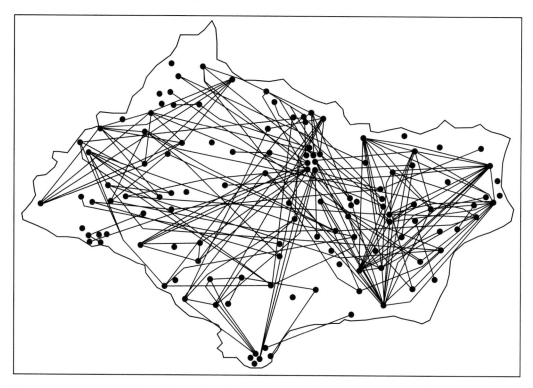

Figure 6.1   Kinship in Llanfihangel yng Nghwynfa, Powys, 1939–40. The lines join households containing persons related to one another in the 'first' and 'second' degree (Source: Rees, 1950, Figure 28, p.76)

minimum services, the hamlets were not in any sense central places proper. As Rees wrote, 'the hearth of the lonely farm itself *is* the social centre' (ibid., p.100). Although there were other studies (Davies and Rees, 1960; Frankenberg, 1966) which presented similar pictures, a warning should be included. Rees was a committed Welshman and perhaps he depicted a condition that he wanted to see, a romantic view of rural cohesion and contentment (see, in contrast, Evans, 1915; Gibbons, 1902).

2.2   THE METROPOLITAN VILLAGE

The second and greatly contrasted study is that of three Hertfordshire parishes by R.E. Pahl, which was published in 1964 under the title *Urbs in rure* [*City in the country*] (Pahl, 1964). The three parishes, Hexton, Watton and Tewin, lay within the London metropolitan fringe. Hexton was still predominantly agricultural; although close to Luton, it had remained isolated and unchanged. But the other two parishes were in marked contrast. Between 1951 and 1961 the population of Hertfordshire increased by 35.7 per cent, 78.7 per cent of that increase being due to in-migration. Here, then, were parishes where the rural past was being fundamentally changed by the impinging suburban present. Particularly significant had been the development of a private residential estate at Tewin Wood, especially due to its closeness to Welwyn Garden City. In consequence, in-migrants dominated the samples that Pahl used in his analysis.

In his conclusion Pahl puts forward four characteristics of this rural–urban fringe, the 'urbs in rure' of his title. The first of these is *segregation*: the building of new private housing estates brought to the countryside the class-segregated areas of the towns. The second is *selective in-migration* in that these areas attracted mobile middle-class commuters who 'live and work in distinct and separate social worlds from the established populations' (Pahl, 1964, p.72). The third characteristic is *commuting*, and the fourth the *collapse of geographical and social hierarchies*. That is, the old social system was transformed by the incomers; their physical mobility meant that they could use the whole fringe virtually as a dispersed city, purchasing goods and services freely and without necessary reference to a formal urban hierarchy.

It is clear that, although in a nominal rural area, the Hertfordshire parishes are a world away from Llanfihangel. Today, these settlements are dominated by what is now known as the 'metropolitan village' – it is the beginning of that phenomenon that Pahl is describing. In moving from one extreme to the other, we cross the divide between rural and urban ways of life which Wirth (1938) tried to demonstrate. But this divide is neither sharp nor clear: hence it has been characterized in the epithet 'rural–urban continuum'.

EXERCISE 6.2

Can you summarize and elaborate on the characteristics of the rural–urban fringe identified by Pahl?

Comment p.224.

The most complete presentation of the rural–urban continuum was offered by Frankenberg (1966). He identified as many as 25 characteristics where the rural condition can be contrasted with the urban (or, as he also termed it, 'the less rural'). There is no space here to describe all these, but the first can act as an indicator. This contrasted 'community', the concept with which this discussion began, with 'association': 'Rural societies have a community nature; people are related in diverse ways and interact frequently'. In contrast, 'urbanized societies have an associative nature. Although there may be a great number of possible relationships, they do not overlap. There is often infrequency of interaction. People tend to feel they have needs, rather than interests in common' (Frankenberg, 1966, pp.286–7). This is perhaps not quite adequate a contrast. It is true that the 'truly rural' have a continual nexus of common interests: that should be evident from the description of Llanfihangel. But urban villagers also can have common interests and can act with considerable vigour over specific issues, usually of the NIMBY (Not In My Back Yard) variety, though the association is normally transitory and breaks apart when the issue is resolved.

2.3   ROLE AND FUNCTIONS OF VILLAGE AND HAMLET

The classic nucleated village up to the early 1800s was a self-sufficient settlement of farmers and agricultural workers, and farmed land was separate from the built-up part. These farm-villages contained only the most basic services such as a smithy, an inn and the church. It was during the nineteenth century that service functions accumulated and goods became shop derived. As that happened, the hamlet and the village became, paradoxically, the lowest ranks in the urban hierarchy with at least one shop (each of the tiny settlements in Llanfihangel had a shop), shop/post office, garage, school and a village hall, as well as an inn and the church or chapel. But limitations were imposed always by the threshold population; that is, the minimum population required to support a commercial service (Chapter 5, section 1.2). Some facilities, of course, were regarded as public services and were not as sharply controlled by such thresholds.

With the increased mobility of the twentieth century, especially with the wider ownership of cars and the advent of mobile shops and services such as the library van, new circumstances have arisen. Four situations can be identified. The first is the standard one in which the village has remained as the lowest level in the urban hierarchy, providing daily and immediate needs (as against the nearest town). The second situation has been termed 'lateral interdependence' (Weekley, 1977), whereby a set of villages provides the essential services without any single settlement having a 'complete' set. Thus, a butcher's shop may be located in one but the post office in another. With present-day mobility, travel between them is virtually problem free. The third situation occurs at the lowest level and in the more isolated areas. In these settlements an element of 'self-sufficiency' still remains and absolute minimum services are available.

These three situations have been markedly affected by the change in the nature of contemporary settlement described earlier. At the highest levels of village growth a fourth situation has arisen, in which some metropolitan villages now have supermarkets and, often, specialized shops, such as garden centres and those dealing in antiques. But, as has been noted, here people can shop over the whole range of the city and its fringe, illustrating the breakdown of geographical hierarchies which Pahl (1964) observed.

In complete contrast, and at the other extreme, rural depopulation has virtually destroyed service thresholds in many areas. A survey of settlements in south-west Wales for the county structure plan examined villages in relation to four selected services – a post office, a primary school and the availability of main sewerage and of a commuter service by public transport. Of the 421 settlements (196 had a population below one hundred), 256 did not have all the four services. The reaction has been not to provide them, because of the cost to public expenditure, and to centralize services based on economies of scale (Carter, 1990, pp.43–8).

This brief survey emphasizes the great variety of character which exists within the general description of 'village' or 'rural settlement'. The one common factor is that, everywhere, the penetration of urban influence is apparent and the so-called 'truly rural' survives only in the most remote and isolated areas.

3 THE CITY: THE TRANSFORMATION OF ITS RESIDENTIAL PATTERNS

Given the improvements in transport and the growing divisions in society by class and ethnicity mentioned earlier, towns and cities experienced a transformation of their internal residential patterns during the nineteenth century. While there is disagreement about the precise timing and the rate of this change (Ward, 1975; Cannadine, 1977), it can be stated that, during the course of the century, towns lost what vestiges remained of their traditional or 'pre-industrial' structures and began to display modern or 'industrial' patterns of residential segregation. In *pre-industrial towns* the affluent lived at or near the city centre, perhaps with their poorer employees living with them in – or behind – their fine town houses. In the *industrial town* the well-to-do left the core to the needs of commerce and industry and looked towards the detached and semi-detached Victorian villas of the suburbs as their favoured residences. In very simple terms, this change has been seen as the demise of the residential patterns associated with Sjoberg's 'pre-industrial city' (i.e. a rich centre and a poor periphery) (Sjoberg, 1960) and the emergence of the twentieth-century city, with its distinctive social 'rings' or zones as set out by Burgess (1967) (i.e. a poor centre and a rich periphery).

Dennis and Clout (1980) have translated some of these changes into spatial models of the pre-Victorian city (Figure 6.2a) and the Edwardian city (Figure 6.2b). In the former, it can be seen that the prestigious main streets were backed by poorer properties; there is also an indication that change was underway with the beginnings of a middle-class suburb and an industrial colony. During the nineteenth century this pattern was gradually replaced by the form shown in Figure 6.2(b), where the core became the central business district with lock-up shops and other

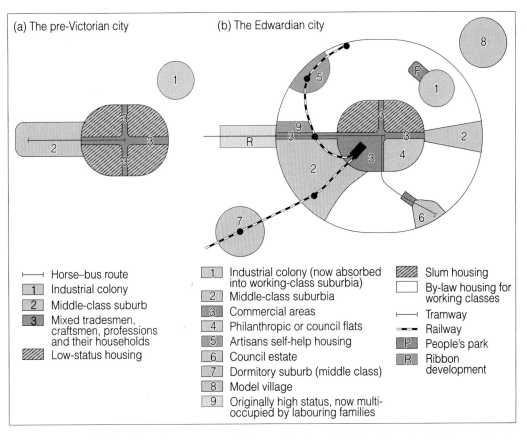

(a) The pre-Victorian city   (b) The Edwardian city

	Horse–bus route
1	Industrial colony
2	Middle-class suburb
3	Mixed tradesmen, craftsmen, professions and their households
	Low-status housing

1	Industrial colony (now absorbed into working-class suburbia)
2	Middle-class suburbia
3	Commercial areas
4	Philanthropic or council flats
5	Artisans self-help housing
6	Council estate
7	Dormitory suburb (middle class)
8	Model village
9	Originally high status, now multi-occupied by labouring families

	Slum housing
	By-law housing for working classes
	Tramway
	Railway
P	People's park
R	Ribbon development

Figure 6.2   A model of evolving urban structures: (a) the pre-Victorian city; (b) the Edwardian city (Source: Dennis and Clout, 1980, Figure 5.7, p.83)

commercial premises and was surrounded by large-scale segregated industrial and residential regions. It can be noted that Burgess's model of the industrial city contained the same basic ingredients as Figure 6.2(b), but they were arranged as concentric zones around the core, as a series of successive rings of low-, middle- and higher-class residential areas outwards towards the edge of the city. Not identified in Figure 6.2 are the ethnic clusters which were characteristic of both Sjoberg's and Burgess' models (see Figure 6.8, p.159).

Another way of looking at the changes between Figures 6.2(a) and 6.2(b) is the elementary model reproduced in Figure 6.3 in which all the activities and personnel of the large household in the pre-industrial town (the workshop and shop, the employees, the employer and his family, and the servants) are separated out in the industrial city into their own distinctive urban regions. What we see is the emergence of large-scale neighbourhoods, each with its own distinctive characteristics brought about by the influences of 'separation' and 'segregation' on both economic activities and people within the built-up area.

While these changes were most marked in large manufacturing centres, it should not be forgotten that Britain's smaller country towns were also subjected to similar processes as, for instance, when the coming of the railway or a local factory spawned a district of working-class terraces, or when the local shopkeepers and professionals vacated their former homes in their central business premises and moved to live in more fashionable houses in select neighbourhoods towards the edge of town.

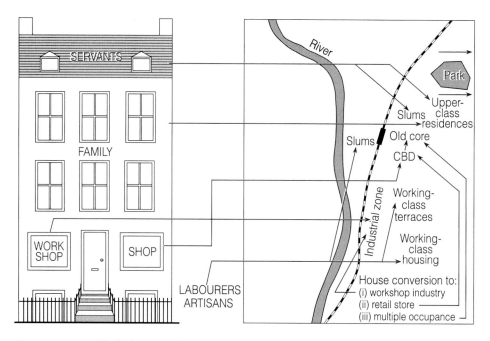

Figure 6.3   A model of urban spatial transformation in the nineteenth century. CBD = central business district (Source: Carter, 1980, Figure 2, p.183)

EXERCISE 6.3

Note down briefly what you think was the most striking difference between the internal residential patterns of pre-industrial and industrial cities.

Comment p.224.

QUESTION FOR RESEARCH

The spatial outcomes from these residential changes were at their most spectacular in large cities. Here distinctive neighbourhoods came to reflect differences of cultural milieu and social class. However, researchers in community history should not be deterred from putting quite small places of, say, around 2,500 population, under scrutiny. The study area – a block of inner-city streets, part of a suburb, a small town – can be defined to reflect changes in social structure, the local manifestations of processes that are more widespread.

---

4   THE NINETEENTH-CENTURY CITY

Using a variety of data sources – CEBs, rate books, trade directories, local surveys and Ordnance Survey maps – geographers and others have tried to reconstruct the residential patterns which emerged in the nineteenth century (Carter and Lewis, 1990, pp.120–47). By the 1870s the processes summarized in Figures 6.2 and 6.3 had produced large-scale segregated districts which were differentiated from each other by class. This is not to claim that these districts were uniformly of a particular status – lower middle class or upper working class, for example – or dominated by a single migrant group: what is fairly clear is that areas had emerged which can be picked out through the analysis of appropriate data as being of a certain standing – and were often labelled as such at the time. A study of Wolverhampton can illustrate the large-scale segregated districts by class that became characteristic of British towns in the second half of the century. Later, we shall look at the influence of ethnicity on the development of social areas.

4.1   SEGREGATION BY SOCIO-ECONOMIC STATUS (CLASS)

In his study of Wolverhampton, Shaw's main source of data was the 1871 census, and this was analysed in conjunction with information on land use and types of housing (Shaw, 1979). It is apparent from the basic land-use data that there was a major contrast between the east and west of the town, with the former dominated by mines and derelict workings, factories and ware-houses and the latter containing much agricultural land and parks. To examine the social and residential mosaic, Shaw superimposed a framework of grid squares on the city, each covering 200 metres on the ground, and collected information on 26 variables from the census for each grid cell. These variables covered a wide range of social, demographic and occupational characteristics of residents – for example, percentage of occupied population in social classes I and II (as defined in the Registrar General's five socio-economic classes of 1951; see Volume 4, Chapter 3, section 2.1.1, on Armstrong's classification), average household size, and percentage of heads of household born in England and Wales outside the local area. Shaw's measures were then mapped and subjected to multivariate analysis to reveal the town's residential structure.

Figure 6.4(a), showing the percentage of household heads in social classes I and II, is one of Shaw's distributions that confirms the east–west dichotomy of Wolverhampton. This is further emphasized by an examination of types of housing, using evidence from maps, documents and field work. Shaw classified residential property into four different size categories, with type A at the one extreme, comprising the smallest cottages and back-to-back houses, and type D at the other, with large detached or imposing semi-detached properties. Types B and C were an intermediate size, with C being mainly 'tunnel back' in terraces. Figure 6.4(b) shows the proportions of types C and D per grid square. What is immediately apparent again is the striking contrast between the east and west, reaffirming the social class distribution above. What these maps reveal is that by the 1870s there were pronounced residential contrasts, with the more rural west attracting the higher social classes in their larger houses and the east dominated by poorer social groups and smaller houses.

While this study lends support to the proposition that cities displayed large-scale segregated districts by the third quarter of the nineteenth century, this is not to say that the small-scale residential segregation, characteristic of pre-Victorian cities, did not survive, especially in and around the central business district. There is some evidence that segregation between upstairs/downstairs, and especially front street/back street, existed in many places, which, at the same time, showed the more modern segregation by locality on their fringes. Inner urban communities may well have been tiny – perhaps a small court or 'rookery' pushed in behind the main street. This residential intricacy is hinted at in a number of studies. Warnes concluded, from his analysis of the 1851 census data for the small town of Chorley in Lancashire, that the 'central area was distinguished by relatively high numbers of the upper three status groups and an unusually low density of the unskilled and the Irish born. To a lesser extent, the areas adjacent to the centre were distinguished by the inverse of the central area's characteristics' (Warnes, 1973, p.183). This suggests the partial survival of a traditional residential structure. Likewise, it has been noted by C.R. Lewis (1979) that, in Cardiff in the middle of the century, the main east–west and north–south streets were favoured by those engaged in shopkeeping and the professions, but these were backed by overcrowded courts. These studies remind us that, while the overall trend was towards the emergence of large-scale segregated residential districts, careful analysis, particularly in central areas, may reveal quite intricate small-scale contrasts.

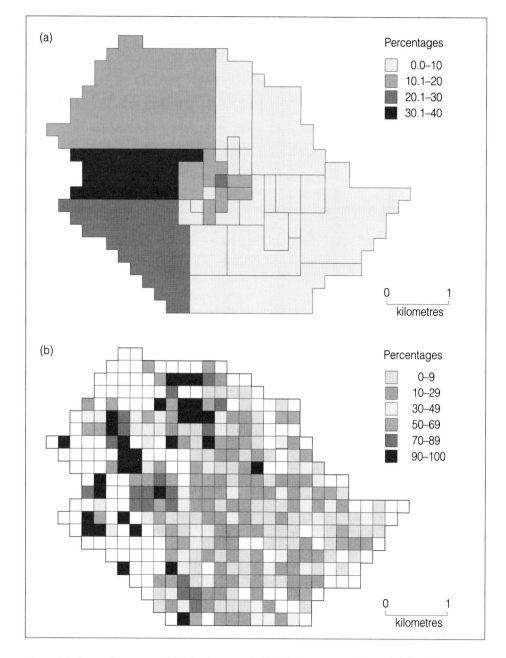

Figure 6.4   Intra-urban patterns in Wolverhampton in 1871: (a) percentage of household heads in classes I and II; (b) proportion of housing types C and D (Source: Shaw, 1979, Figure 4, p.198 and Figure 7, p.204)

The trend towards the segregated areas of our own times has been well demonstrated in case studies of individual residential districts in which a much wider range of evidence has been used. These show that often there was a conscious effort on the part of residents to distance themselves from those whom they regarded as their social inferiors. Hinchcliffe's (1992) study, *North Oxford*, charts the planned development of Norham Manor and Gardens as a high-status residential suburb by St John's College, University of Oxford. Drawing on estate plans, leases and college records, recent field surveys and photographs, this is a splendid example as to the sort of detailed empirical study of street-by-street development that can be undertaken locally.

Two further examples will be taken, the one to illustrate how a landowner responded to the demands of the wealthy for houses in a suburban rural retreat by creating a select community on his estate, and the other to show how differentiation occurred amongst the working classes themselves when skilled artisans tried to demonstrate through their housing that they were a cut above their poorer brethren.

The attempt to create a high-class suburb has been well documented in Cannadine's study (based, in part, on estate records) of the development of Edgbaston in south-west Birmingham (Cannadine, 1980). Between 1810 and 1813 the third Lord Calthorpe and his agent, John Harris, set in train a development scheme designed to appeal to the most wealthy and most important citizens. By the use of restrictive covenants on leases, the aim was to cultivate an exclusive suburb where 'speculative builders, working-class housing, industry, manufacturers and trade were all to be excluded, and the industrial elite of Birmingham were to be welcomed' (Cannadine, 1980, p.93). One measure of the pre-eminence of the citizens of Edgbaston in the life of late nineteenth-century Birmingham is revealed by the concentration of civic leaders who lived in the district (Table 6.1). As Cannadine has indicated, this was a distinctive high-status urban community – a sort of Belgravia of Birmingham.

Table 6.1 Members of Birmingham town council resident in Edgbaston, 1866–1902

Year	Aldermen/total	Councillors/total
1866–67	10/16	17/46
1877–78	11/15	18/47
1881–82	11/16	22/48
1891–92	11/18	19/55
1901–02	10/18	15/53

Source: Kelly's Directories of Birmingham: (1868) p.436; (1878) pp.585–6; (1882) pp.673–4; (1892) pp.732–3; (1902) pp.974–6 (after Cannadine, 1980, Table 23, p.199)

The second case study of segregation by class is Crossick's analysis of 'the labour aristocracy' in his book *An artisan elite in Victorian society* (1978). Using a wide variety of documents – trade union, company, friendly society and local government records – he examined those skilled and relatively well-paid workers who took on the distinctive values, the patterns of behaviour and the social aspirations that distinguished them from the lower tiers of the working class in east London. This stratification between skilled and unskilled men was rooted in the workplace, but it extended beyond, into the general life styles of their families, including their desire – and ability through higher incomes – to move into what were considered to be superior neighbourhoods. Housing was one avenue through which they could express their independence and respectability, and with the building of specifically artisan housing after mid-century, a process of residential segregation occurred.

QUESTION FOR RESEARCH

Crossick (1978) provides numerous pointers to both the changing structures and the processes within artisan communities. There is considerable scope for further detailed local investigations as to changes in patterns of activity amongst families in relation to their involvement in social gatherings, clubs and societies, educational attainment (or aspirations), religious and political affiliations, and so on.

4.2 SEGREGATION BY ETHNICITY

In addition to segregation by socio-economic status, cities displayed quarters which were occupied by minority ethnic groups. Because so many of these incomers were impoverished and lacked urban skills, inevitably they were drawn to the poorest housing – undoubtedly, low socio-economic standing is an important factor in helping to explain the concentration of distinctive groups in specific districts.

Particularly noteworthy in this respect were the large numbers of Irish who flocked to mainland cities after the Great Famine (1847–49) and who occupied 'Little Irelands' of over-crowded and insanitary housing (see Chapter 2, section 4.4). One study, that of Cardiff in 1851 (Lewis, 1980), shows that the Irish, who comprised between 12 and 15 per cent of the town's population, lived in the poorest housing: in the congested courts behind the main streets in the medieval nucleus, such as Landore Court and Kenton's Court, and in the newly constructed terraces of small houses to the south-east of the old town, particularly in Stanley Street, David Street, Mary Ann Street, Love Lane, Little Frederick Street and Newtown.

These areas, characterized by overcrowding and poor sanitation, recorded very high rates of mortality and disease. A sense of community may have been engendered through religion – a Catholic church and school were built between Stanley Street and David Street (G and I on Figure 6.5), right in the heart of the main Irish quarter. Nevertheless, it is difficult to disentangle this sort

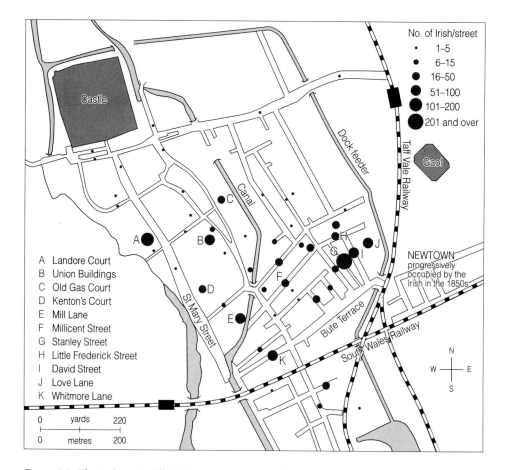

Figure 6.5 The Irish in Cardiff, 1851 (Source: Lewis, 1980, Figure 3, p.22)

of religious cohesion from the grinding poverty they experienced, which, for a long time, trapped the Irish incomers at the bottom of the housing ladder.

However, there are many studies of individual cities which show that groups displayed a strong cultural (religious) identity. For example, in his book *The making of Manchester Jewry, 1740–1875*, Williams (1985), using the surnames listed in city directories to locate Jewish families, explored the distinctive character of the northern sector of the city which developed around its synagogues, schools and other Jewish facilities (for further examples, see Chapter 3, section 2, and Chapter 8). A striking example of spatial segregation on grounds of religion – and one that is remarkably persistent – is provided by Roman Catholicism in Belfast (Jones, 1960). Research on Liverpool has shown that the Welsh, who did not show a marked spatial concentration (though perhaps Everton could be described as the main Welsh district), maintained a clear identity through their nonconformist chapels and their language (Pooley, 1983; see, also, Chapter 2, section 3).

_____ **QUESTION FOR RESEARCH** _____

Studies such as those mentioned above are at a fairly broad scale of enquiry. There is a need for further detailed investigation into the lives of those who lived and worked in these 'ethnic' districts – their places of origin, their cultural traits, their social activities, their marriage patterns and the destinations for their offspring. Over time, did acculturation and assimilation reduce the impact of ethnicity as a factor of residential differentiation?

5 THE TWENTIETH-CENTURY CITY

The trend towards large-scale segregated areas was intensified in the twentieth century through improvements in transport, the steady rise of home ownership on suburban estates, the arrival of further waves of new in-migrants and immigrants, and what was to become a new and significant feature of many places, the building of municipal housing, both in inner districts cleared of substandard property and on green-field sites. In the absence of census information on the composition of individual households, most empirical studies of intra-urban residential patterns have been carried out at a scale of the enumeration district (the small areas used by census administrators), using arrays of variables derived from the decennial censuses. Other data, particularly rateable values, have been employed as indicators of social status, but examples are less numerous in the literature. The details of the techniques used need not concern us here: what is of importance are the insights that have been gained into the nature of the intra-urban residential mosaic.

5.1 SEGREGATION BY SOCIO-ECONOMIC STATUS (CLASS)

A study of Leicester will be briefly outlined to show the spatial framework in which different types of community have developed this century. Lewis and Davies (1974) compiled a data matrix, comprising 56 variables from the 1966 sample census for each of the 143 enumeration districts in Leicester, which was then subjected to multivariate analysis. One of the clear features to emerge from their study was that the variables relating to socio-economic status displayed spatial patterns which brought out the territorial differences between the inner city zone and council estates on the one hand, and private estates on the other. These variations are shown by isopleths (lines joining points of equal value) in Figure 6.6. Here, the status of areas lies between a maximum score of 2+ and the minimum 2– (P and N show the highest and lowest values,

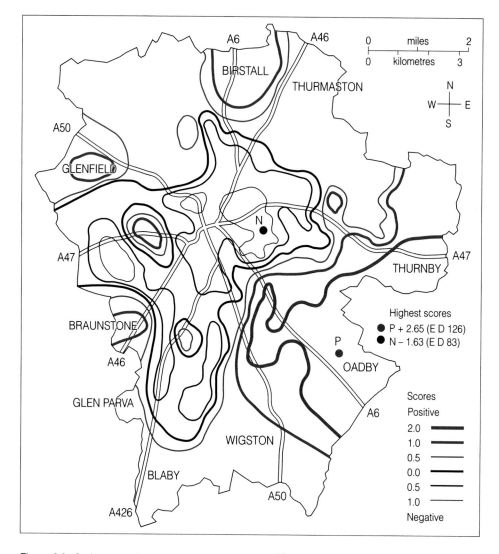

Figure 6.6 Socio-economic status scores in Leicester, 1966 (Source: Lewis and Davies, 1974, Figure 3, p.199)

respectively). Thus, what we see here is the result of further consolidation in the processes of large-scale residential segregation observed earlier for the nineteenth century.

In addition to this sort of aggregate study of an entire city, there are many published investigations of individual residential districts which illustrate the distinctive socio-economic and other features that make them different and give them a particular character. Just as Crossick (1978) examined the life style of artisans in Kentish London in the nineteenth century, so Young and Willmott (1957) have looked at Bethnal Green in east London to highlight the characteristics of a working-class district in post-war Britain; and, whereas Edgbaston was taken earlier as an illustration of suburban development in the nineteenth century, so Willmott and Young's (1960) study of Woodford, east London, could be drawn on to show a particular type of suburban community in twentieth-century Britain. In short, there are numerous studies, based, in part, on in-depth interviews with families, that add flesh to the patterns of residential segregation by socio-economic status revealed by census data.

5.2 SEGREGATION BY ETHNICITY

As in the nineteenth century, ethnicity has continued as a dimension of differentiation within British cities. While a few long-established groups have maintained their distinctiveness, particularly through religious affiliation (e.g. the Jewish population of north-west London and the Roman Catholic/Protestant communities of Belfast), in numbers and concentration these older settlements have been replaced by an influx of new immigrants, especially since the 1950s, from the New Commonwealth. The main immigrant populations have come from the West Indies, India and Pakistan, but individual cities do show small clusters of people from other countries as well.

Numerous studies have been completed concerning the colonization, consolidation and spread of ethnic clusters. Werbner (1979), for example, investigated shifts in Pakistani settlements in Manchester. A series of important studies on the continuity of ethnicity as a factor of residential differentiation in Birmingham have appeared. In the period 1961–66 the numbers of

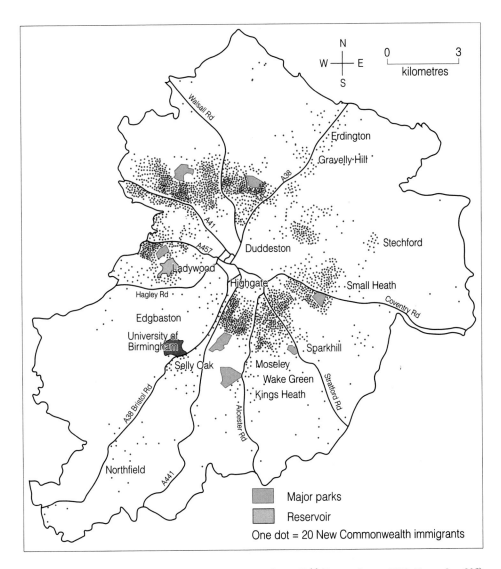

Figure 6.7 New Commonwealth immigrants in Birmingham, 1966 (Source: Jones, 1970, Figure 2, p.205)

immigrants almost doubled from 28,169 to 49,870, amounting to a rise from 2.4 to 4.7 per cent of the city's population (Jones, 1970). This research was based on the analysis, at enumeration district level, of birthplaces as recorded in the 1961 (full population) and the 1966 (sample) censuses.

Jones's maps revealed a pronounced concentration of immigrants in 1961 in a concentric belt, 1.5 kilometres wide, surrounding the core of the city. The dominant feature revealed by his further analysis covering the five years up to 1966 (Figure 6.7) was that the numbers of New Commonwealth immigrants increased most markedly in the areas where they had been most highly concentrated in 1961, and that these same clusters underwent spatial enlargement. From the map, what we see coming into being is a broken ring of social areas dominated by immigrant populations. These particular localities acted as the points of contact for new arrivals and they gradually acquired the appropriate cultural and community facilities. Clearly, this has parallels with migrations discussed elsewhere in this volume – for example, movements of the Welsh to settle in English cities (Chapter 2) and Jewish settlers in London (Chapters 3 and 8).

6 CONCLUSION

This examination of the social geographies of towns and villages has been conducted at the broad scale of enquiry to give insights into some of the major long-term changes that have had repercussions on the structure of communities. First and foremost, during the nineteenth century, Britain experienced massive urban growth which had consequences not only for towns themselves but also for the countryside. Between 1801 and 1911 the balance of population swung from being dominantly rural (66 per cent) to dominantly urban (79 per cent) (Law, 1967), and the shifting and sorting of people that this involved was to have an enormous impact on the structure and social make-up of places at all levels of the settlement hierarchy. Only in more recent times has there been a loss of population from great cities and a drift back to the countryside – the so-called counter-urbanization movement. Against this background our examples have emphasized those factors which have helped to shape the changing social mosaics in rural and urban settings, concentrating, in particular, on the influence of changes in class, ethnicity and mobility.

—————————————— *QUESTIONS FOR RESEARCH* ——————————————

Throughout this chapter the emphasis has been on general trends, trends which can be picked up by you in your own case studies of settlements – and, incidentally, studies that may well contradict some of the points that we have made! Leading on from our discussion we suggest that there are two clear paths of enquiry that you can follow:

1   You can reconstruct the internal socio-economic, family and housing characteristics of a small rural community, or *part* of an urban area in the nineteenth or twentieth century. In the urban setting you must be selective: you cannot study an entire city, but, with some local knowledge, perhaps you can select a block of streets in, say, the expanding urban fringe; or the small terraces associated with a factory; or the courts pushed in behind the main thoroughfares; or an area known specifically, for example, for its Irish or Jewish population. The diagrammatic model of the evolving Victorian city in Figure 6.8 may help you to identify a distinctive district. Detailed analysis of a number of standard data sources will enable you to describe the salient features of your area and to answer specific questions you raise about family structure, ethnicity, occupational characteristics, living conditions, and so on. Some of the sources that you will find most useful include the CEBs (nineteenth century), small area census statistics (twentieth century), trade directories, rate books, electoral registers, local

and Ordnance Survey maps, health and housing reports, registers of deposited house plans, and estate records.

2   You can try to examine the patterns of community interaction and persistence in your selected area. This is something which has not been looked at in any depth in our discussion (though see reference to Crossick's work (1978) in London), but various ways forward are indicated by Dennis and Daniels (1981) (see, also, the summary and discussion in Chapter 9, section 1). Dennis and Daniels show that a very wide range of quantitative and impressionistic evidence can be marshalled to get at the attitudes of, and the relationships between, people in their daily lives in their own communities.

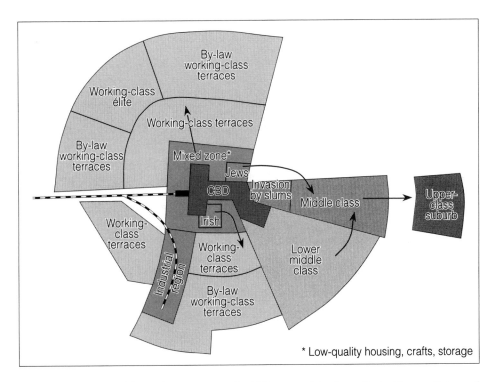

Figure 6.8 A model of the evolving Victorian city. CBD = central business district (Source: Carter and Lewis, 1983, Figure 22, p.90)

REFERENCES

Note: entries marked with an asterisk are suggestions for further reading.

Arensberg, C.M. (1939) *The Irish countryman. An anthropological study*, London, Macmillan.

Arensberg, C.M. and Kimball, S.T. (1940) *Family and community in Ireland*, London, Peter Smith.

Burgess, E.W. (1967) 'The growth of the city', in Park, R.E. and Burgess, E.W. (eds) *The city*, 5th edn, Chicago, IL, University of Chicago Press. (First published in 1925.)

Cannadine, D. (1977) 'Victorian cities: how different?', *Social History*, 2, pp.457–82.

Cannadine, D. (1980) *Lords and landlords: the aristocracy and the towns 1774–1967*, Leicester, Leicester University Press.

Carter, H. (1980) 'Transformations in the spatial structure of Welsh towns in the nineteenth century', *Transactions of the Honourable Society of Cymmrodorion,* pp.175–200.

Carter, H. (1990) *Urban and rural settlements,* London, Longman.*

Carter H. and Lewis, C.R. (1983) in The Open University, *D301 Historical sources and the social scientist,* Unit 15 *Processes and patterns in nineteenth century cities,* Milton Keynes, The Open University.

Carter, H. and Lewis, C.R. (1990) *An urban geography of England and Wales in the nineteenth century,* London, Arnold.*

Crossick, G. (1978) *An artisan elite in Victorian society,* London, Croom Helm.

Davies, E. and Rees, A.D. (eds) (1960) *Welsh rural communities,* Cardiff, University of Wales Press.

Dennis, R. and Clout, H. (1980) *A social geography of England and Wales,* Oxford, Pergamon.

Dennis, R.J. and Daniels, S. (1981) '"Community" and the social geography of Victorian cities', *Urban history yearbook,* pp.7–23. Reprinted in Drake (1994).*

Drake, M. (ed.) (1994) *Time, family and community: perspectives on family and community history,* Oxford, Blackwell in association with The Open University (Course Reader).*

Evans, C. (1915) *My people: stories of the peasantry of west Wales,* London, Melrose.

Frankenberg, R. (1966) *Communities in Britain. Social life in town and country,* Harmondsworth, Penguin.

Gibbons, S. (1902) *Cold comfort farm,* Oxford, Isis.

Hinchcliffe, T. (1992) *North Oxford,* New Haven, CT, and London, Yale University Press.

Jones, E. (1960) *A social geography of Belfast,* London, Oxford University Press.

Jones, P.N. (1970) 'Some aspects of the changing distribution of coloured immigrants in Birmingham, 1961–66', *Transactions, Institute of British Geographers,* 50, pp.199–219.

Law, C.M. (1967) 'The growth of urban population in England and Wales, 1801–1911', *Transactions, Institute of British Geographers,* 41, pp.125–43.

Lewis, C.R. (1979) 'A stage in the development of the industrial town: a case study of Cardiff, 1845–75', *Transactions, Institute of British Geographers* (New Series), 4, pp.129–52.

Lewis, C.R. (1980) 'The Irish in Cardiff in the mid-nineteenth century', *Cambria,* 7, pp.13–41.

Lewis, G.J. (1979) *Rural communities. A social geography,* London, David and Charles.

Lewis, G.J. and Davies, W.K.D. (1974) 'The social patterning of a British city', *Tijdschrift voor Economische en Sociale Geografie,* 65, pp.194–207.

Pahl, R.E. (1964) *Urbs in rure. The metropolitan fringe in Hertfordshire,* Geography Papers No. 2, London, London School of Economics.

Phillips, S.K. (1986) 'Natives and incomers: the symbolism of belonging in Muker parish, North Yorkshire', in Cohen, A.P. (ed.) *Symbolising boundaries: identity and diversity in British cultures,* Manchester, Manchester University Press. Reprinted in Drake (1994).

Pooley, C.G. (1983) 'Welsh migration to England in the mid-nineteenth century', *Journal of Historical Geography*, 9, pp.287–306.

Rees, A.D. (1950) *Life in a Welsh countryside,* Cardiff, University of Wales Press.

Reiss, A.J. (1959) 'The sociological study of communities', *Rural Sociology*, 4, pp.118–30.

Shaw, M. (1979) 'Reconciling social and physical space', *Transactions, Institute of British Geographers* (New Series), 4, pp.192–213.

Sjoberg, G. (1960) *The pre-industrial city, past and present,* Glencoe, IL, Free Press.

Stacey, M. (1969) 'The myth of community studies', *British Journal of Sociology*, 20, pp.134–47.

Ward, D. (1975) 'Victorian cities: how modern?', *Journal of Historical Geography*, 1, pp.135–51.

Warnes, A.M. (1973) 'Residential patterns in an emerging industrial town', in Clark, B.D. and Gleave, M.B. (eds) *Social patterns in cities,* London, Institute of British Geographers.

Weekley, I.G. (1977) 'Lateral interdependence as an aspect of rural service provision: a Northamptonshire case study', *East Midland Geographer*, 6, pp.361–74.

Werbner, P. (1979) 'Avoiding the ghetto: Pakistani migrants and settlement shifts in Manchester', *New Community*, 7, pp.376–89. Reprinted in Drake (1994).

Williams, B. (1985) *The making of Manchester Jewry, 1740–1875,* Manchester, Manchester University Press.

Willmott, P. and Young, M. (1960) *Family and class in a London suburb,* London, Routledge and Kegan Paul.

Wirth, L. (1938) 'Urbanization as a way of life', *American Journal of Sociology*, 44, pp.1–24.

Young, M. and Willmott, P. (1957) *Family and kinship in east London,* London, Routledge and Kegan Paul.

CHAPTER 7

STAYING AND MOVING: LINKS BETWEEN MIGRATION AND COMMUNITY

by Ruth Finnegan (section 1) and Brenda Collins (section 2)

In this volume we have tended to present migration, place and location as separate themes. In reality, of course, the inherent processes, as well as the consequences, are but different sides of the same coin – both for the migrants themselves and for the locations and communities involved.

This chapter pursues some of the more important interconnections between these themes. Migration and place, origins and destinations, movement or staying put, are all aspects that need to be integrated in the local research projects undertaken in family and community history. Section 1 illustrates some of these interconnections through a range of brief examples at the local level, and offers suggestions as to further areas of research.

Hitherto, most of this volume has been concerned with migrant destinations and the ways in which people have settled in new locations and have responded to the new cultural milieu. But, as we see in section 2 of this chapter, the processes of out-movement had consequences, sometimes very profound consequences, in the sending areas. From the mid-nineteenth century onwards the exodus affected many different types of locality, especially in the highland areas – that is, north and west of a line joining the Tees and Exe rivers – and in the western coastal regions bordered by the Atlantic. Section 2, therefore, draws on a number of case studies from Ireland – the country that, in many respects, has experienced the most profound of all such changes – to demonstrate the local implications of sustained out-migration and the use of appropriate analytical approaches. It also presents suggestions for research at the local (micro scale) level that can be taken up elsewhere.

1 HOW DO PEOPLE MOVE AND SETTLE WITHIN LOCAL COMMUNITIES? SOME EXAMPLES AND QUESTIONS

by Ruth Finnegan

Look round you, wherever you live. Towns and villages, suburbs and hamlets – all these local settlements have been created by people staying and moving, perhaps over centuries, perhaps quite recently. One way or another, they can be fitted into the wider contexts explored in Chapters 5 and 6. Our understanding of those aggregate patterns can be complemented by research on how they function in *specific* localities or for *specific* groupings. As Tony Champion urges for the closely related subject of migration, we now need more 'micro-level analysis of processes and conditioning factors' (Champion and Fielding, 1992, p.222). Local settlement patterns, furthermore, are neither static nor permanent. They develop over time, reflecting both specific historical circumstances and the actions of individual people and their families.

There is, thus, scope for research on the dynamics of settlement at a small-scale local level, complementing studies of settlement morphology by some consideration of the active strategies by which people move and settle over time. This section sketches some brief examples. As so often, both the availability and the nature of the sources are relevant for selecting research themes. So the main examples here are from people or groups who in some way stand out either for economic reasons or because they have been labelled by themselves or others as distinctive – and thus are often simpler to track down!

'The poor' can be easier to trace than others – at least when they become embroiled in administrative structures designed to aid or, perhaps, control them. At any rate, this seems to have been so of families who were in contact with the Charity Organization Society (COS), a charitable body whose social workers dealt with poor (but not totally impoverished) families. The COS provided extremely detailed records of individual cases, in part filling the gap in records for the period for which the CEBs are closed to researchers. They document the movements of families who, as Page puts it in his study of families in Edwardian Leicester, were 'not in abject poverty but who had reached a crisis in their household and needed temporary help or assistance' (Page, 1991, p.111).

Do you think the poor would move house more or less than the rich?

One might assume that, in late nineteenth- and early twentieth-century industrial towns in Britain, the poor were the least likely to move. The surprise is that Page's study of 40 COS case histories in Edwardian Leicester reveals a different picture. In fact, one common way in which the poor there adjusted to changes in their social condition was precisely by moving house.

Mostly, this was over very short distances (a short migration distance that, incidentally, recalls the Leicester of the early 1870s – see Chapter 2, section 2.1). A few families managed to move out to the new working-class districts – though these, too, sometimes fell into poverty again. For most, however, movement was within a mere quarter or three-quarters of a mile around the town centre, near local sources of employment. There was a buoyant housing market there due to these constant step-wise movements, with over a third of the population moving at least once a year (Page, 1991, p.112). The moves were one way of coping with poverty: 'For many households, the tenuous nature of domestic budgets meant poverty often led to migration towards cheaper rented property as a means of self-relief from their poverty ... [But] Intra-urban migration was one stage in a downward spiral of poverty and deprivation for poor families' (Page, 1991, p.118). Further local studies might reveal how far this Leicester pattern applied elsewhere. For example, is it true elsewhere that 'the poor were an increasingly mobile element in the social geography of industrializing towns' (Page, 1991 p.118)?

Other researchers have focused on particular categories of people who seem distinctive by their background or culture. It has been noted by historical geographers, as by urban sociologists and anthropologists, that members of minority ethnic groups often congregate in discrete sectors or clusters in urban areas, a distribution that can also influence their later movements (e.g. Boal, 1978; Waterman, 1983; Dennis, 1984; see, also, Chapter 6 above). The resultant studies of residential patterns, and of the effects of how and where people decide to move, have led to interesting – but challengeable – theories about trends and variations which could be followed up in further research.

One illustration can be taken from the Irish in Britain. Research on their nineteenth-century distribution and movements relies largely on birthplace information in the CEBs (only useful, obviously, for first-generation migrants). Thus, Pooley's work on Irish-born migrants in 1871 Liverpool showed a close cluster of poor and unskilled Irish in central and dockside Liverpool – the more skilled groups, however, were spread more evenly over the outer suburbs (Pooley, 1977). A study of 1851 Leeds suggests that, though the Irish were dispersed over many township wards, 80 per cent lived in just three of them (Dillon, 1973). Irish clusters are documented in many other towns too: 'In Cardiff, Falkirk, Leeds, Huddersfield, Bradford and, of course, London, other census-based studies have confirmed that there were urban courts and alleys which were virtually monopolised by the Irish' (Collins, 1993, p.380).

Pooley's study reminds us that we cannot just *assume* segregation, whether for the Irish or any other group. And, indeed, much work remains to be done on specific nineteenth-century localities to discover the detailed patterns of settlement, their relation to local resources (rentable housing, for example, or work within walking distance) and changing patterns over time.

More recent Irish settlers can also be studied, as in the account by King *et al.* (1989) of the 'second wave' of Irish settlement in Coventry, from the 1930s. They exploit published British census data – admittedly only a 'decennial snapshot of the population characteristics of particular areas and communities' (King *et al.*, 1989, p.67), but, since 1961, enlarged by the availability of the Small Area Statistics (see Chapter 1, section 2.2; also, Volume 4, Chapter 3, section 1.5) – supplemented by local church, club and school records; local newspapers; and interviews with local people. These reveal the changing distribution of the Irish-born, and the evolving occupational and social character of this 'community' within Coventry. King and his associates chart the two main routes for Irish settlers in Coventry: one via two inner-city parishes where there was cheap rented property, good Irish contacts, and nearby factories desperate for workers; the other through hostels built near suburban council house developments in the 1940s and 1950s. They go on to comment on changing distribution patterns up to the 1980s. Both Irish-born and second-generation Irish gradually moved further out, leading to a decline in the Irish character of inner city neighbourhoods, subsequently resettled by Asian immigrants. Further research could explore how far such patterns occur elsewhere, whether of the Irish (in so far as they remained distinct) or of other immigrants.

There is research on immigrant settlement *within* Ireland too. One is Waterman's account of Jewish settlements in Dublin (Waterman, 1981, 1983). He explores these in the light of what, he suggests, are the common patterns for immigrant groups (Waterman, 1983, p.55). (These are summarized in Schema A on p.166.)

(a)

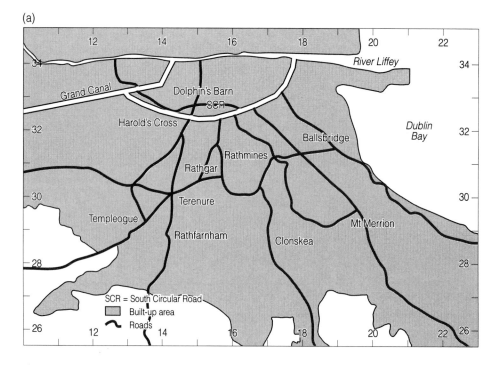

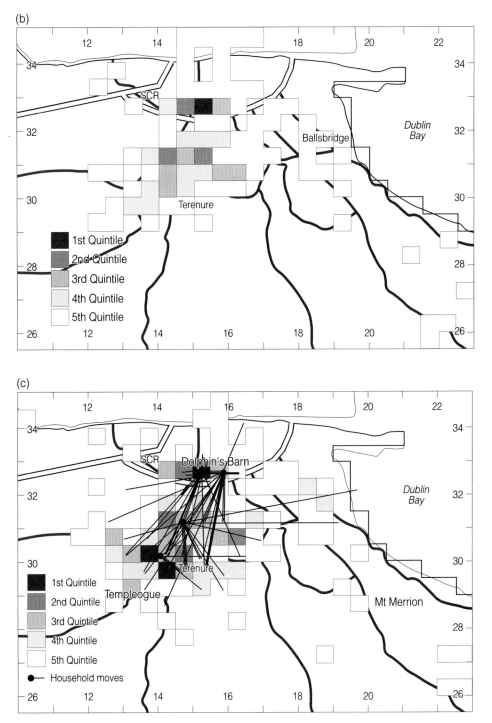

Figure 7.1 Maps showing Jewish settlement and moves in Dublin, 1941–57: (a) (opposite) location map; (b) residential location, 1941; (c) residential location, 1957, and household moves, 1941–57 (sample of the four most active grid squares from which moves originated) (Source: based on Waterman, 1981, Figures 1–4, pp.44–6)

Schema A: Common stages of immigrant settling

1 Initial segregated clustering, partly for social reasons such as the availability of cheap housing or the need for mutual support.

2 Some intra-urban migration but spatially restricted and with some degree of continued clustering even when the original reasons for it are removed.

3 Gradual weakening of the original factors of cohesion.

Using annual reports of the Jewish mutual aid society, synagogue records and personal interviews, Waterman concludes that the processes of Jewish settlement in Dublin did indeed largely follow these phases (Schema A). In the nineteenth and twentieth centuries, immigrant Jews from Eastern and Central Europe settled first in central Dublin on both banks of the River Liffey, close to each other 'for group security and well-being' (Waterman, 1983, p.56). As time went on, prosperous families filtered out into the surrounding suburbs, mainly to two sectors in south Dublin which themselves then became the focus of Jewish institutions and began to attract later immigrants. Up to the late 1950s, residential moves were mainly within these well-defined sectors, but the concentration has grown less marked as the sense of separate cultural identity has declined (see Figure 7.1). There is still some social cohesion, however, through Jewish institutions such as sports club, school and synagogues, and some preference for Jewish families to live close to each other, not only at the macro (or sectoral) level but also at the micro level: the street and neighbourhood (Waterman, 1983, p.67).

With other immigrant groups, too, the basic patterns that Waterman mentions can perhaps be detected in outline – or can they? As in the Dublin Jewish case, there may also be interesting complications, affected by particular cultural traditions, individual decisions and historical circumstances.

There are also studies of immigrants from further afield. One is Pnina Werbner's work on the Pakistani immigrants who first started to move to Manchester from the 1920s (Werbner, 1979, 1990) (Figures 7.2 and 7.3). She reveals not just *static* residential patterns, but the dynamics of settlement and their development over time: first the concentration in 'bachelor houses', then the arrival of immigrants' families. One major source lay in people's memories, supplemented by Werbner's personal observation and by numerical information from the Manchester ratepayers' list and the electoral rolls. Werbner finds a 'fan movement' out from the immigrant enclave, as the first arrivals moved outward to the suburbs, facilitated by their successful entrepreneurship in the local housing market. It was a flexible rather than a permanently closed system, but – as in Wirth's classic work (1928) on Jews in Chicago – those moving out also lost social contacts through living on the periphery. Gradually, however, 'the ghetto is surrounding them once more as other migrants move out of the existing one to join them' (Werbner, 1979, p.385).

This approach could be applied to other localities or groups. Several similar studies have been conducted, particularly for those of Asian origin (see Simmons, 1981) – an attractive topic given the relatively easy identification of Asian names on ratepayers' and electoral lists. Such sources are not without problems, however: the ratepayers' books do not list non-property holders, while electoral registers exclude recent settlers, and are not confined to permanent residents. Census birthplace statistics, too, can be misleading. Nevertheless, such sources do provide background material, and can be supplemented by more detailed oral and localized material, including questions about local perceptions and the more subjective elements of community interaction (see Chapter 9, section 1).

Figure 7.2   A ghetto is not a slum. This quiet street in Longsight, Manchester, houses proud property owners. Neighbourly relations in Longsight are marked by mutual help, sociability and joint participation in domestic rituals (Source: Werbner, 1990, p.297; courtesy of Dr Pnina Werbner, University of Keele)

Figure 7.3   The Central *Jamia* Mosque in Victoria Park, Manchester, built entirely with community funds. Although already too small to accommodate the whole community, it continues to constitute its highest corporate value and remains the focus of intense competition for office (Source: Werbner, 1990, p.299; courtesy of Dr Pnina Werbner, University of Keele)

It soon becomes clear that it is too broad just to speak of 'immigrant settlement', or even about 'black', or 'Asian' settlement patterns in general terms. For there are *different* groupings, arising, for example, from contrasting origins, historical circumstances, religion, a sense of distinctive identity, or traditional family composition. The way is thus open for further research at the micro level on *specific* localities and specific groupings. But the more general theories can still stimulate, providing useful questions for research (see also Schema C in Chapter 3, section 3.3).

There is also the question of how far any particular grouping of people *is* rightly identified as a 'minority ethnic group' or 'community'. Sometimes the answer may seem obvious, especially if there is a common language, religion or origin, tight spatial concentration, or labelling by outsiders. People may be conscious of shared interests or experiences, perhaps because they feel themselves in a precarious, hostile or merely different environment, or because of distinctive values which they treasure. On the other hand, these characteristics are relative rather than absolute features. And (as discussed further in Chapter 9, section 1), just because outsiders, political leaders or researchers attach labels to a group, it does not follow that all those concerned see it the same way or that the labels are necessarily solidly or permanently based. So this, too, leads into questions about people's self-perceptions and their own life experiences. How far *do* they interact socially? What role does a sense of identity play in their decisions about settling together or moving away? How have these processes changed over time?

QUESTIONS FOR RESEARCH

Depending where you live, one or more of the following could form the basis of a research project. Since exploring such questions is time consuming, start with only a *small* locality for intensive study (e.g. a small neighbourhood or even a street). As well as other sources, personal knowledge or contacts are worth capitalizing on.

1   If you live in a locality for which this is appropriate, draw up, as far as you can, a sketch map or plan of the residential distribution of a particular group that interests you and, where possible, mark their movements over time. *Can you relate these to any points in the more general discussion above?* (If you wish, and you have access to appropriate quantitative sources, you could try calculating one or more of: the index of segregation, the index of dissimilarity and the location quotient, and how these varied over time. For these calculations, see Volume 4, Chapter 8, section 9; and, for mapping, Volume 4, Chapter 11, section 2; Mills and Pryce, 1993; also Matthews and Foster, 1989.)

2   Consider a small neighbourhood for which you have access to the nineteenth-century CEBs. Do birthplaces indicate significant amounts of in-migration to the area? Is there clustering or dispersion among people with the same regional birthplace origins? How do these change over time? How do these *relate to the themes considered in this section*?

3   Consider the summaries by either Waterman (1983) (Schema A on p.166 above) or Ballard and Ballard (1977) (Schema B in Chapter 3, section 3.1, pp.94-5) as to the common (but perhaps variable?) phases of immigrant settlement and movement. How far does your own case fit with each or any of these phases?

4   Is it possible to relate any settling or moving patterns you discover to one or more of such other factors as: economic pressures or opportunities; the role of particular cultural traditions or religious institutions; local discrimination; local housing or employment patterns; government migration policies?

5   In what sense – if at all – can the group under examination be called a 'community' and/or a 'minority ethnic group', and has this differed over time? Possible questions to explore could include: degree of residential clustering; amount and nature of interaction (given modern communications this can be extensive, even between dispersed and remote locations); mutual assistance and support; roles of local clubs; perceptions, values or aspirations held

by (some or all of) the people concerned – perhaps changing over time; perceptions, values or aspirations held by others, including politicians and researchers (see also Chapter 9, section 1).

Sources and methods

Many different types of source have been mentioned in this section, but the sources that you will use will vary according to your own situation and topic. Those worth considering include: CEBs (for the nineteenth century); Small Area Statistics (since 1961); published census tabulations of birthplaces for larger areas; in some cases, Charity Organization Society records (not available everywhere – see Volume 4, Chapter 5, section 1; also Page, 1987); electoral registers; ratepayers' books; relevant local large-scale maps, plans, and directories; old and present-day photographs; any relevant personal sources (autobiographies? letters?) to which you have access, and your own knowledge; also, for all the questions (especially for 4 and 5), interviews and oral sources, including existing audio sources. More background on the local area may be gleaned from local newspapers (if only to get some feel for majority perceptions about the people with which you are concerned). There may be specific records about or produced by that particular group, such as mutual aid societies or religious records. (For further information on sources and methods, see Volume 4.)

2 THE IMPACT OF OUT-MIGRATION AND EMIGRATION ON SENDING COMMUNITIES: EXAMPLES FROM IRELAND

by Brenda Collins

Ireland has long been known as a country from which people emigrate. Its population virtually halved between 1841 and 1921, from over 8 million to 4.2 million. This steady loss was connected with a relative lack of urbanization and manufacturing industry. On the whole, in economic terms, Ireland, today, remains comparatively underdeveloped.

This section looks at the residual outcomes in the 'sending' localities from which the migrants came. Thus, the analysis is complementary to Chapter 1, section 3, where the focus was on the migrants themselves and their destinations. Here, the spotlight is on the people and the communities they left behind. How did these continue to function? Assumptions of terminal doom and decline have often been made, typified by Brody (1973), who described a process of demoralization and social atrophy in the west of Ireland. Yet others have suggested that many rural communities have been able to survive by adopting a variety of contingent measures which include part-time farming and state initiatives in the provision of public and private utilities and services (e.g. roads, schools), as well as further out-migration and emigration.

As always, it is helpful to start from some consideration of the social and economic background (you can amplify this by re-reading section 4 in Chapter 2).

2.1 THE RURAL ECONOMY, 1800–41, AND ITS CONSEQUENCES

In the early nineteenth century, poverty spread progressively through the rural population of Ireland as increasing numbers pressed upon limited resources. Farm holdings were subdivided both between farmers and their adult sons, and between tenant farmers and cottiers and others on annual tenancies. This enabled people to marry earlier, thus leading to more families and a greater number of births. Potatoes were adopted as a staple food crop and became a major item in the Irish diet.

Figure 7.4 The emigrants' farewell, 1844 (Source: *Illustrated London News*, 21 December 1844, p.397)

This broad view of the process of Ireland's impoverishment hides uneven regional development within the various regions of the country. There was a west–east divide, a 'dual economy' (Lee, 1971), between most of Munster and Connaught, where the small farmer and cottier class was most numerous and the mass of the people lived on tiny patches of land, and Ulster and Leinster, where the rural social structure was more equitable, with some embryonic modernization. This was typified by the spread of domestic textile production in Ulster and a move from subsistence to market-oriented commodity production in Leinster.

Emigration was one way of relieving the increasing pressures on living standards, but these moves did not have to be permanent. In the period before the Famine, *seasonal migration* had become common (see Chapter 2, section 4). This created a specific framework of living for the families and communities where it became established – mainly in the western counties where farm holdings were smallest (under five acres) and yearly tenancies predominated. Not only were seasonal migrants drawn from particular social groups, but they were likely to be young adult men at the peak of their physical strength when their earning potential was greatest. The wages that they earned in Britain as harvest labourers, and, later in the century, in the construction industry, became a crucial means of providing cash to pay rents on family farms in Ireland. This artificial cushion of support lessened the need for more radical changes and seasonal migration has persisted, as an alternative to permanent removal, in parts of the west – in Co. Mayo and in Co. Donegal – into the twentieth century.

2.2 EMIGRATION AND THE EFFECTS OF THE FAMINE, 1845–49

When the potato crops failed, due to the spread of blight disease, in successive years between 1845 and 1849, the effect upon Ireland was catastrophic. Between 1841 and 1851 the population fell by 20 per cent: about one million people died (see Figure 7.5 for an example in just one family). For those who could afford it, emigration was an alternative, and some 1.25 million people left Ireland between 1845 and 1851 (Figure 7.4). The combined effect of famine mortality and emigration was to restructure Irish rural society. This in turn set in motion major social changes that were to be intensified during the remainder of the century.

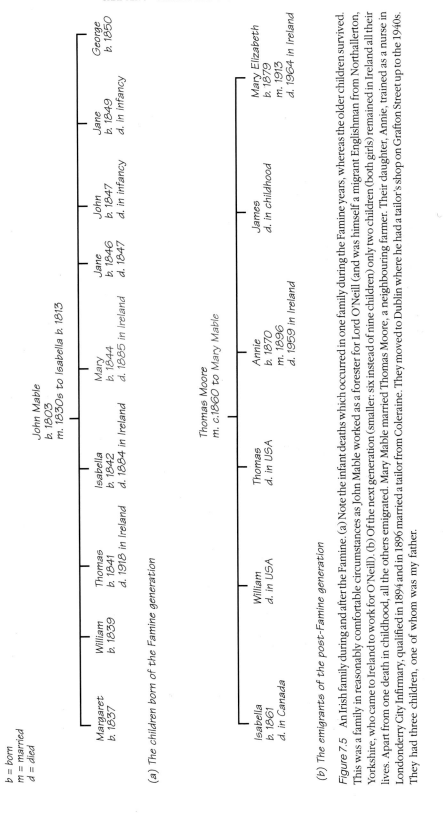

b = born
m = married
d = died

John Mable
b. 1803
m. 1830s to Isabella b. 1813

Margaret	William	Thomas	Isabella	Mary	Jane	John	Jane	George
b. 1837	b. 1839	b. 1841	b. 1842	b. 1844	b. 1846	b. 1847	b. 1849	b. 1850
		d. 1918 in Ireland	d. 1884 in Ireland	d. 1885 in Ireland	d. 1847	d. in infancy	d. in infancy	

(a) The children born of the Famine generation

Thomas Moore
m. c.1860 to Mary Mable

Isabella	William	Thomas	Annie	James	Mary Elizabeth
b. 1861	d. in USA	d. in USA	b. 1870	d. in childhood	b. 1879
d. in Canada			m. 1896		m. 1913
			d. 1959 in Ireland		d. 1964 in Ireland

(b) The emigrants of the post-Famine generation

Figure 7.5   An Irish family during and after the Famine. (a) Note the infant deaths which occurred in one family during the Famine years, whereas the older children survived. This was a family in reasonably comfortable circumstances as John Mable worked as a forester for Lord O'Neill (and was himself a migrant Englishman from Northallerton, Yorkshire, who came to Ireland to work for O'Neill) only two children (both girls) remained in Ireland all their lives. Apart from one death in childhood, all the others emigrated. Mary Mable married Thomas Moore, a neighbouring farmer. Their daughter, Annie, trained as a nurse in Londonderry City Infirmary, qualified in 1894 and in 1896 married a tailor from Coleraine. They moved to Dublin where he had a tailor's shop on Grafton Street up to the 1940s. They had three children, one of whom was my father.

171

Table 7.1 Changes in social structure in rural Ireland, 1845–1910

	Labourers (%)	Cottiers (under 5 acres) (%)	Farmers		Total number of holding
			(5–15 acres) (%)	(over 15 acres) (%)	
1845	44	19	19	18	1,587,000
1851	47	8	18	27	1,070,000
1910	36	8	19	37	820,000

Source: adapted from Lee (1973) p.2

As Table 7.1 indicates, the number of farm holdings declined by over one-third in the 1840s and continued to decline more slowly during the rest of the century. The number of the smallest holdings (those occupied by cottiers) was severely reduced, while larger farms were consolidated. During the second half of the century, farm employment practices began to rely increasingly on family labour. As a result, many landless labourers left the countryside and emigrated. Thus, within the rural communities, farmers, especially those with larger holdings, came to dominate the local social structure. Their influence was all the greater because of the relative lack of industrialization and urbanization in the country as a whole.

2.3 EFFECTS OF EMIGRATION IN THE LATER NINETEENTH CENTURY

Although the rush of the 1840s and early 1850s lessened, people continued to emigrate and in no decade did the numbers leaving fall below 40,000 (again, Figure 7.5 illustrates how this affected one family). However, regional time lags (reflecting the 'dual economy' regions) persisted until the 1870s: the west tended to retain its pre-Famine characteristics of seasonal migration and relatively universal marriage. From the 1880s, however, rates of emigration from the west of Ireland surpassed the other provinces, probably due to the increasing commercial pressure on the small farms in the west. The outcome was to make social and family structures more homogeneous throughout Ireland.

During the later nineteenth century the typical emigrants were likely to be unmarried young adults. Irish men and women emigrated in virtually equal numbers – whether from particular origins or to specific destinations – though in certain decades, such as the 1890s, more women than men left. Emigration had become integrated into the life cycle of individuals as part of the process of growing up.

This continued outflow strengthened the middle classes, especially farmers, who, numerically, had become the largest sector of rural society. They favoured single inheritance and later marriage. By the last quarter of the century the rest of rural Irish society had adopted their values. This inheritance pattern gave a place in rural society to only one son in each nuclear family, and required marriage to a local girl. Farming families tried to consolidate their land-holding positions by a judicious choice of partner, and so the marriage market narrowed. One result was the increased likelihood that, over time, marriages would occur between blood relatives. Also, because marriage was dependent upon succession to the farm, it had to be postponed until the death of the father or until the holding had been relinquished by him. As life expectancy increased, so did the age at marriage in the next generation.

This pattern of family formation also implied celibacy for some. Adult children, who had decided to stay rather than emigrate, waited, often in vain, to find a suitable spouse from a diminishing pool of potential marriage partners. Those who did not marry were reduced to

Figure 7.6 Emigration in the 1930s. The expectation of emigration as a possible option continued well into the twentieth century (Source: Ulster Museum Belfast, Hogg Collection)

subordinate status as servants in the family home or in another household, or they lived solitary lives, marginal to the system of property transmission and powerless in the economic and social life of the community. In contrast, emigration presented numerous opportunities, especially for young women, to mould their own destinies, in livelihood, in marriage and in terms of enhanced social status. An Irish emigrant girl wrote home: 'over in Ireland people marry for riches, but here in America we marry for love and work for riches' (Schrier, 1958, p.6, quoted in Johnston, 1990, p.270).

Thus, the Irish population declined both because emigration siphoned off the young adults who were most likely to contribute to population increase and economic growth, and because of the high rates of celibacy among those who remained. In most other European countries the birth rate at the end of the nineteenth century declined through reductions in family size. In Ireland, family sizes remained large but the rate at which new families were formed was reduced.

2.4 MONEY AND INFORMATION

While limited financial help towards emigration was offered by landlords, philanthropists and the state, the level of assistance was trifling compared with that sent home by emigrants to their families. Official returns indicated that over £34 million were sent back to the British Isles by emigrants between 1848 and 1887, most of it going to Ireland. While some of this 'American money' was used to pay off shop debts, to purchase land, provide marriage dowries and to bolster living standards, a large proportion of the cash came in the form of pre-paid passage tickets. Thus, many Irish emigrants were financed, directly or indirectly, by their fellow country-men and countrywomen who had emigrated before them.

Apart from the finance, emigrants also wrote letters home which exerted a powerful means of spreading further interest in emigration (some examples are given in Volume 1, Chapter 2, section 3). Although some may have exaggerated the benefits of their decision to leave Ireland, others gave practical information on the best ways to travel or the wages that could be earned. Many stressed the new freedoms and opportunities for people to make their own way in life in the new lands.

This dissemination of money and information meant that chain migration was taking place: husbands, for example, sent back remittances to enable wives and children to join them, or one sister or brother in a family financed the travel of another (see Chapter 1, section 3.5). Wider kin or those with an alternative bond, such as church membership, could also be part of the 'chain'. While the initial place of settlement was often a haphazard choice, the chain movement branded each pattern of settlement as distinctive. Thus, extraordinarily localized emigrations did occur: for example, from Co. Tipperary to the Ottawa region in Canada (Elliott, 1988); from Co. Down to Victoria, Australia (O'Farrell, 1984); and, possibly, from a Co. Clare village in the 1930s, 'said, locally, to be supported by the Shanghai police force' (quoted by Foster, 1989, p.369)! In overall terms, chain migration introduced elements of familiarity and desirability into what otherwise would have been an unknown experience for many thousands of emigrants (Figure 7.6).

2.5   LOCAL EXAMPLES OF WIDER THEMES

Thus, as we have seen, the picture was more complicated than one of straight population decline. There is, moreover, much evidence of significant differences within and between the communities of rural Ireland, contrasts which Johnston (1990) suggests are more usually considered to be characteristic of complex urban, rather than rural, societies. It makes sense, then, to examine the truth of the general picture at a local level. The two studies summarized below represent ways in which the impact of emigration upon Ireland can be studied.

'CARRICKBEG', CO. KERRY

The population of 'Carrickbeg' (so named in the study by Breen, 1984) in Co. Kerry declined from about 1,500 in 1841 to just over 1,000 in 1901. There are two contrasting but interdependent patterns of demographic change within this one locality: in the Uplands the population increased from 1841 through to 1881, and in the Lowlands the population declined steadily between 1841 and 1911 (Figure 7.7). Breen suggests that these contrasts superficially resemble the time lag in the patterns of population change between the west of Ireland and the rest of the country. Both were areas of mixed farming, with larger farms employing farm servants common in the Lowland area, and smaller mixed farms in the Upland area, which also supplied farm labour to the Lowlands. The Uplands population increase during the Famine decade appears to have been due to an in-movement of new households to previously uncultivated land as well as to the short-term continued subdivision of land holdings through inheritance. This created a temporary one-generation momentum that persisted until the 1880s. Analysis of the land valuation records of between 1859 and 1917 shows that, in contrast, the population decrease in the Lowlands (leading to emigration) involved, primarily, the non-farming sector; that is, those who did not own land (mainly farm labourers and their families). In the Uplands the same type of loss occurred, though there it was delayed by one generation until after the 1870s.

Drawing on the 1911 census returns to analyse the remaining population, Breen has indicated how family relationships, and the economic and social status of those who moved away, can be linked, locally, to changes in social structure since the 1840s. In 1911 the remaining non-farm groups were of three types:

1   Households headed by farm labourers, probably employed by those from whom they rented a dwelling and land.

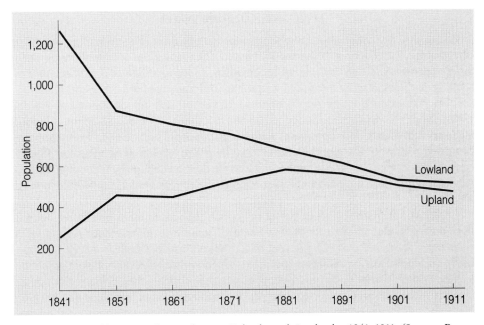

Figure 7.7 'Carrickbeg' population change, Uplands and Lowlands, 1841–1911 (Source: Breen, 1984, p.99)

2   Sub-tenants related to their landlords, commonly as parents, or as uncles or siblings, and occupying a separate house on their land.

3   Those related neither by family nor labour – trades people, small business people and professionals (such as teachers) whose livelihoods, although related to the spending power of the farmers, were not absolutely in their control.

The emigrants during the period 1850–1914 were primarily the younger members of the first two groups: the non-familial farm labourers' families; and the relatives of farmers, including adult dependent children and non-heirs. A switch from arable farming in the Lowlands during the 1850s and 1860s reduced the demand for labour. This may have led to the out-movement of resident married farm labourers as farmers began to employ non-inheriting family labour and unmarried farm servants who lived in. In addition, when required, non-resident casual labourers were now drawn overwhelmingly from the Upland region.

In the 1880s, with falling butter and beef prices, the less valuable (lower rated) Upland farms came under further commercial pressures. Indicative of these pressures are the oral history reports, at the turn of the century, of seasonal migration to north Kerry as an additional support of the small farm economy of the Uplands (see section 2.1 above).

Permanent emigration predominated, however, among the labourers and the non-inheriting members of farming families. Thus, despite the initial internal contrasts between Upland and Lowland areas, by the early twentieth century the outcome was increasing economic and social homogeneity. Due to the substantial out-movements, the family farm became the main form of holding, accounting for between two-thirds and three-quarters of all households. 'Carrickbeg', with all its changes, provides a splendid example, in miniature, of the end results of selective out-migration and economic reorganization on local communities.

LISBELLAW, CO. FERMANAGH

It was not only the rural class structure that changed as a result of emigration. There were also demographic consequences arising from the selective out-movement of certain groups. These aspects are investigated in Vincent's study of marriage patterns, religion and class in Lisbellaw, south Fermanagh, in relation to social inequalities and 'marriage fields' (Vincent, 1983).

The population of the district of Lisbellaw showed a steady decline during and after the Famine: from 3,404 in 1841, to 2,243 in 1851, 1,882 in 1871 and 1,356 by 1901. Farming families made up four-fifths of the population. Farmers usually held land on long leases and they prospered during the rising prices that followed the move to pastoral farming after 1850. In contrast, this change from arable farming reduced the demand for farm labourers, forced some sub-tenants into local wage labour, some to urban migration and others to emigrate to North America.

Of the 664 marriages registered between 1864 and 1920, nearly three-fifths were Church of Ireland ceremonies, 16 per cent Roman Catholic. Somewhat unexpectedly, registry office ceremonies accounted for 13.5 per cent which Vincent ascribes both to mixed marriages between Catholics and Protestants as well as to the large number of small Protestant sects in the locality. Register entries reveal that farming families consolidated their holdings through the marriage of their offspring: fewer than one per cent married a partner from more than ten miles away, and many married within their townland. Marriage exchanges criss-crossed the generations. Non-marrying siblings either acquired a livelihood based on the local towns or emigrated. In contrast, the majority of labourers who married in an area tended neither to have been reared there nor to remain after marriage. In these distinctive ways stability and transiency differentiated the two status groups.

Vincent's analysis of the 1901 census schedules provides a further picture of those who married and stayed in the community and of the implications of the out-movement of non-inheriting siblings. The marrying population was, in fact, the residual element. Only just over half (163 out of 305; 53 per cent) of the households were headed by married couples, another 78 (26 per cent) by widows or widowers. The 41 households headed by bachelors and 13 headed by spinsters were maintained by individuals who do not appear in the marriage records.

Within the farming households, the rarity of households headed by married couples meant that the continuity of farm ownership through inheritance was fragile. Denominational differences compounded this. Just over half the rural farm holdings were held by members of the Church of Ireland. Roman Catholic farmers were both less numerous and less commonly living in conjugal family units. Thus, Roman Catholics accounted for only 28 per cent of the rural farm holdings; and only 40 per cent of their households (26 out of 65 holdings) were headed by married couples with children. Moreover, 18 had no male in the household, five were elderly couples and 11 households were headed by an unmarried person. Thus, disproportionately, the Roman Catholic households contained fewer mechanisms for direct continuity of inheritance.

Vincent relates these distinctive patterns of family structure to the widespread out-migration of adult males and young girls. Paradoxically, whilst their out-movement enabled brothers or sisters to inherit the family farms, their own disappearance from the 'marriage field' reduced that generation's marriage possibilities within the locality as a whole and lessened the likelihood of securing an inheritance pattern from one generation to the next. Within Lisbellaw as a whole, marriage strategies amongst members of the Church of Ireland, although equally constrained by the attitudes towards mixed marriages, meant that there were greater numbers of potential marriage partners. Successful marriages meant, in turn, more children and, in consequence, Church of Ireland families came to dominate the locality.

What conclusions can be drawn from this?

Both these local studies highlight the relationship between the emigration of particular social groups and the social structures of the sending communities. For Breen (1984), the focus is the selective mechanisms amongst the farming families governing the departure of two main sets of people: farm labourers and non-inheriting siblings. Vincent (1983) outlines the even stronger effects of such selective emigration in the particular context of marriage patterns.

Ultimately, selective emigration seems to have led to increasing homogeneity within the communities left behind – whether viewed in terms of social status or family structures. In late nineteenth-century Ireland various legislative policies added further to this homogeneity: the broadening of the franchise in the 1880s, the establishment of representative district councils in 1898, and the land legislation of the period immediately leading up to the First World War whose provisions meant that tenant farmers could buy out their leases and become independent proprietors.

What main themes have emerged?

The main themes and findings can be highlighted in terms of the checklist shown in Schema B. Despite its apparent simplicity, this does provide a useful jumping-off point for further research.

> *Schema B: Some possible features of the impact of out-migration on local communities*
>
> o   A 'culture' of migration, interlinked with local social patterns (e.g. nature of the family, life cycle, inheritance patterns, personal expectations).
>
> o   The economic consequences for the 'sending' community: for example, outlets for those without prospects (given local economic or inheritance patterns), possibility of remittances.
>
> o   The links between the selective emigration of particular groups and the social structure of the local community – increasing inequality and/or changes in social class balance.
>
> o   Increasing homogeneity in local communities over time in terms both of social status and family structures (perhaps, also, due to other factors too?).
>
> o   Links with communities elsewhere through the process of chain migration.

While these studies centre on the impact of movements which individuals initiated, there are other forms of emigration that were to bring profound consequences for the residual communities left behind. In Ireland these included the assisted emigration schemes (used by some owners of large estates as a means of farm consolidation) and government-sponsored emigration (particularly to Australasia), as well as the enlistment of over 300,000 Irishmen in the armed forces during the First World War. This brought extra financial support in the form of allowances to many labourers' households and also exposed Irish families to new and different cultural values.

―――――――― *QUESTIONS FOR RESEARCH* ――――――――

Further small-scale research projects at the local level can add considerably to our understanding of this topic. Emigration is a process that made its impact over time. Therefore this research offers interesting opportunities to combine several different types of historical source materials.

1 The period of greatest significance, from the 1870s onwards, coincides with the much more widespread availability of relevant Irish source material. This includes the printed

census reports and the enumerators' returns of the 1901 and 1911 censuses (see Volume 4, Chapter 3, section 2; and Collins and Pryce, 1993); the land valuation records used by Breen (1984) (available at the National Archives in Dublin and the Northern Ireland Public Record Office in Belfast); and the civil marriage registers used by Vincent (1983), kept by the local registrar. (Since the civil marriage registers may have remained in the hands of the local registrars throughout Ireland and there are no general restrictions on access, they may be available to researchers in other Irish localities.) (Note, also, the links that can be made to the section on emigration discussed in Chapter 2, section 4 in this volume). A massive range of oral history material, covering seasonal migration and other aspects of Irish cultural tradition, is available in the Department of Irish Folklore, University College Dublin (O'Dowd, 1991).

2   Studies that focus on the impact of emigration (and out-migration) on rural communities in other localities could draw on comparable, though not identical, material. It would be interesting to explore how far the various features listed in Schema B also apply outside Ireland (some almost certainly will not, others might), at different periods, or for different circumstances.

3   Inevitably, out-migration and/or emigration brought structural changes in the sending communities elsewhere, especially specific localities in highland Britain. How *similar* were these to the experience of rural Ireland in the nineteenth century? How *different* was the outcome of *sustained and progressive* out-movements? What was the impact of the sudden departure of people – for example, when a local mineral working enterprise was closed down?

3   CONCLUSION

In this chapter we have brought together the migration and settlement themes that earlier, for reasons of presentation, have been treated as separate, though not unrelated, strands. In reality, research on population movements *conducted at the local level* cannot be fully appreciated outside the context of settlement pattern, the physical environment and the social and cultural milieu. The need to bring together and integrate all these aspects is essential within the framework of local studies and in the context of particular communities. Whoever came into contact with a migrant walking on thin air, with no affinity, no attachment to territory, to people, to place! Thus, we hope that you will find that Chapter 7 provides further new perspectives that can be applied to your own work. But, in addition, it can be regarded as having set the scene for Chapter 8, which is an in-depth study of community and territoriality in east London.

REFERENCES AND FURTHER READING

Note: entries marked with an asterisk are suggestions for further reading.

Ballard, R. and Ballard, C. (1977) 'The Sikhs: the development of south Asian settlements in Britain', in Watson, J.L. (ed.) *Between two cultures: migrants and minorities in Britain,* Oxford, Blackwell.

Boal, F.W. (1978) 'Ethnic residential segregation', in Herbert, D.T. and Johnston, R.J. (eds) *Social areas in cities*. Vol. 1. *Spatial processes and form,* London, Wiley.

Braham, P. (ed.) (1993) *Using the past: audio-cassettes on sources and methods for family and community historians,* Milton Keynes, The Open University.

Breen, R. (1984) 'Population trends in late nineteenth and early twentieth century Ireland; a local study', *Economic and Social Review*, 15, 2, pp.95–108.*

Brody, H. (1973) *Inishkillane, change and decline in the west of Ireland*, London, Allen Lane.

Champion, T. and Fielding, T. (eds) (1992) *Migration processes and patterns,* vol. 1, London, Belhaven Press.

Collins, B. (1993) 'The Irish in Britain, 1780–1921', in Graham, B. and Proudfoot, L. (eds) *An historical geography of Ireland,* London, Academic Press.

Collins, B. and Pryce, W.T.R. (1993) 'Census returns in England, Ireland, Scotland and Wales', audio-cassette 2A in Braham (1993).

Davis, G. (1991) *The Irish in Britain 1815–1914,* Dublin, Gill and Macmillan.*

Dennis, R. (1984) *English industrial cities of the nineteenth century: a social geography,* Cambridge, Cambridge University Press.

Dillon, T. (1973) 'The Irish in Leeds 1851–1861', *Thoresby Society Publications*, 54, pp.1–28.

Elliott, B.S. (1988) *Irish migrants in the Canadas,* Belfast, Institute of Irish Studies, Queen's University.

Fitzpatrick, D. (1984) *Irish emigration 1801–1921,* Economic and Social History Society of Ireland, Studies in Irish Economic and Social History.*

Foster, R.F. (1989) *Modern Ireland 1600–1972,* London, Penguin.*

Johnston, J.H. (1990) 'The context of migration: the example of Ireland in the nineteenth century', *Transactions, Institute of British Geographers*, NS 15, pp.259–76.*

King, R., Shuttleworth, I. and Strachan, A. (1989) 'The Irish in Coventry: the social geography of a relict community', *Irish Geography,* 22, pp.64–78.*

Lawton, R. (1987) 'Peopling the past', *Transactions, Institute of British Geographers*, 12, pp.259–83.*

Lee, J.J. (1971) 'The dual economy in Ireland 1800–1850', *Historical Studies*, 8, pp.191–201.

Lee, J.J. (1973) *The modernization of Irish society 1848–1918,* Dublin, Gill and Macmillan.

Matthews, H. and Foster, I. (1989) *Geographical data: sources, presentation and analysis,* Oxford, Oxford University Press.

Mills, D. and Pryce, W.T.R. (1993) 'Preparation and use of maps', audio-cassette 3A in Braham (1993).

O'Dowd, A. (1991) *Spalpeens and Tattie Hokers,* Dublin, Irish Academic Press.

O'Farrell, P. (1984) *Letters from Irish Australia 1825–1929,* Belfast, Ulster Historical Foundation, and New South Wales University Press.

Page, S.J. (1987) 'A new source for the historian of urban poverty: a note on the use of Charity Records in Leicester 1904–1929', *Urban History Yearbook*, pp.59–67.

Page, S.J. (1991) 'The mobility of the poor: a case study of Edwardian Leicester', *The Local Historian*, 21, 3, pp.109–19.

Pooley, C. (1977) 'The residential segregation of migrant communities in mid Victorian Liverpool', *Transactions, Institute of British Geographers*, NS 2, pp.364–82.

Robinson, V. (1992) 'The internal migration of Britain's ethnic population', in Champion and Fielding (1992).*

Schrier, A. (1958) *Ireland and the American emigration 1850–1900*, Minneapolis, MN, University of Minnesota Press.

Simmons, I. (1981) 'Contrasts in Asian residential segregation', in Jackson, P. and Smith, S.J. (eds) (1981) *Social interaction and ethnic segregation*, Institute of British Geographers Special Publication 12, London, Academic Press.

Vincent, J. (1983) 'Marriage, religion and class in south Fermanagh, Ireland, 1846–1920', in Lynch, O.M. (ed.) *Culture and community in Europe. Essays in honour of Conrad Arensberg*, Delhi, Hindustan Publishing Corporation.*

Waterman, S. (1981) 'Changing residential patterns of the Dublin Jewish community', *Irish Geography*, 14, pp.41–50.

Waterman, S. (1983) 'Neighbourhood, community and residential change decisions in the Dublin Jewish community', *Irish Geography*, 16, pp.55–68.

Werbner, P. (1979) 'Avoiding the ghetto: Pakistani migrants and settlement shifts in Manchester', *New Community*, 7, 3, pp.376–89. Reprinted in Drake, M. (ed.) (1994) *Time, family and community: perspectives on family and community history*, Oxford, Blackwell in association with The Open University (Course Reader).*

Werbner, P. (1990) *The migration process. Capital, gifts and offerings among British Pakistanis*, New York and Oxford, Berg.

Wirth, L. (1928) *The ghetto*, Chicago, IL, University of Chicago Press.

PART III

COMMUNITY AND TERRITORIALITY:
AN ILLUSTRATION

❖ ❖ ❖

CHAPTER 8

JEWISH EAST LONDON, 1850–1950

by David Englander

Jacob Amdur was born in Kovno in Lithuania in 1870. Arriving in England in 1893, he settled in the East End of London at 102 Commercial Road, Stepney. He was 23 years old and a butcher by trade. Perhaps he was accompanied by his parents; possibly they followed on. At any rate, Rachel and Elijah Dov Amdur (known to his family as Eli Baer) – recorded in official documents as 'Elliot Bear' – were soon living close by. In 1903 Jacob became a naturalized British citizen. He was described by a police report as 'a respectable man' and was remembered as such by his children. By Sarah Amdur (née Richardson) he had six in all, one son and five daughters. They were a close family. The children saw their grandparents once a week when the youngest would receive a farthing pocket money. As adults, too, the Amdurs saw a lot of each other, meeting at the house of the youngest to talk over the week's events. And so they continued until incapacitated by age and illness. The last of the Amdurs, my mother, died in her eightieth year not far from the Commercial Road dwellings in which she was born.

Not very interesting – or is it? In what respects were the Amdurs typical of the more than 100,000 Russo-Polish Jews who came, mostly to the East End of London, between 1880 and 1914?

At present the question is nigh impossible to answer. Immigrant Jews from Eastern Europe, one authority tells us, are no longer hidden from history. Their past is restored; their story told (Holmes, 1991, p.193). Don't you believe it! The family history of the Jewish immigrant, considered demographically, or as a conjugal group, a locality group, an economic unit, is largely unknown. Myths about the Jewish family exist in place of systematic knowledge on marriage, household structure, kinship relations and residence patterns. Studies of relationships between spouses or between parents and children, on gender roles, on continuities and changes in family behaviour have still to be written. Although knowledge of my own family is fairly minimal, I shall draw upon the life experience of the Amdurs to raise some questions about the shape and character of the world they once inhabited.

The emphasis here is upon spatial patterning in the Whitechapel–Spitalfields district of London, which the Amdurs knew as the 'Jewish East End'. Using contemporary maps and documents, I shall try to chart the growth and development of the largest of London's many immigrant quarters. The use of 'chart' in this context is operational rather than figurative, and I will be making use of the three maps included in this chapter.

_____ *EXERCISE 8.1* _____

The base map shown in Figure 8.1 is your principal activity sheet. Take time to study it carefully. Get to know the district: its administrative divisions (Whitechapel, Spitalfields, Goodman's Fields, Houndsditch, Mile End New Town, Mile End Old Town and St George's-in-the-East. Stepney and Bethnal Green, to which I shall also refer, are just off the map: Stepney to the east, Bethnal Green to the north), and its arterial routes (Whitechapel High Street, Whitechapel Road, Mile End Road, Commercial Road and Commercial Street). Note the location of the railway network and the position of thoroughfares like Leman Street, Cannon Street Road, Brick Lane and Cable Street.

_____

None of these divisions was a 'natural' boundary to prevent the development of human relations and social contacts. But, as we shall see, contemporaries regarded them as important landmarks in their perception of territoriality and in forming judgements about the kinds of behaviour that were considered appropriate and the kinds of contact that could be expected. Our aim, in short, is to create a thematic map of Jewish east London. Information is provided which, when plotted step-by-step as you work through the case study, will build up to form a multi-dimensional areal representation of the religious and cultural life of the immigrant quarter.

This case study raises further questions. The Jewish experience, as presented below, illustrates certain of the key concepts and ideas of community, settlement, cultural distinctiveness, place of residence and territoriality discussed earlier in Chapters 5 and 6. It also underscores the need to consider how the experience of Jewish east London relates to the wider processes of migration, settlement, community creation and identity, and the need to ask how it compares with that of other minority ethnic and religious groups in London or elsewhere.

1 ONE COMMUNITY OR MANY?

The Jews, the oldest settled non-Christian minority religious group in Britain, have maintained a distinctive presence in London ever since the Readmission during the 1650s. In the seventeenth and eighteenth centuries they lived on the eastern fringes of the City of London. Numbers were small (anything between 15,000 and 20,000 persons according to Colquhoun's estimate of 1796) but sufficient to sustain four synagogues – the Spanish and Portuguese in Bevis Marks (established 1702), the Great Synagogue, Duke's Place (1722), the Hambro' in Fenchurch Street (1726) and the New Synagogue in Leadenhall Street (1761) (off map).

The Jewish population lived close by in the adjoining streets and alleys. In due course, pressure of numbers, a growing prosperity and vexatious restrictions on Jewish traders, prompted the eastward movement by some and a westward movement of others. The original nucleus of Jewish settlement was also affected by land-use changes and the transformation of central London from a residential into a commercial district from the 1850s onwards. Our story begins at this point.

What was this original settlement like? How can we find out?

One rich source to which we can turn is the report by Henry Mayhew (1812–87), a remarkable social investigator. His survey of metropolitan street life, *London labour and the London poor*, published in 1851 and reissued ten years later, is a mine of information, not only on Jewish

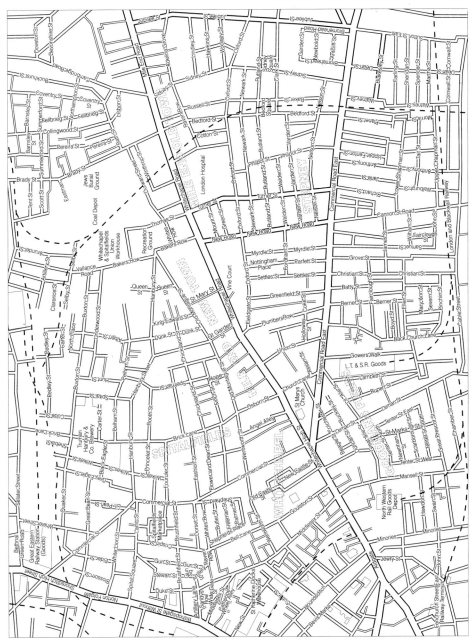

Figure 8.1   Base map showing the core area of Jewish settlement in east London (Source: adapted from a map drawn by G.E. Arkell for Russell and Lewis, 1901)

settlement, but also on other minority ethnic groups such as the Irish and the Italians. Apart from personal observation, Mayhew relied upon interviews with 'gentlemen representatives' of the community and, more unusually, upon the direct testimony of the Jewish street sellers. His engaging and precise portrait of the Jewish quarter can serve as a basis for comparison with the enlarged community that emerged from the mass migrations of the 1880s.

The relevant account for our purposes is in volume 2 of Mayhew's survey. (You may also wish to look this up yourself – it is available in reference libraries: Mayhew, 1861, vol. 2, pp.115–32.) The four salient features of Jewish settlement which struck me in reading Mayhew's account relate to:

1 The occupational peculiarities and narrow economic base of metropolitan Jewry.

2 The expansion of synagogal provision both within and without the eastern fringe of the City.

3 The two distinct settlement centres north and south of Aldgate Pump. The first is made up of a cluster of streets in the Goodman's Fields area to the south of Aldgate and Whitechapel Road; the second takes in the Houndsditch area including Cutler Street in the north-east and extending eastwards beyond Middlesex Street down to Wentworth Street.

4 The extraordinary range of voluntary associations.

EXERCISE 8.2

Identify the area, described in (3) above, on Figure 8.1, perhaps using a highlighter, or shading it lightly.

You will find the map completed, for this and other exercises, on p.225 (Figure 8.7).

Mayhew's observations are consistent with aspects of migration or settling discussed earlier in this book (especially Chapters 1–3). I shall examine each of these features in turn.

The narrow economic base of the Jewish community   The absence of an industrial proletariat and a professional middle class are the most striking features in Mayhew's text. We are plunged into a world of hawkers and pedlars, street sellers and old clothes dealers, craft workers, shopkeepers and diverse petty traders. Mayhew notes, rightly, that the brokers and bankers, who formed the original nucleus of settlement, had decamped. Scholars, indeed, now estimate that as much as one third of London Jewry lived outside the City and East End (Lipman, 1972, pp.43–4).

Synagogal provision   It might be noted that the number of synagogues increased from the original four to eight and that three of the new ones were situated in the West End – in Maiden Lane (Covent Garden); the Western Synagogue in Pall Mall; with the first Reform congregation, the West London Synagogue of British Jews, in Cavendish Square. From the location of these new synagogues we may conclude that the separation of classes affected the Jewish minority as much as the general population and that, by the time Mayhew had put pen to paper, the westward march of the wealthy towards Mayfair and Maida Vale, Bloomsbury and Bayswater, was well under way.

Settlement centres north and south of Aldgate Pump   The human ecology of London Jewry was closely bound up with their occupational structure. The Goodman's Fields area – Great Alie Street, Great Prescott Street, Mansell Street, Leman (pronounced by the locals as 'Lemon') Street, the Minories – was favoured by the upper middle class of wholesale merchants, superior manufacturers and the more substantial retail traders. The centre of the second-hand clothes trade was located in the Rag Fair in Rosemary Lane (Royal Mint Street) near the Tower (off map), and in the markets off Houndsditch in Cutler Street, and in Petticoat Lane (off Middlesex Street). The close connections between work and worship in the evolution of the areas of settlement is suggested by the chronology of synagogue formation: Rosemary Lane (1748); Cutler Street (1790); and Gun Square, Houndsditch (1792).

The smaller manufacturers, who supplied the swag-shops (costermongers) and street sellers with a miscellany of cheap goods, were more widely dispersed.

The Jewish poor are also conspicuous. Mayhew portrays their semi-destitute street life in their wretched homes in the courts and alleys off Whitechapel. But whereas he found street life curious and captivating, in contrast the acculturated Anglo-Jewish community found it repellent and dangerous. Jewish philanthropy, which Mayhew found so striking, in part represented a religious impulse, but it was also a response to the problems posed by the existence of an unruly but highly visible population. To the anxious leaders of Anglo-Jewry the degraded condition and rumbustious life styles of the Jewish populace were perceived as an embarrassment, and as major obstacles to their integration into British life.

Jewish voluntary associations   'I sometimes wish I was a Jew', a non-Jewish fish seller told Mayhew, 'because they help one another … and so thrive where Christians are ruined' (Mayhew, 1861, vol. 1, p.77). Neither Mayhew nor his informant quite grasped that the thrust of Jewish philanthropy was towards the abandonment of the street trades. The Jews' Free School in Bell Lane, founded by Joshua van Oven in 1817, and subsequently supported by the Rothschilds, the efforts of the Jews' Hospital in Mile End and of the Jews' Orphans Asylum in Tenter Street to apprentice boys to useful trades, were part of ambitious programmes designed to replace the nomadic life of the street traders with workshop-based employment. The aim was to transform the Jewish poor into paragons of bourgeois respectability.

We may sum up this discussion by noting that the Jews of London in 1850 were an acculturated, but on the whole an unobservant, community, narrowly concentrated north and south of the Aldgate–Whitechapel Road. Apart from a small incursion into the area around Bishopsgate and Middlesex Street, the Houndsditch settlement to the north did not much extend into Spitalfields. To the south the area of Jewish settlement did not penetrate east of Leman Street into St George's-in-the-East, although, as Mayhew notes, Jewish suppliers maintained a presence in the riverside districts, along with the 'aged and decayed inmates' of the Joel Emmanuel Alms House and the Hand-in-Hand Asylum in Wellclose Square (off map).

The area of Jewish settlement did not expand out in all directions. The expansion of the Jewish quarter in the City seems to have petered out around Goulston Street. Further east, in Mile End, beyond a couple of Jewish hospitals, almshouses and cemeteries, there was little settlement. The opening of the Stepney Jewish Schools in the 1860s marked the beginnings of a new colony around Stepney Green and the Mile End Road. Why Whitechapel and the western part of Mile End were passed over, though, remains unclear. Likewise, we can but note the absence of Jews from the area north of Whitechapel in Bethnal Green.

Before taking leave of Mayhew's Jews, I want to draw attention to certain aspects of the minority population. Mayhew notes, in passing, that the foreign element constituted a fluctuating but significant proportion of the Jewish community. Even if the size is unclear, the observation is a reminder that we are not dealing with an undifferentiated minority, uniform in its tastes, values, attitudes and beliefs. The distinction between native and foreign Jew, implicit in Mayhew's commentary, suggests a community in which one might expect to find considerable variation in the level of acculturation and assimilation. Let us see whether this expectation is justified.

EXERCISE 8.3

Figure 8.2 shows the proportion of foreign-born residents in the various parts of east London and Hackney *before* mass immigration from Eastern Europe had begun. The tables from which the map is derived are reproduced here as Figures 8.3 and 8.4. Contemporaries who imagined the East End to be a homogeneous immigrant quarter might have been surprised by the information shown in the tables. Why? Keep your explanation brief: a dozen lines or so will do.

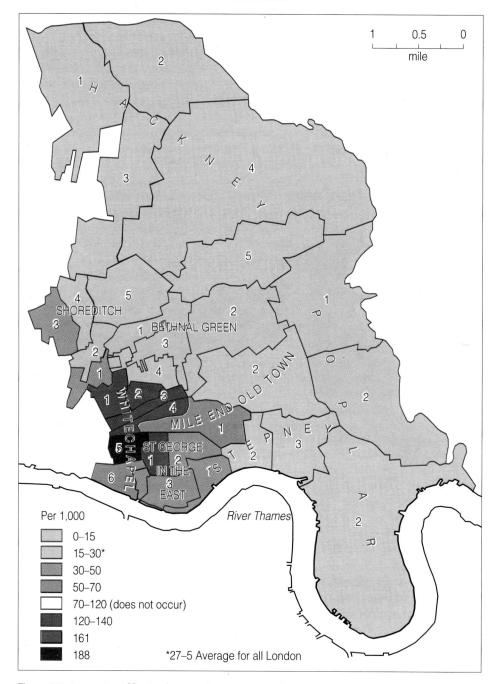

Figure 8.2   Proportion of foreign-born residents in east London and Hackney, 1881. Registrars' districts are named and subdistricts numbered, in agreement with the census tables, 1881 (Source: Booth, 1902, vol. 3, pp.100–1)

Number of Persons born out of the United Kingdom living in the various Sub-Registration Districts of East London and Hackney, 1881.

Sub-Registration Districts.	Born in the British Colonies and Dependencies.	Born in Foreign Countries.		Total	Percentage of Population
		British Subjects	Foreigners		
Spitalfields	41	241	3455	3737	16·15
Mile End New Town	19	41	2034	2094	13·53
Whitechapel, North	13	36	1318	1367	13·67
Whitechapel Church	38	86	836	960	12·82
Goodman's Fields	26	58	1747	1831	18·85
Aldgate	84	32	270	386	6·32
St. Mary	39	208	2020	2267	12·46
St. Paul	73	235	605	913	4·43
St. John	57	92	140	289	3·44
Shadwell	53	124	236	413	4·09
Ratcliff	58	51	137	246	1·52
Limehouse	106	120	335	561	1·75
Mile End Old Town (Westn.)	91	163	2255	2509	6·6
Do. do. (Eastern)	167	304	610	1081	1·6
Bow	111	148	235	494	1·33
Bromley	214	274	328	816	1·27
Poplar	304	186	1015	1505	2·73
Holywell	20	24	226	270	3·66
St. Leonards	21	36	127	184	1·23
Hoxton New Town	55	119	316	490	1·63
Hoxton Old Town	29	48	193	270	0·96
Haggerston	74	94	259	427	0·92
Hackney Road	42	74	176	292	0·98
Bethnal Green	98	154	298	550	1·15
Do. Church	41	45	146	232	0·77
Do. Town	28	37	305	370	1·97
Stanford Hill	83	47	34	164	1·77
West Hackney	165	190	421	776	2·06
Hackney	428	322	763	1513	1·97
South Hackney	130	140	327	597	1·50
	2708	3729	21,167	27,604	3·21

Figure 8.4   (Source: facsimile extract from Booth, 1902, vol. 3, p.113)

Number and Country of Birth of persons of foreign birth and nationality enumerated in Registration Districts of East London and Hackney, 1881.

	Whitechapel	St. George's-in-the-East	Stepney	Mile End Old Town	Poplar	Shoreditch	Bethnal Green	Hackney	Total
Russia	835	164	22	136	59	30	57	29	1332
Poland	4458	402	8	757	33	83	197	26	5964
Sweden and Norway	68	152	50	18	297	19	2	43	649
Denmark	19	23	17	8	52	11	8	29	167
Holland	1850	243	40	379	70	41	65	182	2870
Belgium	37	65	8	72	14	13	5	66	280
France	116	23	77	49	101	54	36	173	629
Germany	1805	1493	326	1212	659	708	451	929	7583
Austria-Hungary	224	77	12	117	19	40	14	58	561
Switzerland	15	7	1	9	9	22	6	51	117
Spain and Portugal	11	12	19	5	43	6	5	24	125
Italy	16	29	15	5	37	29	21	29	181
Greece	3	13	1	1	12	1	—	9	40
Turkey and Roumania	9	4	—	7	6	4	9	8	47
China	2	—	35	—	35	—	—	3	75
Others in Asia	—	17	3	1	—	—	1	2	24
Africa	8	—	3	2	—	—	3	1	17
United States	170	35	64	85	109	60	43	120	686
Others in America	3	6	4	2	22	—	3	21	61
Country not stated	6	—	3	—	1	—	1	—	11
Born at Sea	5	—	—	—	—	—	1	1	7
Total	9660	2765	708	2865	1578	1121	925	1804	21,426

Figure 8.3   (Source: facsimile extract from Booth, 1902, vol. 3, p.112)

It will be seen that, in 1881, the ratio of foreign-born to the general population was highest in east London and Hackney. The whole district of east London and Hackney contained c.27,000 foreign-born persons, or 3.25 per cent of the total population. The corresponding percentage for the whole of London was 2.75 per cent. It will also have been noted that Germany was easily the largest contributor to the foreign population of the Metropolis. As the tables in Figures 8.3 and 8.4 show, there was no district in east London without a large German contingent. The pronounced Polish presence, though, will not have been missed. Unlike the widely dispersed Germans, the Poles were concentrated in a small area. Whitechapel alone contained 4,458 Poles out of a total of less than 6,000 in Tower Hamlets, mostly engaged in tailoring and bootmaking. Whitechapel, too, was home to some 835 Russians as well as a substantial Dutch community. The Dutch, a contemporary observed:

> ... are mostly Jews, but the colony is a longer established one than that of the Polish Jews, as is shown both by the proportion of males to females, and a comparison of numbers with older census returns. A thousand of this birth and nationality were recorded, in 1881, in three of the Census collectors' [i.e. enumerators'] books alone in the district of Spitalfields, out of a total of 1850 in the whole of Whitechapel, and no less than half of these were then engaged in the cigar making.

(Booth, 1902, vol. 3, pp.102–3)

You will note, too, that the foreign element diminishes in all directions as we depart from the centre of Whitechapel.

German immigrants included a large proportion of non-Jews; Russians, Poles and Dutch settlers, by contrast, were overwhelmingly Jews. Their presence underscores an important feature in the make-up of the minority. The Jews of London, as Mayhew suggests, may well have been an increasingly settled population, but, as the census data show, their expansion was not due to natural increase alone. Continuous immigration not only supplied significant increments to the ever-growing proportion of native-born Jews, it introduced fresh sources of religious and cultural diversity and also served to sustain Jewish separatism. As one mid-Victorian commentator put it: 'this large admixture tends to keep up the distinctions between Jews and Englishmen, which but for that circumstance would be hardly perceptible' (Anon., 1865, p.582).

To conclude, Jewish east London, before the advent of mass immigration from Eastern Europe, contained a Jewish minority that was far from homogeneous. The variety was noted in the 1880s when the Jewish community came under close scrutiny. Arkell, who interviewed Woolf Cohen, a master tailor at 77 Leman Street, on 29 February 1888, remarked: 'An ordinary observer would not suspect he was a foreigner, as his appearance and speech were English'. Of Mr Price of Wood Street, Spitalfields, whom he interviewed three weeks later, he wrote: 'This man is a jolly "John Bull" type of man with but little of the characteristics of the Jew', quite unlike those encountered in Petticoat Lane where 'on every side may be seen the pallid Jewish features, whether of the German, the Pole or the Russian; half-starved or under-nourished, and barely clad ...' (Booth Collection, A19, fos. 74, 97; A23, fo. 92). But, as I have suggested, such differences were not new. Whether the sources of differentiation are such as to enable us to speak in the plural of the Jewish communities of east London, with significant cultural distinctions, is something which could form the basis of a worthwhile research project. All I am seeking to do at this stage is to signpost diversity and dynamism. Cockney Jews, Russian Jews, Dutch Jews, German Jews and Polish Jews together suggest a multi-national minority religious and ethnic group characterized by differing degrees of acculturation and assimilation.

2   STUDYING THE GEOGRAPHY OF SETTLEMENT

There is a variety of methods which can be applied to study the growth of the Jewish quarter. Some, like the CEBs, will already have suggested themselves; others might include the use of Jewish trade directories, scrutiny of synagogue membership lists and the formation of new congregations, the location of trade union locals, friendly society branches, cultural institutions, and so on. Drawing on such a multiplicity of sources, we should be able to plot the development of the Jewish East End.

Charles Booth pioneered social analysis, street by street, for his great inquiry *Life and labour of the people in London* (Booth, 1902), useful not just for the Jewish settlement but for many other areas of London too (and, once again, available in some reference libraries). With evidence drawn from police officers, teachers, clergy, local administrators, social workers and, above all, from the school attendance officers, Booth had created a detailed poverty map which classified streets by colour according to social class (see Volume 4, Chapter 4, section 6, Figure 4.11).

EXERCISE 8.4

George Arkell, who had prepared the maps for the Booth survey, applied the same techniques to illustrate the development of Jewish east London for the Toynbee Hall inquiry of 1899 (published as *The Jew in London: a study of racial character and present-day conditions*, London, 1901, and written by Charles Russell and H.S. Lewis, as part of Toynbee Hall's investigation into the problems and prospects thrown up by Jewish immigration from Eastern Europe). His map, published in 1899, of which an extract is reproduced here as Figure 8.5, has been praised by one historical geographer as 'an objective survey of the extent of Jewish settlement in east London' (Smith, 1988, p.204). It requires careful attention. Before you scan it, though, read the explanatory notes printed below. Then, briefly make a note of the relevance of these to the information displayed in Figure 8.5.

The map of Jewish East London has been prepared to show the extent of the Jewish settlement, which has grown up around the old Ghetto by the City walls, and also the proportions of Jew and Gentile resident in the district ...

The information possessed by the London School Board, covering the whole area of the inquiry, would, it was thought, form the best basis for a comparative statement ... The School Board Visitors' schedules contain particulars of all families with children of school age, and the officers make a note of all infants as possible future scholars, so that, practically, information was available respecting all families with children under fourteen years of age.

These particulars have been taken out, street by street, the Jewish families being distinguished from the non-Jewish. The characteristics of the Jews are many and distinctive; Christian [sic] name and surname, the school to which the children go, the observance of the Jewish holidays, etc.; all these tokens are so clear that it proved comparatively easy to discriminate.

(Russell and Lewis, 1901, pp.xxxiii–xxvi)

Figure 8.5   This map shows the proportion of the Jewish population to other residents of east London, street by street, in 1899
(Source: adapted from a map drawn by G.E. Arkell for Russell and Lewis, 1901)

The status of the information supplied by the School Board Visitors, and Booth's assumptions and procedures with respect to the evaluation of their evidence, have been queried by modern scholars (O'Day and Englander, 1993). As you can see, Arkell, his faithful assistant, shows the same tendency to convert personal impressions into social facts and to generalize from a non-random sample to the whole of the population. Are not Jewish-like names, school attendance and the observance of Jewish holidays questionable criteria for the identification of distinctively Jewish and non-Jewish streets? It is almost certainly true that, to have confidence in Arkell's subtly shaded percentages, we need, at the very least, to test the reliability of the streets he identifies against other independent sources. Such a test would be, in itself, a worthwhile project. For the moment, though, we must not be beguiled by the cartographic techniques that have been used. As with any documentary source, these types of map need to be handled with caution.

EXERCISE 8.5

Examine closely, in the context of Mayhew's written descriptions of the Jewish colony in the 1850s (see section 1), the immigrant quarter as depicted on Arkell's map (Figure 8.5). To what extent does the Arkell map record the following:

1   The intensification of the area of settlement?

2   Extensions to the Jewish areas?

Even from a quick glance it is clear that the immigrant quarter had grown in breadth and depth since Mayhew's day. The map shows the spread of the Jewish population beyond the original area on the eastern boundaries of the City into Whitechapel, Spitalfields, St George's-in-the-East and Mile End, and to Stepney and Bethnal Green. Jewish east London, at the close of the century, was an area of 1.5 square miles with a peak population of around 125,000. Let us now consider the territorial distribution of the people, to see when these changes occurred.

Intensification of the area of settlement   First, we should note that the expanding immigrant population (there were between 2,000 and 5,000 new arrivals each year) was not evenly spread throughout the area. In 1881, 77 per cent of the Russians and Poles in London lived in the Whitechapel, St George's-in-the East and Mile End Old Town Poor Law Unions; ten years later the proportion was 82 per cent. The rise in the percentage of foreigners in the population between 1891 and 1901 was from 24 to 39 per cent in Whitechapel; 5 to 12 per cent in Mile End Old Town; 16 to 29 per cent in St George's-in-the-East and 2 to 4 per cent in Limehouse (off map). As the late V.D. Lipman remarked, Jewish concentration 'might be compared to a cistern into which the inflow exceeded the outflow' (Lipman, 1954, p.94).

Extension of the area of settlement   The newcomers, as Figure 8.5 suggests, were prone to cluster close to the original area of settlement. It will be seen that, in an area covering roughly three-quarters of a square mile in Whitechapel and St George's, nearly all the streets were classified as half-Jewish; and in respect of one-quarter of the streets, 95 per cent of the population was reported as Jewish. The chronology of settlement formation is comparatively easy to establish. 'Whitechapel', said a report of 1884, 'has never thoroughly recovered from the overcrowding that arose when, night after night, wagon loads of poor Jews were brought up from the docks, where they had just arrived, still panic-stricken, from Russia' (Anon., 1884). And it never did recover.

The wagons were busy in 1886 to convey the influx that followed the expulsion of the Poles from Prussia. They rolled even more hectically in 1891–92 after the mass expulsions from

Moscow and Kiev. They were at their busiest, however, after the Kishinev *pogrom* of 1903 and the Russo-Japanese war of 1904. The new arrivals, settling in the streets adjoining the original Jewish quarter, soon constituted a solid block that extended from the eastern fringes of the City, through Houndsditch and Middlesex Street to Commercial Street. To the north of the Whitechapel Road, the movement was eastwards from Spitalfields to Mile End New Town. 'The newcomers', said a contemporary description:

> ... *have gradually replaced the English population in whole districts which were formerly outside the Jewish quarter. Formerly in Whitechapel, Commercial Street roughly divided the Jewish haunts of Petticoat Lane and Goulston Street from the rougher English quarter lying to the east. Now the Jews have flowed across this line; Hanbury Street, Fashion Street, Pelham Street, Booth Street, Old Montague Street, and many other streets and lanes and alleys have fallen before them; they fill whole blocks of model dwellings ... and they live and crowd together, and work and meet their fate almost independent of the great stream of London life surging round them.*
> (Booth, 1902, vol. 3, pp.103–4)

Thereafter the newcomers began to fan out, moving along an arc that stretched southwards through Whitechapel, took in the western tip of Mile End Old Town, and extended down to the north-western portion of St George's-in-the-East.

Cross with me now into the triangle bounded by the Mile End Road (on the north), Commercial Road on the south and Jubilee Street on the east (Figure 8.5 again). Mind where you step. The horses are messy as well as dangerous! Note the high proportion of streets classified as between 75 and 100 per cent Jewish. The opening of new synagogues – in Fieldgate Street, Philpot Street, Nelson Street and Jubilee Street – between 1900 and 1914, and the formation of Sephardish congregations, suggest that all these streets comprised the principal area of Jewish settlement, comparable to that of Spitalfields. Across Commercial Road in St George's-in-the-East, the Judaization of the streets was equally dramatic. Whereas in Mayhew's time the main nucleus of Jewish settlement did not extend east of Leman Street, the map in Figure 8.5 shows the in-filling in the square bounded by Cannon Street Road in the east and Cable Street in the south. Clearly, as Arkell's map shows, the mid-century gap between Mile End Old Town and the western nuclei of settlement had been closed.

3   COMMUNITY CREATION

So far I have described the territorial distribution of Jewish settlements.

How, though, can these spatial patterns be explained?

Some general considerations are suggested in a contemporary account published in the *Sunday Magazine*, an 'improving' journal for the respectable middle classes. Mrs Brewer, the author, however, was decidedly unconventional in her approach. 'Generally', she remarked:

> ... *when writing of a people, attention is drawn almost exclusively to what we term the upper classes, for as a rule it is they who appear to make history. This example I cannot follow ... . It is of my visits to the immigrants and to the poor resident Jews that I desire to speak ... Too much has hitherto been written from hearsay, and the Jews feel they have suffered from this practice.*
> (Brewer, 1892, p.18)

Her informed and sympathetic portrait of the 'Jewish colony' appeared in the 1890s (but can now be consulted in the reprint in Englander, 1994). Let us consider what it tells us about the impact of the Jewish religion upon the pattern of Jewish settlement.

It is the centrality of religion which I found most striking in her account. Orthodox Judaism is seen as more than just a religion. Its rituals and rules, Mrs Brewer rightly remarks, inform everyday life. The old saying that 'it is not the Jews who have kept the Sabbath but the Sabbath that has kept the Jews' is readily confirmed in her observations on the ways in which Sabbath observance intensified labour, defined work and leisure, and dominated the home environment. Her fine evocation of the special atmosphere created by the lighting of the candles at the Friday night meal pinpoints important sources of family solidarity and Jewish identity. The proximity of the synagogue, noted in passing, was the foundation on which all of this rested. Prohibition of the use of any form of transport on the Sabbath and on Holy Days made it essential for the Jews to live within walking distance of a synagogue. Jewish settlement reflects this pedestrian requirement.

Other considerations, apart from Sabbath observance, included burial provision; medical aid and charitable assistance; suitable schooling for children; ritual baths for female purification; special arrangements for the slaughtering of meat and poultry; and the supervision of butchers and bakers according to Jewish Law. In a liberal democratic society, where Jewish communal organization was a voluntary affair, the infrastructure of the faith required a certain minimum population threshold for the community to be viable in economic terms. The Jewish quarter, though it had no formal territorial boundaries or legal status, thus possessed an identifiable presence which contemporaries readily recognized. And so, with Mrs Brewer, we encounter the vigilant *shomer* (i.e. supervisor/inspector) policing the butcher shops of Wentworth Street; we visit the first 'Jewish' Board School in nearby Old Castle Street, where the benevolent Mr Levi combats poverty as much as ignorance; and we call in at the nearby Jews' Free School to catch the lunch-time Hebrew classes. Here, too, lessons are not disturbed by the rumble of empty stomachs. Necessitous scholars, Mrs Brewer tells us, 'can go up-stairs to the kitchen and have a cup of hot milk and a piece of bread for their breakfast'. Taking our leave, we make our way along Whitechapel to visit the Rothschild Wards at the London Hospital where the Jewish sick were cared for. Philanthropy, we learn, was not always sufficient and Jewish recovery retarded where beds were wanting and Jewish patients had to be placed among the gentiles. Cemeteries, Mrs Brewer notes, were available at West Ham and Willesden for those who did not recover!

Apart from the network of synagogues and their attendant support systems, Mrs Brewer identified a number of other factors that helped to consolidate the sense of identity and community amongst Jewish immigrants.

Employment, language and culture were distinctive features that bound together members of the Jewish community. What was the significance of each of these?

Employment   Mrs Brewer rightly notes the predominance of tailoring in immigrant employment. The street trades of Mayhew's day have been replaced by an industrial proletariat. With the flash of the needle and the whirr of the sewing machine she evokes the domestic workshops of Old Montague Street where people sewed as if their lives depended on it – as indeed, they did! Apart from ready-made clothing, immigrants were readily found in bootmaking and in cabinet-making. Jewish industry concentrated on trades in which capital and skill requirements were minimal and cheap labour plentiful, and in which homework, the application of simple hand-driven machinery and the subdivision of labour made it possible for London employers to compete effectively with the factory-based manufacturing industries of elsewhere. 'Sweating' is simply the term which historians now use to describe this particular industrial strategy.

Jewish concentration in these trades, however, was more than just a simple reflection of the position of the immigrant worker in the labour market. As Mrs Brewer observes, labour recruitment and settlement formation relied upon the processes inherent to chain migration (Chapter 1, section 3.5). She notes that most of the passengers arriving by the Hamburg steam boat were met at the quayside 'by relations already established here'. And writing of the tailors of Old Montague Street, she tells us that 'many of the immigrants had letters to the people living there'. Armed with an introduction from family and friends, invariably the newcomer turned to the *landsmannschaften* – the support network of religious and voluntary associations transplanted from the same village or district in Eastern Europe. These bodies, as we shall see, played significant roles in the processes of adjustment, acculturation and in the geography of resettlement.

The immigrants, as I noted earlier, were anything but an undifferentiated mass. Mrs Brewer clearly thought that some were superior sorts fallen on hard times – apart, that is, from 'the rough element who come here from Amsterdam'! But the tendency to identify with *landsmen* (i.e. natives of the same locality) evidently was pronounced. 'The Polak' (Polish Jew), wrote one contemporary critic, 'imagines himself superior to the *Litvak* (Lithuanian Jew) and their antipathy is so great that a Polish swain will never be found paying court to a *Litvatchschki* [sister or daughter to a Litvak]' (Smith, 1899, p.433).

No doubt, the status distinctions based on place or origin were important, but those which once separated the Ashkenazi from the Sephardi, for example, had lost much of their force through intermarriage and business ties. Evidence for this comes from an analysis of the marriage registers at the Spanish and Portuguese Synagogue at Bevis Marks in London. Similar studies need to be undertaken of marriages among the Jewish immigrants from Eastern Europe. You might have imagined that Jacob Amdur would have married a Lithuanian at the Kovno Synagogue at Catherine Wheel Alley. Not so. By marrying Sarah Richardson he joined a family of English Jews. Moreover, it was the 'Englishness' of the Richardsons that was transmitted through the children and grandchildren. The Amdur sisters, whose conversations still ring in my ears, never spoke of the Lithuanian origins of their father and grandparents. Until I looked at the naturalization papers at the Public Record Office for the purpose of this chapter, I was quite unaware of these particular origins.

Language   It is the language of the immigrants, Mrs Brewer tell us, which defines the area of Jewish settlement and creates the initial impression of being in some distant territory. Shopkeepers with unpronounceable names selling goods advertised in an incomprehensible language, and, above all, the locals gabbling in an unknown tongue, made for a strange sense of isolation and curiosity. It also gave rise to some degree of hostility.

Misunderstandings, conflict and consternation were unavoidable where English was neither spoken nor understood. A Polish girl who got lost and became confused was taken by the police to an asylum for the insane; a rabbi who went to a register office to make enquiries was married by mistake and had to seek an annulment! Effective policing, too, was impossible where the people spoke little English and the police spoke nothing else (Englander, 1992, pp.97–8). Mrs Brewer, a German speaker, experienced few language difficulties. Others found communication much more trying. A witness before the Select Committee on the immigration of foreigners was asked if he agreed with the statement '… but for the street architecture one might easily imagine the place to be the busy quarters of an Eastern town'. The respondent, a local man, in accounting for Jewish concentration, explained:

> … the Jew is naturally attracted to that situation where his language is understood, and where his requirements would be understood, just as you find is the case in Saffron-hill with the Italians, and in Soho with the French … . It is only natural that they would go where they could talk to people, and where their talk would be understood.
>
> (Parliamentary Papers, 1888, qq.2829–30)

Yiddish today, like Latin, is an academic rather than a living language. The everyday idioms and expressions, that once filled the air in Spitalfields and Whitechapel, have given way to a much more formal bookish knowledge of Yiddish, which makes up in cultivation what it lacks in spontaneity. In Mrs Brewer's day, though, Yiddish was the most audible expression of a distinctive and vibrant culture. The religious dimension was pronounced. The *mezuzah*, displayed on the door-post of every house, she recalls, is 'one of the first things which struck my notice'. Equally memorable is the *sheitel*, the 'ugly brown wig' worn by Orthodox married women, which she notes, with approval, is increasingly being repudiated by their younger and better acculturated sisters. And, had she been present during the festivals of *Purim* or *Simchat Torah,* no doubt she would have drawn attention to the processions and celebrations that enlivened life in the immigrant quarter. This, then, is a comparatively safe environment, relatively isolated from the world outside by the sheer density of numbers, bound together by a common language.

Culture   Mrs Brewer's account, alas, neglects the secular culture of the immigrant quarter. The versatility and creativity of the newcomers was, however, embodied in an assertive, ethnically based, popular culture which still awaits its historian. Here, we can do no more than map the contours. Self-generated social institutions were manifold. Some, like the 15,000-strong Jewish Friendly Societies movement, were as much concerned with the allocation of social honour as with the provision of social insurance. Its east European origins and *landsmannschaft* connection was affirmed in the Plotusk Jewish Friendly Society and in variants from such places as Cracow, Warsaw, Denenburg, Kutno, Dobrin, Lublin, Zhitomir and Stedletz. These, at any rate, were deemed respectable. The same could not be said of the various clubs, meeting halls, trade union branches and coffee shops that sprang up. Some were barely disguised gambling dens; others combined politics with entertainment. The pious condemned them; the police were vigilant. Special Branch, which kept the East End under close surveillance during the First World War, noted the concentration of political dissidents. 'A considerable number', said a report on 'Russian revolutionary matters':

> *... can be found at the New Home Restaurant, 3 Great Garden Street; Ladies Tailors Trade Union, 10 Great Garden Street; the Local No. 9 of the I.W.W. [International Workers of the World] No. 76 Great Tongue Yard, Whitechapel; ... the New York Restaurant, 128 Whitechapel Road; the Parisien Restaurant, 162 Whitechapel Road. No. 3 Great Garden Street is best attended on Saturdays and Sundays from 2 to 10 p.m., and at 10 Great Garden Street, Saturdays and Sundays between 3 and 8 p.m. The other addresses any evening.*
>
> (Quoted in Englander, 1994, pp.105–6)

Sometimes religious and secular cultures were too close for comfort. The policing difficulties of the district were much aggravated by disturbance due to the conflict between the secular and the spiritual (Englander, 1994).

Clubs, societies, coffee houses, cafés and restaurants, though they opened and closed with a startling rapidity, provided one source of sociability, the streets another. 'Wentworth Street in full swing', writes Mrs Brewer, '... is a sight worth seeing'. And while her account conveys something of the excitement of its crowded shops and barrows, it does not penetrate beyond the human aggregate to explore the conversations and encounters that were taking place. Had she paused to listen, she would almost certainly have discovered that, apart from the exchange of goods and services, information was being transmitted on private concerns and public affairs and that the interactions between customer and retailer involved considerably more than a commercial transaction. Shopkeepers and their customers, as neighbours and *landsleit* (families from the same town or village in Russian Poland), often acted as informal agents with respect to the collection and distribution of charity and other forms of assistance. These sorts of activities, though under-represented in our documentary sources, can be pursued in the oral history archives that recently have been created (Kushner, 1992). In many cases, too, they are still part of living memory. I write here from personal experience of the family butcher shop in Hope Street in which, as a small boy, I passed much of my time in the 1950s (not unlike that shown in Figure 8.6). The customers, I recall, were large, middle-aged, formidable ladies, virtually all of them the daughters of immigrant parents, who sat on a long bench propped against the wall, drinking

Figure 8.6 The photograph shows my second cousin, Esther Amdur, and her husband, Abraham Rafer, with their son, David (aged 2), outside their butcher's shop in Hessel Street, 1911. Esther's father, Nathan (Jacob Amdur's brother), came to England in 1891 and was also an East End butcher. Abraham Rafer (Roife) was born in Wolgaporna, Russia, in September 1879. He came to England alone, *c.*1902, and got a job with a butcher for two shillings and six pence a week, plus lodgings. Later he brought over a sister from Russia (Source: London Museum of Jewish Life)

large cups of tea, smoking cigarettes and discoursing on this, that and the other. The purchase of meat seemed to be a secondary affair by comparison with the energy devoted to the discussion in hand. Also, I remember, from time to time one of them would bring in bundles of neatly laundered cast-offs from her grandchildren for my benefit.

What other forms of sociability might you expect to have found?

The streets of London's Jewish East End were not only filled with shoppers. The corner of Black Lion Yard (adjacent to Great Garden Street) and Whitechapel High Street was also the location of the *hazar markt* – in direct translation the 'pig market', but in reality the hiring market where unemployed tailors and bootmakers stood around on a Saturday morning hoping to negotiate an engagement for the coming week. Once the Sabbath was over, though, Whitechapel High Street and Commercial Street became the resort of promenading couples, courting and displaying, and of young people socializing and having fun. Those who had saved their coppers might catch a show at one of the local Yiddish theatres or playhouses – and of these there were many.

--- ***EXERCISE 8.6*** ---

Here is a brief, and probably incomplete, list of those Yiddish theatres and playhouses. On your map (Figure 8.1, p.183), highlight the streets on which they could be found:

> Hebrew Dramatic Club, Princes (subsequently Princelet) Street, Spitalfields
>
> Pavilion Theatre, Whitechapel (corner of Baker's Row and Whitechapel Road)
>
> East London Theatre, Fieldgate Street, Whitechapel
>
> York Minster Music Hall, Philpot Street, Whitechapel
>
> Grand Palais, Commercial Road (east of New Road)
>
> Stamford Theatre, Shoreditch High Street (actually off map to the top left-hand side, but included here to give a fuller idea of the extent of the theatres)
>
> New Yiddish Theatre, Osborn Street (Whitechapel end of Brick Lane)

Completed map (Figure 8.7) p.225.

4 IMMIGRANTS AND THE HOST COMMUNITY

Having looked in general terms at the forces making for Jewish concentration, I want now to narrow the focus to identify certain internal and external influences upon the physical environment. First, I shall explore the significance of *landsleit* (people from the same village or region) in the formation of the immigrant quarter, and then I will look at the role of antagonism against the Jews in defining the zone of settlement.

What further sources and indicators can be used in the exploration of ethnic segregation?

Beatrice Potter's study of the Jewish community, contributed to *Life and labour of the people in London* (Booth, 1902, vol. 3, pp.169–73; reprinted in Englander, 1994, pp.197–9), is particularly helpful. Noteworthy are her observations on the role of the *chevroth* (religious confraternities) in preventing the disorientation of migrants. Contemporaries were agreed that, their ragged appearance notwithstanding, immigrant Jews were not part of the 'rough' or 'dangerous classes'. Although, occasionally, their assumed political radicalism gave cause for concern, the people from the Pale of Settlement (i.e. the designated territories within the Russian Empire where Jews were compelled to reside and work) were not, in general, to be found among the rootless, disorganized elements of the population.

Although Potter's researches were published at the close of the 1880s, it would be wrong to conclude that the *chevroth* had, simply, been transplanted from Eastern Europe during that troubled decade. Bearing in mind the importance of immigration from Europe before 1881 (see Chapter 1, section 4; Chapter 3, sections 1 and 2), it will come as no great surprise to learn that the *chevra* is first found in 1853 in the form of the *Chevra Manahem Abelim Hesed Ve'Emeth* (Society of Kindness and Truth). In essence a friendly society combined with a synagogue, this was founded by 50 Dutch Jewish workers to provide funeral and mourning facilities. Subsequently, the range of its services was enlarged and, in 1870, it became the Sandys Row (Artillery Lane) Sephardi Synagogue. The Germans followed suit with the *Chevra Bikur Cholim,* founded in Old Broad Street (now Broadgate, off map) in 1858, and later removed to Spital Square. There were similar congregations in Old Castle Street, Goulston Street, New Court (Fashion Street), White's Row, Wide Gate Street, Artillery Lane and Mansell Street. In all, there were in east London in 1870 at least 20 *chevroth*. It has been estimated that all these minor congregations accounted for more than 2,500 seat-holders and that, combined, they supplied the social and religious requirements of upwards of 10,000 souls (Lipman, 1954, pp.71–5).

Why, you may ask, did the newcomers not join established City synagogues? The answer is straightforward. The immigrant poor found membership of the major synagogues prohibitively expensive, they found the service deficient in warmth and spirituality, and they resented the Jewish native élite that monopolized the status-bearing rituals and ceremonies. The *chevra,* by contrast, as Beatrice Potter rightly recognized, represented a self-creating, self-supporting and self-governing alternative that endowed participants with a sense of dignity and independence, and gave scope for the acquisition of social honour.

Attached to the *chevra* was the *Beth Hamerdrash*, a study circle for adults, and the *cheder*, a class for the instruction of the young. Here, under the guidance of the *melammed* (teacher), the sons of the ghetto could learn Hebrew (the language of public worship) and the elements of Judaism. In sharp contrast, daughters were neglected. Jacob Amdur's five daughters were all fluent in Yiddish, but the son alone was able to follow the service of the synagogue. Immigrant women relied upon the *Beis Rachel*, a popular prayer book, written in Yiddish, with commentaries and legends.

The *chevroth*, then, were something more than social or voluntary associations for devotional purposes. To thousands of newly arrived Jews the *chevra* was, in Gartner's phrase, 'the primary cell of their social life' (Gartner, 1973, p.187). Like the friendly society movement mentioned earlier, the *chevra* had a *landsmannschaft* character that made for the reproduction in Whitechapel of the relationships characteristic of the *shtetl* (small village town). Beatrice Potter held some strange ideas about Jews – her picture of impoverished immigrants as Talmudic types ever ready to engage in scholarly disputation is, I think, rather fanciful. But she is correct in her observations on the importance of the *chevra* as a social, spiritual and cultural shock absorber. 'Usually,' she writes somewhat ungrammatically, 'each Chevras is named after the town or district in Russia or Poland from which the majority of its members have emigrated; it is, in fact, from old associations – from the ties of relationship or friendship, or, at least, from the memory of a common home – that the new association spring' (Englander 1994, p.198).

How many *chevroth* were there? Where were they situated? Unfortunately, Potter, precise in so many respects, is vague both on numbers and their distribution. Thirty or forty, she states, were scattered around the Jewish quarter. These, she adds, had been persuaded to federate by the Anglo-Jewish leadership, anxious to prevent the development of a secessionist immigrant community based on groups of small synagogues that were automonous. The Federation of Synagogues had been formed in 1887 on an initiative of Samuel Montagu, the observant bullion broker, and Liberal Member for Whitechapel, and provided generous financial assistance for the improvement of synagogal facilities. In general, Montagu sought to expose the 'foreign Jew' to the beneficent influence of the English (Alderman, 1987). A glance at the affiliates of the Federation and their addresses should give us some idea of the distribution of the East End *chevroth*.

―――――――――――――― *EXERCISE 8.7* ――――――――――――――

Have a look at the list of synagogues listed in Table 8.1 below and, on your map (Figure 8.1, p.183), mark their street locations.

Table 8.1 List of synagogues compiled from *Laws and bye-laws of the Federation of Synagogues*, London, N.P. Valentine, 1895. Copy in Booth Collection, B.197, fo. 33

'Peace & Tranquillity' Mansell Street Goodman's Fields	'Crawcour' Fieldgate Street Whitechapel	'Mile End New Town' Dunk Street Mile End New Town
'Peace & Truth' Old Castle Street Whitechapel	'Jerusalem' Union Street Whitechapel	'Mikrah' Fashion Street Spitalfields
'Polish' Cutler Street Houndsditch	'Eye of Jacob' Artillery Street Houndsditch	'Bikkur Cholim' Spital Square Spitalfields
'Sons of Covenant Friendly Society' Hope Street Whitechapel	'Kalischer Synagogue' Great Alie Street Goodman's Fields	Spital Street Spitalfields
'United Brethren of Konin' Hanbury Street Mile End New Town	'Bikkur Cholim, Sons of Lodz' New Castle Street (removed to Goulston Street) Whitechapel	New Road Mile End
'Suwalki' Hanbury Street Mile End New Town	'Warsaw Synagogue' Gun Street (off Artillery Street) Spitalfields	Vine Court Whitechapel
'United Kalisher' St Marks Street Goodman's Fields	'Kindness and Truth' Sandys Row (Artillery Lane) Houndsditch	Princes Street (marked Princelet Street) Spitalfields
'Voice of Jacob' Pelham Street Mile End New Town	'Kovno' Catherine Wheel Alley Houndsditch	Scarborough Street Goodman's Fields
'Holy Calling Benefit Society' New Street Houndsditch	'Love and Kindness' Great Prescott Street Goodman's Fields	Greenfield Street Whitechapel
'Holy Calling Benefit Society' Fashion Street Spitalfields	'Chevra Shaas' Old Montague Street Whitechapel	St Mary Street Mile End New Town
'House of David United Brethren' Fieldgate Street Whitechapel	'Kebel Hassidim' Old Montague Street Whitechapel	

Completed map (Figure 8.7) p.225.

It is important to remember that the 32 synagogues shown above only include affiliates of the Federation of Synagogues and the list, therefore, is incomplete. Among places of worship not included are the ultra orthodox secessionist congregation, the *Machzigei Hadath* (Upholders of the Law) situated at the corner of Fashion Street and Brick Lane. Still, the table does several things: it conveys some idea of the prominent position occupied by religious institutions in the culture of the immigrant population and underscores the point, made earlier, that to pray together Jews had to stay together. It also supplies an instructive comparison with the roles of nonconformist chapels in the Welsh migration and settlement process (discussed in Chapter 2, section 3). The inclusion of congregations such as the *Bikkur Cholim* in Spital Square, and those of Mansell Street, Fashion Street and Old Castle Street, indicates a certain continuity with mid-Victorian Jewish immigration, and mention of the 'Polish' Synagogue in Cutler Street connects us with earlier migrants. It also suggests a prima facie case for thinking that the *landsmannschaften* did constitute an organizing principle of immigrant settlement in east London. This is something which can be taken further. Documentary evidence containing the names and addresses of members of certain of the minor synagogues and friendly societies is available and could be explored to identify residential patterns and see how far spatial relations were influenced by place or origin (Kushner, 1992).

We should not assume that the Jewish East End was uninfluenced by the wider society. Quite the contrary. Antagonism between native (i.e. British born) and long-settled Jews and immigrant Jews, recorded by Potter in connection with the *chevroth*, represented something more than just an internal struggle for power and position. More alarming were the political implications of further mass immigrations and the ways in which the settlement in east London was evoked in the creation and definition of a specifically 'Jewish Question'. The fears of Anglo-Jewry's acculturated élite were not without substance. The growth of Jewish east London, as we shall see, was not free from trouble. From such concerns emerged a comprehensive strategy of 'Anglicization' supported by a dense and overlapping network of Anglo-Jewish communal institutions – lay, ecclesiastical, educational and philanthropic – devoted to the socialization of the immigrant masses. Not only was Yiddish to be abandoned; the newcomers were expected to quit the congested quarters in Whitechapel and Spitalfields and remove to the outlying suburbs where cultural resistance was more difficult to sustain. A Jewish Dispersion Committee was appointed in 1902 to organize their departure. Once again, we may note the instructive comparison with the social networks amongst Welsh nonconformist congregations in London and Liverpool (Chapter 2, section 3).

EXERCISE 8.8

Charles Booth, in his surveys in *Life and labour of the people in London*, likened the coming of the Jews to the slow rising of a flood (Booth, 1902, 3rd ser., vol. 2, p.3). Is this an accurate description of the settlement formation process? Look now at the Arkell map (Figure 8.5, p.190). Does it confirm or deny Booth's statement? Itemize, in no more than a dozen lines, what Arkell's map tells us about the Judaization of the streets of east London.

In the first place, probably you will have noted the existence of certain non-Jewish enclaves in the core area of settlement. There was a solid Christian presence off Lolesworth Street and Thrawl Street, in Whitechapel, and along Whitechapel High Street and the western tip of Commercial Road; there were no Jews in Dorset Street, nor in the Peabody buildings in Commercial Street; and even in the courts and alleys to the south of Old Montague Street, Jews were conspicuous by their absence. In some parts of Mile End New Town, but principally around Albert Dwellings and the blocks north of Hanbury Street and south of Underwood Street, there was little Jewish settlement.

The second feature, which requires comment, concerns the outer limits of Jewish settlement. These are sharply drawn. Not many Jews lived in the riverside districts beyond Cable Street; Bethnal Green, too, remained largely resistant to Jewish settlers. The demolition of the notorious slum in the vicinity of Old Nicholl Street in Bethnal Green (off map), the area fictionalized as the Jago, and its replacement by the London County Council's Boundary Street Estate during the late 1890s, attracted some Jewish settlement, especially in Church Street and Calvert Avenue (off map). The third of the Amdur sisters, Leah Stein, occupied No. 32 Laleham Buildings (on the Boundary Street Estate), where, with neighbours Kitty and Solly Benjamin and Mrs Levy (a widow with whom all seemed to have an intense love–hate relationship), they constituted a distinct 'Jewish' bloc. But, in general, Jews did not settle in appreciable numbers north of the line of the Great Eastern Railway until after the First World War.

What are we to make of all of this information? Is Jewish immigration and settlement appropriately described as 'an irresistible flood carrying all before it'? The imagery certainly conveys a sense of the dynamism and fluidity that were characteristic of the making of Jewish east London, and this is important. But does it explain the segregation process – why some streets succumbed while others resisted, and how settlement barriers came to be fixed in one direction rather than another? But should we not try to avoid language that is loaded? Is not the flood analogy suggestive of social disaster rather than a host–minority relationship, the character of which has yet to be established?

Booth's terminology, in my view, conceals more than it reveals. The Arkell map (Figure 8.5, p.190) seems to indicate numerous points of contact between the minority and majority populations, both within the Jewish East End and on its periphery. Some were conflictual. Tension between the immigrant and the indigenous populations arose over jobs and housing, life-styles and language. Impoverished homeworkers, interviewed by Booth or his associates in 1888, were particularly resentful. Mrs Lee, a tailoress of 50 James Place, Devonport Street, Commercial Road (off map), 'spoke bitterly of the Jews ... When you go to the warehouse they are there, a whole row of them, ready to take everything'. But it was their depressing effect upon earnings that so infuriated Mrs Goodey, a trouser machinist, when interviewed in her home at 46 Wilson Street, Stepney (off map): 'The Jews had caused the fall in prices,' she grumbled, 'everytime the work comes in they take off a $\frac{1}{2}$d. or 1d. off the price' (Booth Collection, A19, fos. 101, 115).

Shopkeepers and costermongers were also hostile. Apart from weekday competition, they suspected that minority claims for Sunday opening were nothing but a cunning attempt to create a Jewish trading monopoly. Others condemned Sunday trading as being anti-Christian and anti-social. Anglican clergy were particularly critical. Before the coming of the Jews church attendance was difficult; afterwards it seemed impossible. The displacement of the church-going population had lowered the income of the clergy and the subscriptions on which church work depended. Missionary work among the Jews, for those who had the heart to undertake it, was not merely ineffectual, it did much to excite religious and ethnic antagonisms (Englander, 1988).

The influence of inter-communal conflict on the spatial patterning in Jewish settlement in east London was well reported by journalists and social investigators. At the beginning of the 1890s Booth invited selected members of the London police to assist with the revision of the Poverty Map of 1889. For this purpose the metropolis was parcelled out into a number of beats, each patrolled conjointly by interviewer and respondent. Not only were police officers required to identify the so-called 'Jewish streets', they also presented much incidental information as to the character and make-up of the community. 'During these walks', wrote Booth, 'almost every social influence was discussed, and especially those bearing upon vice and crime, drunkenness and disorder' (Booth, 1902, final volume, p.136).

Inevitably, problems of peace-keeping directed police attention towards the processes of ghetto formation. Police observation, however, presented the growth of the area of settlement, not as the expression of a slow-forming deluge, but as a negotiated process.

The assertion of Jewish territoriality was contested, street by street, by an indigenous population that was alarmed by the inflationary effects of immigration on rented accommodation. Peace reigned only in those streets in which the issue had been decided. Where native and immigrant lived side by side, uncertainty persisted with 'friction and quarrels the inevitable result'. In streets colonized by Jewish immigrants as well as by in-migrants from Ireland, tensions ran high. Thus, Duke Street and Black Lion Yard, with their ethnically mixed populations, were both considered dangerous, and Spring Gardens (between Hanbury Street and Old Montague Street), with its mixture of poor Jews and Irish, was said to be 'a rough place for the police'. The trend, though, was towards complete territorial segregation: streets tended 'to become all Jew or remain all English' (Englander, 1989, pp.551–71).

Street supremacy, once established, was not usually subject to further challenge. Shepherd Street, where the 'Jews have been turned out by a set of rough English and Irish', was one of the few streets to have changed hands twice. In general, the non-Jewish population appears to have relied upon spontaneous and unorganized forms of intimidation to prevent Jewish settlement. Chief Superintendent Thomas Arnold, head of H. Division (Whitechapel and Spitalfields), told the select committee on foreign immigration that Jews were frequently assaulted by 'the lower order of British roughs' (Englander, 1994, p.96). It is possible that much of the apparently mindless Jew-bashing, reported by police and others, is better understood as the expression of a defensive territorialism that came most readily to the poor and politically marginalized classes (see Boal, 1976; Huttman et al., 1991; Timms, 1971). Note, too, the observations of Carter and Lewis in this volume (Chapter 6, sections 4 and 5).

Violence, however, was only a part of the repertoire of resistance. Popular hostility could be mobilized in more subtle ways. An example of this comes from the 'model' dwelling of Katharine Buildings in the East End (further described in Volume 1, Chapter 5) which the Abrahams family left after two weeks because, said Hyman Abrahams, 'the children of the buildings hated them as Jews' (O'Day, forthcoming). In the core area of the settlement locality, too, the tendency was towards segregation. The lodging house population of Flower Street, Dean Street and Thrawl Street, which survived well into the inter-war years, was given a wide berth. The Amdur sisters spoke of the inmates as the worst kind of *goyim* (gentiles). These people – described as 'low-lives', 'louse-bags', *novkes* (prostitutes), 'Irish' and worse – were remembered as quarrelsome and violent. 'You should have heard the screams, David. It made your blood freeze!' The Amdurs' experience was by no means uncommon. Their memories, as Jerry White's oral history of Rothschild Buildings in Wentworth Street has shown, were shared by others of that generation (White, 1980, pp.121–8).

——————————————————— *EXERCISE 8.9* ———————————————————

Read the following extracts from the local newspaper, the *East London Observer*, and the Toynbee Hall Inquiry into the *Jew in London* (Russell and Lewis, 1901). How do these reports qualify the account given above?

Rent Riots in Ernest Street

The position in regard to Ernest Street, Stepney, is unique. So strong, indeed, is the local feeling that, at present, a number of houses are empty because incoming tenants are seriously threatened if they take the house at the higher rent their lives won't be worth many years purchase. Some of the houses are already wrecked, windows and doors are broken and burst; the surrounding population is in a general state of ferment, and the evictions which take place daily only tend to fan the flame. In essentials a Judenhetze [hatred of Jews] prevails, and though we do not believe there is anything more than a local significance, it is of course quite obvious that such a feeling ought not to be encouraged, because, although its beginning may be small, like a rivulet, its ending may be great.

(East London Observer, c.1899, reprinted in Englander, 1983, p.121)

Anti-Jewish Feeling

In those districts on the edge of the foreign quarter, where the native population is thus being driven out, there is naturally a considerable amount of hostile feeling. And seeing that the method by which this victorious progress is achieved commonly consists in paying abnormally high rents, and defraying the expense, in defiance of all laws of decency and sanitation, by taking in a sufficient quantity of lodgers, the indignation which is aroused is by no means groundless or unjust. At the present moment this is the most widespread and acute grievance against the foreign element; and it … opens up some very serious questions.

(Russell and Lewis, 1901, p.16)

Clearly, these extracts identify housing struggles and the price of accommodation as the prime generator of inter-communal conflict. The period of mass immigration, coinciding with an intensive burst of street clearances and other 'improvements', had a devastating effect upon the stock of housing. Overcrowding and rents shot up in response to the particular pressures exerted by the immigrants upon an already tight housing market. And, as rents rose, tension mounted.

Both accounts also direct attention towards the localization of conflict on the periphery. Ernest Street, it will be noted, was on the frontier of the Jewish East End, lying just beyond Stepney Green, south of the Mile End Road off White Horse Lane (off map to the east). The Booth inquiry received similar testimony. Booth's police collaborators acknowledged the existence of exclusion zones which Jews entered at their peril. The slums around the Old Nicholl in Bethnal Green, before the clearances for the Boundary Street Estate, was one such quarter. 'No Jews have set their foot in this district', said Sergeant Trench, 'They would not dare to, they would be so roughly handled' (Englander, 1989, p.564). The Royal Commission on Alien Immigration, too, heard evidence that native resistance to Jewish encroachment was fiercest in these frontier districts. Jews who tried to settle in the riverside areas, it was claimed, were likely to get their heads kicked in (Englander, 1994, pp.92–3). One might also note the location of anti-Jewish disturbances during the First World War in Blythe Street and Teesdale Street (known locally as 'Jew Island') to the north of Old Bethnal Green Road (off map) (Englander, 1991, pp.113–16).

5   CONCLUSION

What conclusions should we draw from all of this? One scholar, who has made a long-term study of the significance of political violence in east London, has suggested that the incidents described above are evidence of an enduring racially exclusive vigilantist culture which took shape during the years of Jewish immigration from Eastern Europe (Husbands, 1982, pp.3–6). More research needs to be undertaken before the argument is self-standing. Too little is known about the social dynamics of the inter-communal street confrontations, about the urban ecology in which they occurred, and about the status and character of the local expulsionists. Looking at the Arkell map (Figure 8.5, p.190), one is struck by the variable outcome of all these considerations. I wonder, too, whether in areas like south-east Spitalfields, where aggression had failed, did residents quickly develop avoidance strategies? And whether, in effect, these regulated relationships between what had become the Jewish majority and the indigenous minority?

5.1 DISPERSAL OF THE JEWISH COMMUNITY

One strategy, which I have not as yet considered, was simply to quit the area. Until now, my emphasis has been on the formation of the Jewish East End. It should not be forgotten that, while the inflow exceeded the outflow, the migration of Jews to the suburbs of north-east and north-west London was already advanced *before* the outbreak of the First World War, and became even more so in the years that followed (Lipman, 1962–67, pp.78–103). Acculturation and embour-geoisement were reflected in significant changes in the spatial distribution of the community, above all in the abandonment of the Whitechapel ghetto. Whereas, in 1889, 90 per cent of the Jewish population lived in east London, only 60 per cent did so 40 years later. By then an 'E.1' address was the hallmark of social failure: those with a 'Bishopsgate' telephone number claimed it was for business only; those without a telephone kept *stum* (silent)! The destruction of the built environment and the dispersal of the community during the Second World War completed the process. By 1949 the East End accounted for less than a tenth of London's Jewish population. Numbers dwindled rapidly thereafter. The *mikvahs* (ritual baths) closed, the synagogues were relocated, kosher butchers retired and cultural life collapsed. Jewish east London, which once seemed so permanent, had lasted less than one hundred years. Like all Jews, the Amdurs were affected: one moved to Stamford Hill, one to Hackney, and one retired to Brighton. The eldest and the youngest sisters remained. Their children, however, left the area and, in doing so, they left behind the identity that went with it. Jacob and Sarah Amdur had nine grandchildren. Seven of the nine had children, and all but two of them married non-Jews. Today, they live in California, New York, Indiana, Grenoble, Hertfordshire, Maidstone and, also, in Milton Keynes.

5.2 ONLY CONNECT ...

Jewish east London, as presented above, raises more questions than it answers. What I have tried to do is to map the pattern of Jewish settlement and indicate some possible connections between community and social geography. 'Only connect', the epigrammatical expression of the 1960s, remains a useful injunction which underscores the import-ance of contextualization both in terms of what is known and what needs to be discovered.

_____ *EXERCISE 8.10* _____

By way of conclusion, I should like you to look back over Volume 2 and consider the following questions:

1   What bearing does our case study in this chapter have on the discussion in Chapter 6 (sections 4.2 and 5.2) on ethnicity as a factor of residential differentiation?

2   To what extent does this study of Jewish east London confirm more general patterns and processes concerning residential segregation and immigrant groups?

3   What similarities and differences can you identify between:

(a)   the Pakistanis in Manchester (discussed in Chapter 7, section 1; also in Werbner, 1979);

(b)   the Irish in Cardiff (see Chapter 6, section 4.2); and

(c)   the east London Jews as given above?

4   Bearing in mind our discussion of the genesis of a racially vigilantist counter-culture in east London, you might like to reflect upon the interaction of minority religious and ethnic groups within the wider society and the ways in which new community identities can be formed within the receiving population. (This would make an exciting project!)

Some migrants arrive from overseas, most from inland. Few of us, I suspect, are from families that have been rooted to the same spot for more than two or so generations. Sooner or later we all become migrants. The example of east European Jewry, which I have chosen to examine, indicates some possible connections involving the settlement of one particular minority and the formation of local identities and communities.

Inevitably, reasons for differences, separation and conflict occupy much space – both in contemporary observation and in memory – but they should not obscure the dynamic nature of identity formation and the ways in which this is influenced by wider social processes. There are two points to remember here: (1) we are as much concerned with traditions of tolerance as with charges of racial antagonism; and (2) you need not be a member of a minority ethnic or religious group to relate to a particular neighbourhood or community.

QUESTION FOR RESEARCH

That being so, you might care to consider how your own life experiences compare with mine. Start with your own family, its myths and memories, and try to locate its movements in time and space. Map the area in which your people settled and try to identify the personal and institutional networks they either helped to sustain or created. Ask yourself: 'How far did the interaction of family and environment lead to the construction of a distinctive and coherent outlook?'. Account for the circumstances of the formation of this outlook. Compare your own approaches and findings with those presented in this chapter (and elsewhere in this volume). Examine the local records available in your public library or archive office. Some are remarkably rich in newspapers, census returns, documentary collections and oral records. If the latter are insufficient, why not collect your own material?

NOTE ON ORIGINAL AND MANUSCRIPT SOURCES

Jacob Amdur's petition for naturalization with police observations (see p.181) is to be found at the Public Record Office in HO 144/718/110316. The naturalization files at the Public Record Office are indexed by name and year and include information on the applicant's nationality, place of birth, parents, age, occupation, civil status and place of residence in the previous five years. Materials relating to the survey of *Life and labour of the people in London* are included in the Booth Collection, British Library of Political and Economic Science, London.

REFERENCES AND FURTHER READING

Note: entries marked with an asterisk are suggestions for further reading.

Alderman, G. (1987) *The Federation of Synagogues, 1887–1987,* London, Federation of Synagogues.

Anon. (1865) 'The Jewish community in England', *Chambers' Journal of Popular Literature,* pp.582–6.

Anon. (1884) 'Report of Lancet Special Sanitary Commission on the Polish colony of Jew tailors', *The Lancet,* 3 May, pp.817–18.

Boal, E.W. (1976) 'Ethnic residential segregation', in Herbert, D.J. and Johnston, R.J. (eds) *Social areas in cities.* Vol. 1 *Spatial processes and form,* London, Wiley.

Booth, C. (1902) *Life and labour of the people in London,* 17 vols, London, Macmillan.

Booth Collection, London, British Library of Political and Economic Science.

Brewer, Mrs (1892) 'The Jewish Colony in London', *Sunday Magazine*, xxi, pp.16–20, 119–23, reprinted in Englander (1994).

Buckman, J. (1983) *Immigrants and the class struggle: the Jewish immigrants in Leeds, 1880–1914*, Manchester, Manchester University Press.[*]

Drake, M. (ed.) (1994) *Time, family and community: perspectives on family and community history*, Oxford, Blackwell in association with The Open University (Course Reader).

Englander, D. (1983) *Landlord and tenant in urban Britain 1838–1918*, Oxford, Clarendon Press.

Englander, D. (1988) 'Late Victorian Jewry', in *A331 Religion in Victorian Britain*, audio-cassette 2, side 2, AC1183, Milton Keynes, The Open University.

Englander, D. (1989) 'Booth's Jews: the presentation of Jews and Judaism in *Life and labour of the people in London*', *Victorian Studies*, xxxii, pp.551–71.

Englander, D. (1991) 'Police and public order in Britain, 1914–1918', in Emsley, C. and Weinberger, B. (eds) *Policing Western Europe: politics, professionalism and public order, 1850–1940*, New York, Greenwood.

Englander, D. (1992) 'Stille Huppah (Quiet Marriage) among immigrant Jews in Britain', *The Jewish Journal of Sociology*, xxxiv, pp.85–109.

Englander, D. (1994) *A documentary history of Jewish immigrants in Britain, 1840–1920*, Leicester, Leicester University Press.[*]

Fishman, W.J. (1988) *East End 1888*, London, Duckworth.[*]

Gartner, L.P. (1973) *The Jewish immigrant in England 1870–1914*, 2nd edn, London, Simon Publications.[*]

Henriques, U.R.Q. (ed.) (1993) *The Jews of South Wales: historical studies*, Cardiff, University of Wales Press.[*]

Holmes, C. (1991) 'Historians and immigration', in Pooley, C.G. and Whyte, I.D. (eds) *Migrants, emigrants and immigrants*, London and New York, Routledge. Reprinted in Drake (1994).

Husbands, C.T. (1982) 'East end racism 1900–1980: geographical continuities in vigilantist and extreme right-wing political behaviour', *London Journal*, viii, pp.3–26.

Huttman, E.D., Blauw, W. and Saltman, J. (eds) (1991) *Urban housing: segregation of minorities in Western Europe and the United States*, Durham and London, Drake University Press.

Kushner, T. (ed.) (1992) *The Jewish heritage in British history*, London, Frank Cass.

Lipman, V.D. (1954) *A social history of the Jews in England 1850–1950*, London, Watts.

Lipman, V.D. (1962–67) 'The rise of Jewish suburbia', *Transactions of the Jewish Historical Society of England*, xxi, pp.78–103.

Lipman, V.D. (1972) 'The development of London Jewry', in Levine, S.S. (ed.) *A century of Anglo-Jewish life*, London, United Synagogue.

Mayhew, H. (1861) *London labour and the London poor*, 4 vols, London, Griffin, Bohn.

O'Day, R. (forthcoming) *Potter, Pycroft and Paul: the sweet trinity and Katharine Buildings, 1885–1890*.

O'Day. R. and Englander, D. (1993) *Mr Charles Booth's inquiry: life and labour of the people in London reconsidered*, London, Hambledon.

Parliamentary Papers (1888) xi; (1889) x *Report of Select Committee on Emigration and Immigration (Foreigners) with Minutes of Evidence*.

Russell, C. and Lewis, H.S. (1901) *The Jew in London: a study of racial character and present-day conditions*, London, T. Fisher Unwin.

Smith, D. (1988) *Maps and plans for the local historian and collector*, London, Batsford.

Smith, J. (1899) 'The Jewish immigrant', *Contemporary Review*, lxxvi, pp.425–36.

Timms, D.W.G. (1971) *The urban mosaic: towards a theory of residential differentiation*, London, Cambridge University Press.

Werbner, P. (1979) 'Avoiding the ghetto: Pakistani migrants and settlement shifts in Manchester', *New Community*, 7, 3, pp.376–89. Reprinted in Drake (1994).

White, J. (1980) *Rothschild Buildings: life in an East End tenement block 1887–1920*, London, Routledge and Kegan Paul.

Williams, B. (1976) *The making of Manchester Jewry 1740–1875*, Manchester, Manchester University Press.[*]

PART IV

REFLECTING ON THE ISSUES

❖ ❖ ❖

CHAPTER 9

COMMUNITY AND COMMUNITY HISTORY

by Ruth Finnegan (section 1) and W.T.R. Pryce (section 2)

1 COMMUNITY: WHAT IS IT AND HOW CAN WE INVESTIGATE IT?

by Ruth Finnegan

How do we investigate community history? Some points will already be obvious: that we need to move beyond individual people or families to study the relationships between them, that communities involve change, movement and migration, not just stability. We can also try invoking some of the more explicit theories about the history of communities in the nineteenth- and twentieth-century British Isles, or about the history of community more generally.

Among such theories, one common image is the 'Golden Age' myth: that communities in the past, unlike now, were harmonious and stable, part of a world we have lost. In fact, however popular this theory, like the somewhat similar nostalgic vision of the 'traditional' family, it turns out to have little, if any, support in historical terms (see, for example, the discussion in Anderson, 1983). Conflict, movement and change are to be found in earlier centuries too, not least in the Victorian era where the 'Golden Age' is sometimes assumed to be located!

A more acceptable generalization is of a gradual change over the centuries (especially the last two centuries) from typically isolated, self-sufficient and close-knit communities to a stage marked by increased population movements, diversity, urban and industrial settings, and fewer stable personal ties. The disruption caused by the Industrial Revolution is often seen as the watershed in this development from 'pre-industrial' to 'industrial' communities.

This long-established theory has attracted wide support, and is alluded to and developed at various points earlier in this volume (e.g. Chapter 6). There are counter-arguments too. Some scholars are sceptical about claims about universal or simple consequences from industrializ- ation (e.g. O'Brian and Quinault, 1993; Jackson and Moch, 1989; Anderson, 1983), or see the more extreme versions of this theory as just another version of the same old Golden Age myth.

A more specific generalization concerns the history of working-class communities in Great Britain. Community studies of both villages and working-class areas within towns in the 1950s (see Frankenberg, 1966) seemed to demonstrate the persistence of vital and autonomous working-class communities right into the twentieth century, based on close personal and family relationships. Others question the conclusions and methodology of such research, however, or suggest that such communities resulted from particular economic and demographic conditions which 'only really emerged even in limited areas of the country in the late nineteenth century and ... were already disappearing when first "discovered" by the sociologists of the 1950s' (Anderson, 1983, p.3).

A final view is that, at root, there have been no *essential* changes at the community level – people still interact, live, love, quarrel, further their own interests, just as they always have. And yet, against that, have there not been successive influential changes over the last two centuries in demographic, economic, political, communication, or residential patterns, affecting the constraints and opportunities within which people live in communities? (See earlier chapters in this volume on the effects, for example, of population movements, urbanization, or the emerging patterns of settling and moving and their dynamics over time; also Mills, 1993.)

These various theories are still the subject of discussion and controversy. What *is* clear, however, is the need for research on *specific* localities or groups in order to throw light on these and similar generalizations. This is where small-scale projects can play an important role. But to engage in such research effectively – both enhancing our understanding of the differences and similarities over territorial space and time, and interacting with the general theories – we need to look a bit more closely at that central term 'community'. For, unless we know what it means, it is scarcely easy to investigate its history!

1.1   SO WHAT DO WE MEAN BY 'COMMUNITY'?

Like 'family', the word 'community' sounds simple. A general definition might be 'an area of social living marked by some degree of *social coherence*. The bases of community are *locality* and *community sentiment*' (quoted in Frankenberg, 1966, p.15). Fine, as far as it goes. But look more closely. There are, in fact, a number of different, if overlapping, senses here (see Schema A).

> *Schema A: Some meanings of 'community'*
>
> 1   A locality (perhaps the most common meaning).
>
> 2   Some grouping sharing common interests, not necessarily localized.
>
> 3   A locality or grouping bound by close ties, such as kinship or neighbourliness.
>
> 4   A sense of belonging together.
>
> 5   A claim or invitation to observe common ties or interests.

We need to sort these out, not only to avoid confusion but also, more positively, because each meaning points to *different* – and interesting – questions for investigation.

1   *A locality.* This is certainly one central meaning, both in this volume and elsewhere. You will recall the many examples of localized communities, towns and subtowns (Chapter 5); villages, hamlets and suburbs (Chapter 6); rural Irish communities (Chapter 7); Jewish east London (Chapter 8); and perhaps the shifting and only partially localized community of Pakistani immigrants in Manchester (Chapter 7; Werbner, 1979). Further examples could be a parish; an Irish townland; a ward within a town; or just a set of buildings, or a single street – involving a study of social make-up either at one point in time, or the changes through many years.

2   *Some grouping sharing common interests.* Dispersed occupational, cultural or religious groupings are also referred to as 'communities' (e.g. the 'academic community', 'ethnic' communities, the 'Welsh community' in Liverpool or London – see Chapter 2). Such usages do *not* necessarily entail spatial closeness.

3   *A locality or grouping bound by close ties, such as those of kinship or neighbourliness.* This sense, too, is a common one. It recalls, as well, Tönnies' famous depiction of *Gemeinschaft* as the warm, personal 'community', contrasting with the artificial, impersonal *Gesellschaft* or 'association' (see Bell and Newby, 1971, p.23 ff.). This meaning also raises researchable (if complex) questions. How far *are* people integrated by kinship links, friendship, common interests, mutual support? Are such ties based on consensus or harmony? And can internal conflict (or, indeed, external threat) be one kind of community tie?

4   *A sense of belonging.* This overlaps other meanings, but emphasizes the *subjective* side of shared identity – people's ideas and feelings. Thus, for some scholars, what makes 'community' is not physical contiguity or even shared interests, but the perceptions and symbols people share (Cohen, 1985; Strathern, 1981). Or, in the words of the Punjabi Muslim poet Iqbal, a community is 'born' when it reaches a state of 'self-consciousness' (quoted in Werbner, 1990, p.1). This meaning opens up questions about whether this 'sense of belonging' differs for different individuals or groupings even within the same 'community', or at different times or situations (well demonstrated, for example, in Townsend and Taylor, 1975; also in studies of 'ethnic' identity such as Werbner, 1990).

These last two senses often imply 'community as a Good Thing'. There are overtones of well-being, harmony and closeness. It is thus sometimes tempting for researchers and participants alike to use the word 'community' when they want to project an idealized image (subliminally perhaps!) rather than *investigate* whether there really was consensus and affection, and in what way. This leads on to the final meaning of 'community'.

5   *A claim or exhortation to observe common ties or interests.* If community partly rests on people's relative and subjective belonging, it follows that 'communities' can be created through people *becoming* aware of these links. A feeling of shared community can thus *emerge* out of particular experiences: whether because of some conflict with others, the heightening of consciousness through political actions, or new ways of classifying particular categories of people. Researchers themselves can 'create' community by their questions and conclusions! So, too, can people narrating and crystallizing their experiences through 'community publishing' or oral history collecting (see Bornat, 1992).

In one way such creations are fictions. They prove neither the prior and permanent existence of an explicit community, nor total agreement among its members. On the other hand, such creative fictions represent a normal human process through which people, now and in the past, have (sometimes in both senses of the word) forged their links or their common interests – whether middle-class residents in a modern 'garden village' suburb, the 'community' of 'the Irish' in nineteenth-century North America or the Irish in twentieth-century Coventry (King *et al.*, 1989), or the many examples described in this volume. Once again, the poet Iqbal pertinently speaks of a community 'creating its own history [out of] a thousand images' (quoted in Werbner, 1990, p.1) – just as British Pakistanis in Manchester 'create their community out of their shared memories, their myths, about the early years of their migration to Manchester. Their community is born out of their common perceptions of the society in which they live' (Werbner, 1990, p.1).

Indeed, perhaps all communities are continuously '*becoming*' rather than 'being' (to adapt Werbner's comment, 1990, p.2). Investigating this process over time for a specific case could be an interesting research topic: how community awareness arose or diminished, or how a 'community myth' emerged from particular events and interests.

Sometimes this 'warm' sense of 'community' is harnessed to bring pressure on people in the form of political or religious rhetoric designed to emphasize links precisely because they are *not* as strong as the speakers wish; or to promote a homogeneity that not everyone actually agrees about (think of labels like 'the Jewish community', 'the Asian community' or 'the Roman

Catholic community'). Invoking 'community' like this is sometimes just wishful thinking, but can also be a direct attempt at political mobilization or manipulation. Either way, researchers should not be misled!

A given place or group may be a community (more, or less) in several of these senses simultaneously. Still, never assume that, once you have said 'community', *all* the meanings automatically apply. Rather, use the term as the jumping-off ground for *investigating* different possibilities and for spotting just which meaning is the focus of your own research, or the research of someone else. Being aware of these varying aspects of 'community' alerts you to use the term not only critically – being sceptical, for example, of the rhetoric underlying objective-sounding statements about 'communities' – but also constructively for research.

1.2   THE RELATIVITY OF COMMUNITY

If the first lesson is the need to unpack and investigate different senses of 'community', there is also a second and extremely important point. A 'community', it turns out, is not something clearly demarcated, of which people either are or are not members. As will by now be obvious, people are simultaneously attached to many localities: their own neighbourhood, street, ward, town, region, nation, continent; and probably to various interest groups too – a church, occupational group or whatever. They belong to *several* communities, and perhaps different ones at different times or for different purposes.

Interesting questions thus arise about people's multi-community membership. Who lives where, how close, how permanently, interacting with whom? Are some members of a 'community' absent (emigrants or out-migrants perhaps), but still in touch? Are there circles of 'community', nearer and further? Have new modes of transport and communication over the last two centuries changed the scale of 'local'? In any given case the answers may not be obvious – and could repay investigation.

It could even be asked how far *any* communities are fully bounded or definitive units. Keith Robbins put it well when discussing 'the identity' of nineteenth-century Britain, and the relationships between England, Scotland and Wales: 'It is an oversimplification ... to take borders and frontiers too seriously. There were many "Norths" and many "Souths" and the boundary was not fixed. Different criteria ... produce different "frontiers"' (Robbins, 1988, p.6; Colley, 1992).

It is tempting to reify a locality – or a group of people – by labelling it 'a community', implying something permanent, exclusive and separate. But even within a 'single' community there will be *internal* divisions, and differing groups who at various times belong together more, or less, or in differing senses – well exemplified in the study by Phillips (1986) of natives and incomers in Muker parish, North Yorkshire. There are also the other, overlapping, communities at various levels – local, regional, national, occupational, religious – to which, again, people more or less belong, depending on their viewpoints, their own movements and their situations at any given point of time. And each of these levels may influence their actions and perceptions (for further comments in the context of local history, see Phythian-Adams, 1991; Schürer, 1991; Mills, 1993).

There are important historical questions here. For the community identity of a particular locality or group will vary over *time*. Active social ties or a sense of belonging may become weaker (or stronger) over the generations. The extent of internal heterogeneity or of population stability may change. So that which is a 'community' at one time may not be so at another – or anyway, not in the same sense. These dynamics of change provide a further set of research questions.

1.3 STUDYING COMMUNITY AND COMMUNITIES

Precisely because it *is* an emotive and ambiguous concept, it is particularly interesting to investigate in what sense some specific area or grouping could be called a 'community', and how this has changed over time. Some practical suggestions for such research are put forward in the paper by Dennis and Daniels (1981) on the social geography of Victorian cities, laying out specific characteristics for researchers to investigate. Rather than taking 'community' as a once-and-for-all entity, Dennis and Daniels break it down into a series of possible characteristics (summarized in Schema B: though initially developed for Victorian cities, their scheme could also be applied to small towns and villages, and to other periods).

Schema B: Indices of 'community'

o   Residential stability.

o   Distance between residence and workplace.

o   Kinship and marriage links.

o   Affiliation with local clubs, churches and other interest groups.

Source: based on Dennis and Daniels (1981)

Such indicators have their ambiguities, and need to be interpreted with caution. But as the authors argue, 'the more indices of community life that are available the more advantaged we are to assess the significance of any one' (Dennis and Daniels, 1981, p.19). All are, in one way or another, susceptible to enquiry using sources such as the census, directories, ratebooks, business records, church and club records and yearbooks, supplemented by literary accounts, or local newspapers (we might also add maps and photographs, and, for more recent periods, oral sources). Their list also gives a framework for linking with comparative researches on other localities.

--- *EXERCISE 9.1* ---

Look back at Schema A on p.210. How far do Dennis' and Daniels' indices in Schema B fit with the five meanings there?

Not surprisingly, many of the same ideas recur. Kinship and shared interests surface in each. Residential stability links with the idea of locality. A 'sense of belonging' might be partially translated into Dennis' and Daniels' fourth indicator. Putting the two schemas together reinforces, again, the multiplicity, and also the overlap, within the simple-sounding term 'community'.

How about applying these ideas to the study of a particular community (in any of the above senses)? The following exercise gives one example.

--- *EXERCISE 9.2* ---

Go back to Chapter 8 and make brief notes on how far and in what sense you would consider Jewish east London a 'community' by testing it against the indicators and meanings in Schemas A and B here (there is some further background in Chapter 3, section 2). The answers are left to your judgement.

You were probably unable to find all the answers (a need for more research perhaps?). But practising this kind of analysis should take you further than just revising the themes of one illustrative case study. It should also help to equip you for the demanding – but enjoyable – task of investigating some community of your own choice, drawing on your own sources.

QUESTIONS FOR RESEARCH
---

1   Can any or all of the indicators in Schema B be investigated for either a given locality or a non-localized community using sources accessible to you? If so, how do your conclusions compare with findings from elsewhere (e.g. in this volume, or in Dennis and Daniels, 1981)? Do your investigations make you want to refine your own definition of 'community'?

2   Test out the hypothesis (Dennis and Daniels, 1981, p.8 ff.) that: 'Short-distance and circular mobility is characteristic of nineteenth-century working-class areas' by examining relevant sources for a small locality (see, for example, Chapter 2, section 2.1). If the hypothesis turns out *not* to apply, that is worth discovering too! Are there variations with area or date?

3   How far can a project in which you are interested be illuminated by analysing it in terms of some or all of the meanings or indicators of 'community' discussed above?

Your sources and methods will vary with your particular case and question, but may well include: CEBs; church and club records; electoral rolls and ratepayers books; directories; newspapers and other literary sources; and, for recent examples, oral sources. Make your research manageable by taking a *small-scale and limited community.*

Other hypotheses or questions could be derived from the discussion above; from Dennis and Daniels (1981) or Phillips (1986); or from Questions for Research earlier in this volume (you may now find the earlier chapters on migration taking on new relevance).

The questions raised by looking closely at 'community' can encourage both more precise and more imaginative research into the history of social groupings, whether locally or non-locally based, as well as giving the opportunity of relating this to work by other scholars. The final point, then, is that researchers into community history need both to be aware of the wider theories and debates, *and* to relate them to small-scale and specific studies, deepening our understanding of the differing ways in which people live together now and how they lived together in the past.

2   CONCLUSIONS

by W.T.R. Pryce

In making the transition from family history to community history we have surveyed a large number of different analytical methods and approaches. In consequence, the main themes of this volume are characterized more, perhaps, by their variety and differences than by concentration on just one or two particular research techniques. Constant throughout, however, is our concern with the need to conduct *local* studies in particular communities, on a scale that is manageable for the lone researcher drawing on local resources. Because worthwhile original contributions can be accomplished at the micro level of research, this is our deliberate decision. But, at the same time, we have placed considerable emphasis on the need to set small-scale investigations in a wider context. Taking a major theme from this volume and, in the context of your own research project, making it your own, must be regarded as an essential aspect of your work.

No research project in family and community history should ever be allowed to glide into a siding – or perhaps, dead-end buffers! – simply due to the short focus of its conception or its domination just by the specific and the unique. In this book we have provided you with numerous direction indicators. And when it might be wise to proceed with caution in certain directions, we have included some warning signals. In providing you with a choice of different tracks on which to run, we have taken you to some major research junctions that can provide ideas for a number of different itineraries. Here and there we have made suggestions for a change of emphasis; or, alternatively, we have pointed to opportunities for a switch of direction that could lead to substantially new and original lines for further investigation.

Some research projects may turn out to be like main-line journeys, contributing directly to the scholarly literature on major topics. Others, in their own ways just as valid, will be more akin to branch-line excursions. In drawing on existing knowledge in history or from one or other of the social sciences, these latter routes might take you through old research landscapes, or, perhaps, through familiar areas that now, in the light of new ideas, appear to have gained a certain freshness and new meaning. Whichever path you find yourself following, we hope that the advice and guidance offered in this volume will help to make your journey an informed one.

As stated in the Introduction, our exemplars and case studies have been drawn from published work on many different locations within the British Isles, including Ireland. Indeed, because of the substantial contribution made by the Irish people to so very many aspects of life, we feel that it would have been quite inappropriate to have excluded the important Irish dimension. On the other hand, we are conscious that not every region within any of the countries of the United Kingdom or in Ireland is represented in this volume. In some cases this may be because research on a particular locality has still to be undertaken. Yes, openings do exist for further work which, in some circumstances, will turn out to be a new and original contribution. As pointed out in the previous section, a very substantial need still remains for conclusions derived from the study of one specific locality or community to be tested and verified elsewhere.

Our selection of case studies has been guided, to a considerable degree, by the research completed up to the date of writing. Nevertheless, the volume of published work is such that we have had to be very selective as to which localities to include and which to leave out. This has been forced on us by our aim to provide you, our readers, with a wide range of exploratory themes; an adequate consideration of the sources that are available, and their limitations; and an unambiguous demonstration of the effectiveness of appropriate analytical techniques.

All these considerations lead up to that important question: 'What, in the end, do we mean by community history?'.

Community history, because it deals with localities, and the people of localities, is a form of local history. It deals with families, groups, organizations and institutions in their specific *local* settings, in context. Drawing, as it does, on the insights from a number of related academic disciplines, community history is, in itself, a distinctive form of interdisciplinary scholarship. Thus, in this volume we have been able to savour some of the approaches used in historical geography (a discipline that focuses on the study of changing locational features, spatial linkages and inter-dependencies over time). Hence, in some of its manifestations, community history takes the form recognized in other arenas as the historical geography of specific *localities*. Similarly, the perspectives of the historical demographer bring a concern for *local* population structures and their changes over time; the historical sociologist and the social anthropologist endow community history with a concern for groups in a particular *locality* or *community*, as well as the study of relationships within and between communities over time or at one specific date in the past; the economic historian provides a focus on *local* aspects of economic activities, occupational structures and industrial development; whilst the social historian deals with social processes in the *community* and *local* institutions in all their considerable variety. Many of these distinctive strands are interwoven through our illustrative case studies.

Human settlements and communities are endowed with their own inherent dynamic; and population movements, in all their different forms, are of considerable significance in generating changes over time. So, whilst being aware of the different contributions made by traditional specialist academic disciplines, because their emphasis is on the study of localities or specific groups and changes over time, we can state that the end result is what we now refer to as community history.

Thus, community history explores the ways in which communities and their institutions change – and are changed – over time. It deals with the impact of wider influences and the ways in which groups and communities are created and maintained, ways in which they are changed and how, ultimately, they may sink into decline. In the past, population transfers into an area, or out from an area, have been of considerable significance in promoting and then maintaining the dynamics of change – both in terms of the social make-up of communities and for the diffusion of new ideas and attitudes.

Volume 1 of this series dealt both with family history and with the history of the family. In this, the second volume, we have shown how community structures, territorial affiliation, migration and the nature of cultural institutions contribute to the building of a sense of community; and how these considerations affect manifestations of community and community history. All these matters lead us on to recognize the need for further in-depth treatment of the social, cultural and institutional aspects of community. These topics receive further exploration in the themes covered in Volume 3 of this series.

REFERENCES AND FURTHER READING

Note: entries marked with an asterisk are suggestions for further reading.

Anderson, M. (1983) 'What is new about the modern family?', Occasional Paper 31, *The family*, London, OPCS, pp.2–16. Reprinted in Drake (1994).

Bell, C. and Newby, H. (1971) *Community studies: an introduction to the sociology of the local community*, London, Allen and Unwin.*

Bornat, J. (1992) 'The communities of community publishing', *Oral History*, 20, 2, pp.23–31.

Bulmer, M. (1985) 'The rejuvenation of community studies? Neighbours, networks and policy', *Sociological Review*, 33, pp.430–48.*

Cohen, P. (1985) *The symbolic construction of community*, London, Tavistock.*

Colley, L. (1992) *Britons: forging the nation, 1707–1837*, New Haven, CT, Yale University Press.

Day, G. and Murdoch, J. (1993) 'Locality and community coming to terms with places', *Sociological Review*, 41, pp.82–111.*

Dennis, R. and Daniels, S. (1981) '"Community" and the social geography of Victorian cities', *Urban History Yearbook*, pp.7–20. Reprinted in Drake (1994).*

Drake, M. (ed.) (1994) *Time, family and community: perspectives on family and community history*, Oxford, Blackwell in association with The Open University (Course Reader).

Frankenberg, R. (1966) *Communities in Britain*, Harmondsworth, Penguin.

Harper, S. (1989) 'The British rural community: an overview of perspectives', *Journal of Rural Studies* 5, 2, pp.166–84.*

Jackson, J.H. and Moch, L.P. (1989) 'Migration and the social history of modern Europe', *Historical Methods*, 22, pp.27–36. Reprinted in Drake (1994).

King, R., Shuttleworth, I. and Strachan, A. (1989) 'The Irish in Coventry: the social geography of a relict community', *Irish Geography*, 22, pp.64–78.

Mills, D. (1993) 'Community and nation in the past: perception and reality', in Drake (1994).*

O'Brian, P. and Quinault, R. (eds) (1993) *The Industrial Revolution and British society*, Cambridge, Cambridge University Press.

Phillips, S.K. (1986) 'Natives and incomers: the symbolism of belonging in Muker parish, North Yorkshire', in Cohen, P. (ed.) *Symbolizing boundaries*, Manchester, Manchester University Press. Reprinted in Drake (1994).*

Phythian-Adams, C. (1991) 'Local history and national history: the quest for the peoples of England', *Rural History*, 2, 1, pp.1–23.

Robbins, K. (1988) *Nineteenth-century Britain, England, Scotland, and Wales: the making of a nation*, Oxford, Oxford University Press.

Schürer, K. (1991) 'The future for local history: boom or recession?', *The Local Historian*, 21, pp.99–108.

Strathern, M. (1981) *Kinship at the core: an anthropology of Elmdon, a village in north-west Essex in the nineteen-sixties*, Cambridge, Cambridge University Press.*

Townsend, A.R. and Taylor, C.C. (1975) 'Regional cultures and identity in industrialized societies: the case of north-east England', *Regional Studies*, 9, pp.379–93.

Werbner, P. (1979) 'Avoiding the ghetto: Pakistani migrants and settlement shifts in Manchester', *New Community*, 7, 3, pp.376–89. Reprinted in Drake (1994).

Werbner, P. (1990) *The migration process. Capital, gifts and offerings among British Pakistanis*, New York and Oxford, Berg.

EXERCISES: ANSWERS AND COMMENTS

Note: details of references mentioned in this section are given at the end of the appropriate chapter.

Exercise 1.1

Migrated: emigrated: emigrated.

Exercise 1.2

1   In general, migrants are elderly (false), single (often true), badly educated (not necessarily so), skilled (often true).

2(a)   *Direct methods* of measurement use data that indicate the movements of the migrants themselves; that is, those who change residence across a migration-defining boundary (boundary recognition varies with scope of the research project).

2(b)   *Indirect methods* use estimates inferred from the differences between the observed change in population and changes due to natural increase between specific dates, or measures based on significant differences between local and national sex ratios.

3   The birthplace tables in the published reports suffer from a number of problems. For example: (1) only life-time migration is recorded – that is, places of birth and enumeration – but none of the intermediate places where a migrant lived during his or her life-time; (2) there is little or no cross-tabulation of birthplaces with other census data. In addition (not mentioned in section 2.2 of the text), there is the fact that (3) different territorial units are used in 1851 (but not subsequently) to present the data on birthplaces (counties) and areas of enumeration (registration districts).

Exercise 1.3

The decision to migrate is usually taken at a significant point in the life cycle – for example, at marriage, on getting a new job, on retirement, following the death of a husband or wife. You will probably find this in your case. Initially, each move might seem to have had a single cause – a push or a pull perhaps? After reflecting a little more, probably you have found that the situation was more complicated – hence our decision to score the 'pushes' and the 'pulls' as complementary factors, each being counted as a vector of 10 (the total of the scores).

Exercise 1.4

1   The first task would be to change the named components in each of the boxes. This demands a full understanding of both the general context (the 'environment') and the specific setting in which a particular set of migration flows is operating. The various links can then be customized to meet the particular context of the research.

2(a)   The systems approach can be used as a tool for sorting out relationships within a particular context – once the basic detective work on the sources has been completed and the appropriate statistics analysed.

2(b)   The systems approach can be an enabling device, helping to draw our attention to new sources, new lines of research, new explanations.

Exercise 2.1

Here are two examples of other migration themes that can be examined using data contained in the CEBs:

1   Migration status and the numbers of persons in the nuclear family (see Schürer, 1991, pp.124–5).

2   Migration status and family typology; for example, simple nuclear, extended or joint families, multiple-family households, etc. (see Volume 1, Chapter 3, section 2).

Exercise 2.3

1   Our first question is not easily answered but the most likely explanations for *net* population increases, as far as research to date shows, are:

o   continuing early marriage;

o   increases in the birth rate;

o   a decline in the death rate or levels of morbidity;

o   improved diet and nutrition;

o   environmental and medical improvements.

Of course, these obvious factors conceal others that need to be taken into account, including changes in sex ratios, increased fecundity, increased family size – and a host of economic and cultural considerations.

2   Demographic growth had a profound effect on migration, primarily because increased numbers put pressure on already stretched resources. This was masked for a while by improved food supply, but when this broke down, inevitably, it increased the nature of migration, temporary at first, then permanent. It also generated emigration, which generally increased (though in cycles) as the nineteenth century progressed.

Exercise 2.6

1   Most, perhaps all, of them.

2   Perhaps the role of women, and local landholding and family patterns (though these are covered in a general way by 'economic and social factors'). You may have identified others.

Exercise 2.7

Poor Law records

Topographies/printed records

CEBs

Directories

Estate/land grant records

Lists of distinctive names (e.g. Irish surnames)

Ordnance Survey Memoirs (Ireland)

Ships' passenger lists/ships' manifests

Membership records (e.g. Welsh chapels, trade unions, etc.)

Birthplace tabulations in published census reports

Electoral registers/poll books

Property valuation and rate lists

Rentals

Marriage registers

Burial registers

Memoirs

Oral history

Exercise 2.8

1   d, f.

2   d, e, f.

3   d, e.

4   b.

5   b, c.

6   a, d.

7   a, e, f.

8   e.

9   a, b, c, d, e.

10   e, f.

11   e.

12   f.

Exercise 3.1

Common patterns that you might have noted were:

1   Marriages and births of the first child in the same year for Friedrich Hermann (16 April 1847 and 19 July 1847); Hermann Kurt (1 May 1873 and 15 August 1873) and Kurt Heinrich Hermann (16 February 1899 and 25 November 1899). It seems more likely than not that the first two of these were pre-maritally conceived births (see Volume 1, Chapter 3, section 1.1).

2   Marriage at very similar, and relatively later, ages (Friedrich Hermann was 27, Hermann Kurt 26 and Kurt Heinrich Hermann 26). Reasons for this might be to do with the length of apprenticeship and perhaps a need to find a livelihood of equal status with that of the father.

3   Three generations of furriers in Germany – and four, if you include Charles, born in London. This could demonstrate the importance of family tradition in this form of craft-based livelihood.

4   The Anglicization of the name – extremely common in both the First and Second World Wars for obvious reasons. Why did Hermann Schulze choose the name Shelley? The story which has come down in the family is that when he went to change his name, he was told that Shaw, Short and Shelley were names he could choose from (as being close to Schulze), so he picked Shelley!

5   Bankruptcy – possibly more common among immigrants than among the indigenous population. There were certainly a large number of foreign names in the lists of those declared bankrupt about this time.

Exercise 3.2

In general, emigration was very much an option for young, newly married couples in the Germany of 1899, as it was in many other countries. In particular, the 'push' and 'pull' factors (see Chapter 1, section 3.2) which are common and which operated in the case of Hermann Schulze, could be summarized as follows:

Push factors

1   The obligation of military service. At least two of his brothers, Max and Kurt, did do national service; his youngest brother, Hans, followed Hermann to England and was interned as an alien on the Isle of Man during the First World War since, unlike Hermann, he was not naturalized.

2   Decline (relative or absolute) of a small town in a rural area.

3 (Possibly) decline in an industry which was not highly mechanized. While furs remained in fashion more or less until after the Second World War, processing furs became less labour intensive. Since it was conducted on a small scale, statistics and data on the fur trade are scarce.

4 The strict moral code which pertained in the Germany of that time.

5 The possibility that Hermann was expelled by his family as a 'bad lot'.

Pull factors

1 Possible evidence here is the suggestion that there might be a family connection with London. Since Hermann himself spoke little English on arrival (and his wife never learnt very much), it seems likely that his personal links with England had not been close. This does not mean, however, that some family or business links did not exist.

2 Emigration to England was not only a relatively popular option, but may well have been seen as an opportunity for upward mobility and self-improvement – the chance to achieve independence and do well.

Exercise 3.3

You could divide your answer into positive and negative points. These are the ones I came up with:

On the positive side

1 In spite of his bankruptcy, Hermann Schulze stuck to his trade and appears to have supported a second wife and child by it. He achieved modest success, becoming a Freemason and making friends in his adopted country.

2 Abramson (1992, p.11) has advanced the theory that the true rewards of the almost inevitable hardships of emigration (Russian Jewish in his example) are not realized for several generations. This suggestion appears to be borne out in the case of Hermann Schulze. In section 2, Peter Braham examines his grandfather's emigration in the context of Abramson's hypothesis.

On the negative side

1 He experienced personal tragedy (bankruptcy, the death of a comparatively young wife of cancer).

2 It could be suggested that the experience of emigration to a foreign country might be blamed for the marital infidelity (more unusual, perhaps, in 1915 than today) and his casting of his young sons on the world (the younger was 15 and almost completely blind). Such behaviour could be ascribed, as in other cases, to the psychological effects of emigration.

Exercise 3.7

Newspapers; records of particular institutions; government records; diaries; letters; maps; photographs; oral sources (both already recorded, and still to be sought out); and records specific to a particular category (in the Jewish case the Memorial Books – for other groups there might or might not be alternative sources). Also note the uses of secondary sources: in the Jewish case these are particularly numerous (e.g. Gartner, 1960; Burman, 1982; Fishman, 1975, 1988; Williams, 1976), but for many groups something at least can usually be discovered and is worth searching for.

Exercise 3.9

1 Here are some obvious headings for comparison or contrast between different immigrant groups:

o *Who came and how:* as independent individuals? as young fathers (or mothers)? sending for children later? step-wise? as established families? stage in life cycle?

o *Households:* at first living with relatives, or in bachelor houses or hostels? in a full (or fragmented?) family unit? later on in nuclear – or in extended – households?

o *Residential patterns of settlement:* segregated? clustered? dispersed? changing?

o *Links with area of origin:* advice and assistance? 'myth of return'?

Some further potential headings are touched on, but not followed up (perhaps you can find out the answers?):

o *Social, political, economic background:* push factors in place of origin? a culture of migration? pull factors in new country? chain migration?

o *Occupation/livelihood:* typical job(s) associated with particular immigrant groups? changing or diversifying over time?

o *Cultural institutions* (e.g. clubs, churches): providing assistance for recent immigrants? a focus for cultural identity?

o *Reaction of resident and majority population:* neutral? hostile? mixed?

o *Development of ethnic or other group identity:* at once? in second generation? enhanced by experience of living in foreign, even hostile environment? rejected by individuals on their way out or up?

o *Second generation changes.*

2 Almost every phrase is significant!

(You will find that this kind of analysis of taped or written life stories could turn out to be one useful way into a migration project: you would then need to go on to check from other evidence – including further life stories – how typical the individual experiences were.)

Exercise 3.10

1 Your answer will be personal to you. But here are some worth considering:

o The various concepts introduced in Chapter 1 (e.g. chain migration, 'push and pull', intervening obstacles and opportunities) and the way they can be applied to a range of otherwise very different cases.

o Significant factors to investigate both in a single study and as the basis of comparison are given in Schema A in section 4.2 of Chapter 2 (pp.56–7), and in the answer to Exercise 3.9 above. Also try extending your matrix for Exercise 3.9 to the case studies in Chapter 2 and sections 1 and 2 in this chapter; and, later, to examples from Chapters 7 and 8. This will help to alert you to themes and questions for your own research (no doubt you will find some more worth pursuing than others).

2 Not all the categories apply to the Chapter 3 case studies – but filling in as many entries as you can should again alert you to interesting questions.

Exercise 4.1

1 Contrasted shadings: red lines for men, black lines for women.

2 Vertical lines represent excess ratios in 1851, horizontal lines are used for 1801.

3   The location of the exposed coalfield; parish (in capital letters) and township (in lower case letters – a subdivision of a parish); parish churches (crosses) and/or major industrial villages (dot symbols); names of parishes with declining populations before 1851 (in red); parish (continuous lines) and township (dotted lines) boundaries are all shown distinctively. The parishes with no significant differences in terms of sex ratios are not shown, thus focusing our attention on the all-important areas for in- or out-migration.

Exercise 4.2

For a 20 per cent sampling fraction we take every fifth household ($100 \div 5 = 20$). Thus, the schedule numbers will be 8, 13, 18, 23, 28, 33, 38.

Exercise 4.3

1   Denbigh 830; Holywell 1,296; Llanrhaeadr 498.

2   Llanarmon 7 per cent; St Asaph 11 per cent. These are point estimates.

3   Holywell 8±1.51 per cent; Llanrhaeadr 11±2.80 per cent.

4   In Holywell 8 per cent of the *sample* population had been born in neighbouring parishes, but at the 95 per cent confidence level the actual percentage of the *whole* population would have been between 6.49 and 9.51 per cent (i.e. 8–1.51 = 6.49; 8+1.51 = 9.51). This range is the standard (or sample) error.

At Llanrhaeadr the corresponding figure lay somewhere between 8.20 and 13.80 per cent.

5   Generally, the larger the sample, the smaller the sampling error. Note, size here is the *actual number of individuals* in the sample (e.g. Holywell 1,296 persons), not the percentage they represent of the total population.

Exercise 5.1

(a), (d), (f), (h), (i), (k) and (m).

Exercise 5.2

1   *Low centrality:* low status, everyday needs, cheap goods, small catchment area, low population threshold.

2   *High centrality:* expensive goods, market town, scarcity, high demand, goods and services of 'high range/order'.

3   *Not relevant:* isotropic surface, yeomen, hexagonal shape.

Comment: 'isotropic surface' and 'hexagonal shape' are theoretical properties of the Christaller model. These do not exist in reality (see Schema B, pp.123–4). 'Yeomen' is included in the list to see if you can practise discrimination!

Exercise 5.3

Your lists should have reflected:

o   Particular central place activities that existed at a specific date or within the stated time periods.

o   Regional location.

o   The relative importance of the selected town in relation to other centres.

Although the majority of your indicators will have general applicability, probably some will be specific to your selected centres and particular local circumstances.

Exercise 6.1

It can be shown that changes in these factors had a significant impact on the evolving social structure of rural and urban communities: different classes sought to establish their own identities and to distance themselves from each other in settlements; immigrant ethnic groups displayed distinctive traits which set them apart from the indigenous population; and improvements in transport facilitated the outward spread of towns and cities and eventually opened up the countryside to commuters.

Exercise 6.2

Pahl noted four distinctive features, which may give you pointers for your own projects:

1 The emergence of residential areas segregated by class.

2 The selective in-migration of middle-class residents.

3 Commuting.

4 Widespread mobility amongst newcomers, leading to the breakdown of traditional shopping and social patterns.

Exercise 6.3

There was a marked contrast in the locations occupied by the different social classes: in the pre-industrial city, the centre was occupied by the most wealthy citizens and the periphery by the poorest residents, whereas in the industrial city the poor lived near the centre and the better-off at the periphery.

Exercises 8.2, 8.6 and 8.7

For the answers to these exercises please see Figure 8.7 opposite.

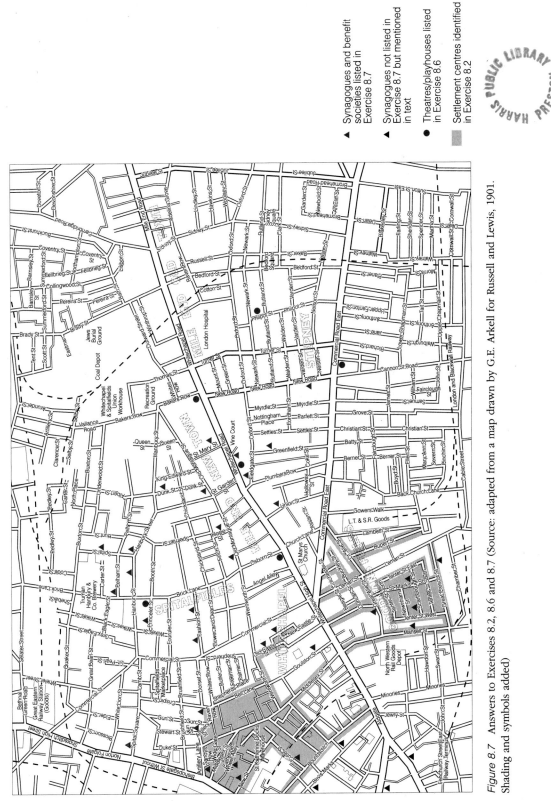

◀ Synagogues and benefit
    societies listed in
    Exercise 8.7

◀ Synagogues not listed in
    Exercise 8.7 but mentioned
    in text

● Theatres/playhouses listed
    in Exercise 8.6

▨ Settlement centres identified
    in Exercise 8.2

Figure 8.7 Answers to Exercises 8.2, 8.6 and 8.7 (Source: adapted from a map drawn by G.E. Arkell for Russell and Lewis, 1901. Shading and symbols added)

ACKNOWLEDGEMENTS

Grateful acknowledgement is made to the following sources for permission to reproduce material in this book:

Chapter 1

Text

Pryce W.T.R. (1993) 'Migration: some perspectives', in Rowlands J. (ed.) *Welsh family history: a guide to research*, (Aberystwyth), Association of Family History Societies of Wales.

Figures

Figure 1.4: Mabogunje A.L. (1970) 'Systems approach to a theory of rural–urban migration', *Geographical Analysis*, 2, Ohio State University Press; Figure 1.5: Barraclough G. (ed.) (1978) *The Times atlas of world history*, Times Books, a division of HarperCollins Publishers; Figure 1.6: Segal A. and Marston L. (1989) 'Maps and keys – world voluntary migration', *Migration World*, no. 1, 1989, vol. XVII, published by The Center for Migration Studies of New York, Inc.; Figure 1.7: Glamorgan Archive Service.

Chapter 2

Figures

Figure 2.3: adapted from Pritchard R.M. (1976) *Housing and the spatial structure of the city*, Cambridge University Press; Figure 2.4: Pooley C.G. (1983) 'Welsh migration to England in the mid 19th century', *Journal of Historical Geography*, 9, pp.287–305, Academic Press Ltd; Figure 2.6: Jones E. (1985) 'The Welsh in London in the 19th century', *Cambria*, 12, no. 1; Figure 2.7: National Library of Wales; Figure 2.11: Withers C.W.J. and Watson A.J. (1991) 'Stepwise migration and Highland migration to Glasgow, 1852–1898', *Journal of Historical Geography*, 17, pp.35–55, Academic Press Ltd; Figure 2.12: Mitchell B. (ed.) (1989) *Irish emigration lists 1833–1839*, Genealogical Publishing Company.

Tables

Table 2.6: adapted from Withers C.W.J. and Watson A.J. (1991) 'Stepwise migration and Highland migration to Glasgow, 1852–1898', *Journal of Historical Geography*, 17, pp.35–55, Academic Press Ltd; Table 2.7: adapted from Fitzpatrick D. (1985) 'A curious middle place', in Swift R. and Gilley S. (eds) *The Irish in the Victorian city*, Croom Helm.

Chapter 3

Figures

Figures 3.1, 3.2: courtesy of Monica Shelley; Figure 3.3: Negative D1589, ref. MR.4.H7 Plate 5, Royal Geographical Society, London; Figures 3.4, 3.5: courtesy of Mrs Ray Braham; Figure 3.6: Kurzweil A. (1980) *From generation to generation: how to trace your Jewish genealogy and personal history*, William Morrow and Company Inc.; Figure 3.7: (top right): photo Tim Smith/Guzelian/Bradford Heritage Recording Unit; (bottom left): Ethnic Communities Oral History Project; (bottom right): Alex Schweitzer/Age Exchange Theatre Trust; Figure 3.8: adapted from *Oral History*, 20, 2, Autumn 1992, Oral History Society / courtesy of Pauline Taylor, Suffolk County Council Libraries & Heritage; Figure 3.9: adapted from Alladina S. and Edwards V. (eds) (1991) *Multilingualism in the British Isles*, 2, Longman Group UK Ltd.

Chapter 4

Figures

Figure 4.1: National Library of Wales; Figures 4.2, 4.5: adapted from Pryce W.T.R. (1975) 'Patterns of migration and the evolution of culture areas: cultural and linguistic frontiers in northeast Wales, 1750 and 1851', *Transactions, Institute of British Geographers*, 65, pp.79–107, The Institute of British Geographers.

Chapter 5

Figures

Figure 5.1: adapted by the author from Patten J. (1972) 'Village and town', *Agricultural History Review*, vol. 20; Figure 5.2: Dickinson R.E. (1934) *Economic Geography*, 10, p.179, Economic Geography, Clark University; Figures 5.3 (Great Britain), 5.4: Langton J. and Morris R.J. (1986) *Atlas of industrializing Britain*, Methuen and Co.; Figure 5.3 (Ireland): Graham B.J. and Proudfoot L.J. (eds) (1993) *An historical geography of Ireland*, Academic Press Ltd; Figure 5.5: reproduced by permission of Solomon & Whitehead (Guild Prints) Ltd. NB: prints of this painting are available from the aforementioned company; Figure 5.7: reproduced from Everitt A. *Journal of Transport History*, 3 (1979), by permission of Leicester University Press (a division of Pinter Publishers Ltd), London. All rights reserved; Figures 5.8, 5.9: Greaves B. (1968) *Methodism in Yorkshire 1740–1851*, unpublished PhD thesis; Figure 5.10: Green F.H.W. (1950) 'Urban hinterlands in England and Wales: an analysis of bus services', *Geographical Journal*, 116, pp.64–8, Royal Geographical Society; Figure 5.11: adapted from Carter H. (1965) *The towns of Wales: a study in urban geography*, University of Wales Press; Figure 5.12: adapted from Odell P.R. (1957) 'Urban spheres of influence in Leicestershire in the mid 19th century', *Geographical Studies*, 2, © Professor P.R. Odell; Figure 5.13: Lewis C.R. (1975) 'The analysis of changes in urban states: a case study in mid-Wales and the middle Welsh borderland', *Transactions, Institute of British Geographers*, 64, The Institute of British Geographers.

Chapter 6

Figures

Figure 6.1: Rees A.D. (1950) *Life in a Welsh countryside*, University of Wales Press; Figure 6.2: Dennis R. and Clout H. (1980) *A social geography of England and Wales*, Pergamon Press, © Richard Dennis and Hugh Clout; Figure 6.3: Carter H. (1980) 'Transformations in the spatial structure of Welsh towns in the nineteenth century', *Transactions of the Honourable Society of Cymmrodorion*, pp.175–200; Figure 6.4: Shaw M. (1979) 'Reconciling social and physical space', *Transactions, Institute of British Geographers*, New Series 4, The Institute of British Geographers; Figure 6.5: Lewis C.R. (1980) 'The Irish in Cardiff in the mid-19th century', *Cambria*, 7; Figure 6.6: Lewis G.J. and Davies W.K.D. (1974) 'The social patterning of a British city', *Tijdschrift Voor Economische en Sociale Geografie*, 65, pp.194–207, Royal Dutch Geographical Society; Figure 6.7: Jones P.N. (1970) 'Some aspects of the changing distribution of coloured immigrants in Birmingham, 1961–66,' *Transactions, Institute of British Geographers*, 50, The Institute of British Geographers.

Chapter 7

Figures

Figure 7.1: adapted from Waterman S. (1981) 'Changing residential patterns of the Dublin Jewish community', *Irish Geography*, 14, The Geographical Society of Ireland; Figures 7.2, 7.3: courtesy of Dr Pnina Werbner, University of Keele; Figure 7.5: courtesy of Brenda Collins; Figure 7.6: Ulster Museum Belfast, Hogg Collection; Figure 7.7: Breen R. (1984) 'Population trends in late nineteenth and early twentieth century Ireland: a local study', *Economic and Social Review*, 15, 2, pp.95–108, The Economic and Social Research Institute.

Chapter 8

Figures

Figures 8.1, 8.5: adapted from a map drawn by G.E. Arkell for Russell C. and Lewis H.S. (1901) *The Jew in London: a study of racial character and present day conditions*, T. Fisher Unwin; Figures 8.2, 8.3, 8.4: Booth Rt Hon. Charles (1902) *Life and labour of the people in London*, Macmillan; Figure 8.6: London Museum of Jewish Life.

Exercises: answers and comments

Figure

Figure 8.7: adapted from a map drawn by G.E. Arkell for Russell C. and Lewis H.S. (1901) *The Jew in London: a study of racial character and present day conditions*, T. Fisher Unwin.

Covers

Front (clockwise from top left)

Shell fish at cottage door and ladies working: The Sutcliffe Gallery; Children gleaning at harvest time: Rural History Centre, University of Reading; Two men, one with child in arms: Northamptonshire Libraries and Information Service, Local Studies Department, copyright: Mr S. Tapp; Envelope containing Joseph Hartley's letter of 27 August 1861: courtesy of Michael Drake; Raunds – Peace Day 1919: Northamptonshire Libraries and Information Service, Local Studies Department, copyright: Mrs P. Keedle; Emigrating family on ship: from Bigger D. and McDonald T., *In sunshine or in shadow*, Belfast, Friars Bush Press; Aerial view of West London.

Back (clockwise from top left)

Three ladies in Llanfair Caereinion, Powys, *c.*1900: courtesy of the late Miss Blodwen Jones, from Pryce W.T.R. (1991) *The photographer in rural Wales*, Llanfair Caereinion, The Powysland Club; The Llanfair Light Railway: recently arrived train from Welshpool, 1905: courtesy of Dr W.T.R. Pryce; The Doms family, Belgian refugees, 1914: Bedfordshire County Record Office; Aerial view of Kettering: Northamptonshire Libraries and Information Service, Local Studies Department; Evacuee children: *Derby Evening Telegraph*; 'Joyce Wright writes home': extract from an evacuee's letter from the Second World War: from Wicks B. (1988) *No time to wave goodbye*, Bloomsbury Publishing Ltd; Park scene with swings: Northamptonshire Libraries and Information Service, Local Studies Department, copyright: Mr Frank T. Thompson.

INDEX